God's Highway Project

A Study of the Book of Isaiah
(Isaiah 40-66)

by
Christy Voelkel

Copyright © 2026 by Christy Voelkel

Scripture taken from the New King James Version®. Copyright © 1982 by Thomas Nelson. Used by permission. All rights reserved. Unless otherwise noted, all Scripture cited in this study is from the NKJV.

Scriptures passages have been copied from the online Bible reference source, Blue Letter Bible (www.blueletterbible.org) using its copy feature.

Strong's Hebrew Lexicon definitions from Blue Letter Bible. Web. September 2023.

Table of Contents

Introduction	vii
Lesson 1: Preparing the Way (Isaiah 40:1-5)	17
Lesson 2: The Comfort of Empowerment (Isaiah 40:6-31)	23
PART 1	**31**
Lesson 3: The Power of Fear (Isaiah 41)	33
Lesson 4: The False Comfort of Partiality (Isaiah 42)	43
Lesson 5: The Comfort of Validation (Isaiah 43)	53
Lesson 6: The Promise of Prosperity (Isaiah 44:1-23)	59
Lesson 7: The Comfort of an Ever-present God (Isaiah 44:24-28)	69
Lesson 8: The Glory of the Savior King (Isaiah 45)	77
Lesson 9: The Comfort of Laying Down Burdens (Isaiah 46)	91
Lesson 10: The Comfort of Vengeance (Isaiah 47)	99
Lesson 11: The Comfort of God's Sovereignty (Isaiah 48)	109
PART 2	**125**
Lesson 12: The Stumbling Block of Despair (Isaiah 49)	127
Lesson 13: The Comfort of One Who Has Been There (Isaiah 50)	143
Lesson 14: The Pursuit of Righteousness (Isaiah 51:1-8)	153
Lesson 15: Facing Fury (Isaiah 51:9-23)	161
Lesson 16: The Comfort of the Good News (Isaiah 52:1-12)	171
Lesson 17: The Glory of the Sacrifice (Isaiah 52:13-15)	179
Lesson 18: The Way Out of a Crooked Place (Isaiah 53)	193
Lesson 19: The Stumbling Block of Shame (Isaiah 54)	203
Lesson 20: Redefining Abundant Life (Isaiah 55)	217
Lesson 21: The Promise of Equality (Isaiah 56:1-12)	229

Table of Contents, cont.

PART 3	247
Lesson 22: The Reward of Peace (Isaiah 57)	249
Lesson 23: The Practice of Letting Go (Isaiah 58)	255
Lesson 24: The Comfort of Confession and Closure (Isaiah 59)	267
Lesson 25: Out of Darkness, Into Light (Isaiah 60)	279
Lesson 26: Comfort Fulfilled (Isaiah 61-62)	285
Lesson 27: The Treading of the Winepress (Isaiah 63-64)	295
Lesson 28: The Final Recompense (65-66)	301
Conclusion: God's Highway Project	311
The Prophetic Timeline	317

*In loving memory of a beloved student,
Mrs. Cheryl Bowman,
who passed into the arms of her Lord the week I was
preparing to teach on the practice of letting go.*

Introduction

We live in a world full of broken people, broken families, and broken communities, but the brokenness is, to a great extent, self-inflicted. News stations and social media bombard us daily with profane, hate-filled protests and manipulative even fraudulent social messaging. Those who put themselves forward as our visionary leaders cry, "Peace, peace!" where there is no peace and speak great swelling words of emptiness, as the apostle Peter described it (2 Peter 2:18). Our social values have become so eroded and twisted that our culture is now characterized by violence, corruption, miscarriages of justice, sexual immorality, disregard for the sanctity of life, and a growing resistance to God and His values. The erosion has made its way even into our church body. Should we be surprised that a general oppressiveness and sense of powerlessness has beset us in this generation?

It isn't hard to see the societal fallout from this. In the midst of all the external conflict, we grapple with the internal conflicts caused by fear, despair, self-pity, shame, destructive anger, and withdrawal into silence—all reactions that come with feeling powerless. Victims take justice (as they see it) into their own hands, seeking their own solutions to escape the oppression or, at least, cope with it. Some have let their victimization so define them that they never escape that identity. Many who aren't victims themselves choose to identify with victims out of sympathy and outrage, and thus, embrace the victim identity as well. Our culture has increasingly glorified a victim-centric mentality, often vindicating the abused by enabling and even encouraging them to become abusers themselves.

These are the problems with which we grapple on a personal, day-to-day level. They are the problems we face when we go out into our world to minister to victims of abuse or those simply overcome by hopeless circumstances. This is our modern culture, and it is going to get worse. We know from Scripture that as the End Times draw near, both physical and spiritual oppression will abound more and more.

Sounds pretty bleak, doesn't it? It was pretty bleak for Israel in the book of Isaiah, as well. She, too, was suffering from societal brokenness and the host of issues it caused, all of which stemmed from her broken relationship with God. Sadly, it would take even more suffering under the oppressive hands of Babylonian captors before she would come to the end of her tether and seek a solution from God.

God made a way out of bondage for Israel (and through Israel, a way out for the rest of us). The solution rests in returning to Him—to His vision of life, His values, and His way of thinking and acting—and therein lies the rub. Returning to God requires a reversal of course on Israel's part and an upending of life as she had known it. It means letting go of a world of fleeting pursuits for the promise of enduring peace and prosperity in a kingdom that hasn't been realized (even today). As it is for Israel, so it is for those of us struggling with brokenness in life, often at the hands of the world but sometimes by our own hand.

But good news! There is hope! However, the journey back to wholeness and well-being is a daunting one, so much so that in the aftermath of Babylonia's demise, most of Israel chose to remain in that place of exile rather than return to God and kingdom. In the same way, many people today choose to remain in their bondage and brokenness rather than go through the process of being dug out of the pit in which they find themselves physically, spiritually, mentally, and emotionally. It takes faith to make the return journey, but for those who persevere, there is the assurance of well-being, peace, and a vast, eternal reward.

Before we dive into the Biblical text, let me frame it for you with some information about Isaiah in general and the themes for the study. (Please note: all Bible verse referenced in this study are taken from the New King James Version, unless otherwise noted.)

About the Book of Isaiah

Isaiah was a prophet sent to the southern kingdom of Judah. His time of prophesying spans the reign of four kings, as introduced in Isaiah 1:1:

> "The vision of Isaiah the son of Amoz, which he saw concerning Judah and Jerusalem in the days of Uzziah, Jotham, Ahaz, and Hezekiah, kings of Judah." – Isaiah 1:1

We know from 2 Kings 17 that the northern kingdom of Israel fell to the Assyrians in Isaiah's days, during the reign of King Ahaz of Judah. Isaiah prophesies that the same fate will befall the southern kingdom of Judah at the hands of Babylonia—not a very popular message. According to tradition, Isaiah died at the hands of Hezekiah's son, King Manasseh, by being sawn in two.

Isaiah's prophetic book is broken into two main sections that mirror the Bible as a whole:

- **Isaiah 1–39** addresses Israel before the Babylonian Captivity while she is still living in the land of Israel. Isaiah saw the downfall of the northern kingdom of Israel in Ahaz's day and warned against the same fate looming on the horizon for the southern kingdom of Judah. The first 39 chapters are very much like the 39 books of the Old Testament in their message of condemnation and judgment.
- **Isaiah 40–66** fast forwards to a picture of Israel at the end of the Babylonian Captivity. The setting changes and so does the tone of the message. The last 27 chapters, like the 27 books of the New Testament, are filled with comfort, hope, reconciliation, and a vision of a future kingdom. For the purpose of this study, we are picking up in the "New Testament" half.

Peaks and Valleys on the Prophetic Time

As God reveals Israel's future return in Isaiah 40-66, He marks some historical high points along the way, which we might envision as mountain ranges with successive peaks (see chart on the next page)

1. The first and closest mountain range on the horizon is the **Babylonian exile.** Isaiah 40 opens at the peak of Israel's oppression, when God reveals His plan to bring His people out of exile and bondage.
2. The second, more distant mountain range marks the rise of the Persian Empire, which succeeds the Babylonian Empire in the historical timeline. The peak point in Isaiah's vision is the commissioning of **King Cyrus of Persia**.
3. The third distant mountain range rises in the time of the Roman

Empire and peaks at the commissioning of the sin-bearing **Servant.** This is the Servant's first advent in history.

4. The final, furthest mountain range is the age of **the Servant's kingdom** which is established at the time of His second advent. As Isaiah sees it, this is the pinnacle achievement in regard to Israel's restoration.

From where Isaiah stood on the plains of time looking up at these mountain ranges of historical eras, these peak events seemed closely stacked on one another, but in reality, each mountain range is separated by valleys of time.

1. The Babylonian Captivity lasted for 70 years before Cyrus came on the scene.
2. The valley between Cyrus of Persia and the (first) coming of the Servant in the days of the Roman occupation lasted a little over 500 years. That valley encompassed the rise and fall of Persia and Greece before Rome took over the empire.
3. The last and current valley is the Church Age. As we will see in this study, Isaiah foresaw that the Gentiles would be brought into the Servant's kingdom. What he didn't foresee was that God would make an age of it. We are currently living in the valley of time between the first coming of the Servant-King and His second coming when He will establish His kingdom.

God's Highway Project encompasses the full journey from exile to that future kingdom. It is doesn't end with Israel's release from the Babylonian Captivity. That was only a minor step in the greater on-going journey.

That is the historical framework for Isaiah 40-66. Now let's look at the narrative structure of the text itself.

The Narrative Structure of Isaiah 40–66

Overall, the body of the text is encompassed by an inclusio. Simply put, an inclusio is a repeated verse or phrase that is found at the beginning and end of a selection of text and sets up the theme for that selection, kind of like bookends that encompass books on a particular topic. Here in Isaiah 40-66, we have a dual inclusio. The first inclusio frames the theme of preparing the way. We see the repeated phrase in Isaiah 40:3,

> *"The voice of one crying in the wilderness: 'Prepare the way of the LORD; make straight in the desert a highway for our God.'"* – Isaiah 40:3 (emphasis added)

and again in Isaiah 62:10,

> *"Go through, Go through the gates! Prepare the way for the people; Build up, Build up the highway!..."* – Isaiah 62:10 (emphasis added)

There is a second inclusio that frames the theme of reward. The repeated phrase is found in Isaiah 40:10,

> *"Behold, the Lord GOD shall come with a strong hand, and His arm shall rule for Him; Behold, His reward is with Him, and His work before Him."* – Isaiah 40:10 (emphasis added)

and again in Isaiah 62:11,

> *"... 'Say to the daughter of Zion, "Surely your salvation is coming; Behold, His reward is with Him, and His work before Him."'"* – Isaiah 62:11 (emphasis added)

Thus, we have an overall, two-fold theme of preparing the way and the determination of reward that runs through God's redemptive plan as described in Isaiah 40-66.

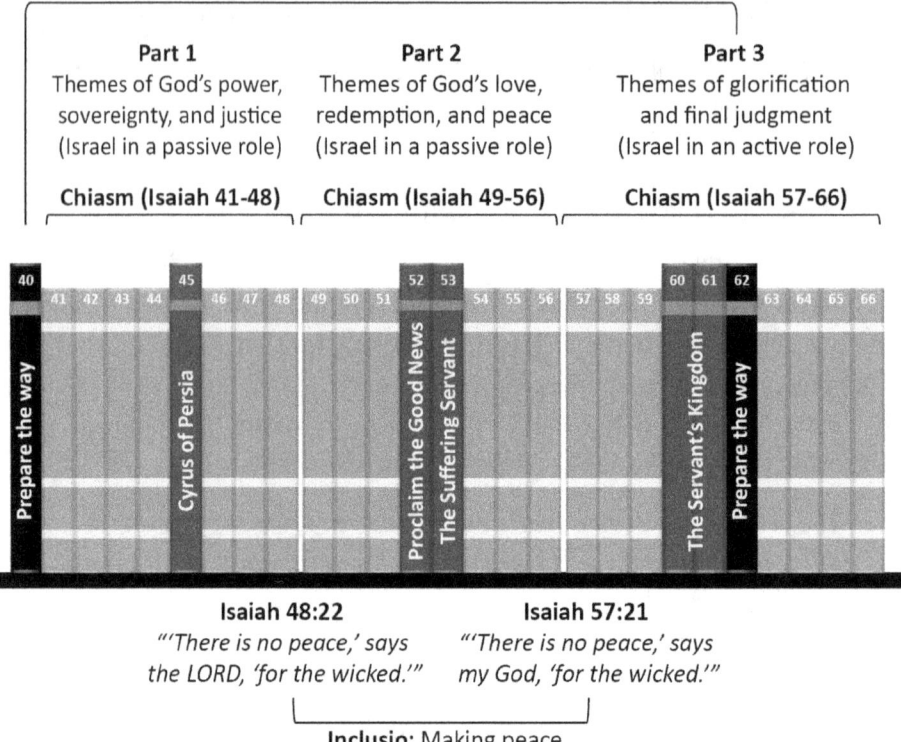

The overall body of chapters is sub-divided into three main parts:

- **Part 1 (Isaiah 40–48)** focuses on the themes of God's sovereignty, power, and justice, with the focal point being the commissioning of Cyrus in Isaiah 45. In this section, Israel is cast in a very passive role. She can do nothing to effect her own release from bondage, and her only action is to bear witness of God's work on her behalf.

- **Part 2 (Isaiah 49–56[1])** focuses on the themes of God's love and grace in His effort to redeem His people. Again, Israel is cast in a

---

[1] My break between Parts 2 and 3 differs from Jewish commentaries, a difference which I base on the chiastic structures of the overall text rather than the repetitive verses at the end of Chapters 48 and 57. According to the side notes in my Tanakh, Jewish scholars separate the parts at the repetitive verses, which form an inclusio with the theme of peace for Part 2. Adele Berlin and Marc Zvi Brettler, editors ; Michael Fishbane, consulting editor. The Jewish Study Bible: Jewish Publication Society Tanakh Translation. (Oxford ; New York : Oxford University Press, 2004), 882, commentary in side note for verse 22.

very passive role of simply having to believe and accept God's and the Servant's effort on her behalf.

- **Part 3 (Isaiah 57–66)** changes tone rather dramatically. Where Israel had remained passive in Parts 1 and 2, her actions are now addressed as God weighs her heart and finds it lacking. This final part opens with a delay in the restoration process until her heart and actions are corrected, then moves into the final glorification of the righteous and judgment of the wicked. Chapter 62 is the focal point of this part and contains the closing bookend for the inclusio in Isaiah 40.

Parts 1, 2, and 3 are each arranged in a chiasm. A chiasm is a way of structuring an argument by building the argument, point by point, to a key thought, and then revisiting the opening arguments, point by point, with closing arguments. The closing arguments are paired with the opening arguments in such a way as to resolve them, reverse them, or expand them with new information. The chiastic structure lends a sense of an almost courtroom-like setting as arguments develop in stages.

- **The chiasm of Part 1** encompasses the arguments in Isaiah 41–48. The focal point of that chiasm is the commissioning of Cyrus in Isaiah 45.

- **The chiasm of Part 2** encompasses the arguments for God's love and revolves around the redemptive death of the Sin-bearing Servant in Isaiah 51–53. The focal point of the chiasm is the command to proclaim the good news in Chapter 52. The "good news" is the ultimate comfort to which God's comforting effort is building, and that command is housed between the picture of God pouring out the cup of wrath on Israel in Isaiah 51 and the Sin-bearing Servant taking that cup in her place in Isaiah 53. (Note: Many commentaries say that the death of the Sin-bearing Servant in Isaiah 53 is the high point, but I am going to respectfully disagree with that. While the Servant's work is the crux of the redemptive effort overall and Isaiah 53 is the pivotal, central chapter in the spread of chapters we are covering, it is not the apex of the chiasm. The chiasm focuses on the command to us to proclaim the good news as the key effort when offering comfort.)

- **The chiasm of Part 3** revolves around the picture of the Servant's realized kingdom, which is the end of "the way" toward which we have been preparing. It is also where the determination for reward is discussed.

The chiastic structures are very important because they help define the main thrust of the section and identify its focal point. The pairing of opening and closing arguments in the structure also set up important comparisons that the author wants us to consider. At the beginning of each part, I will lay out the chiasm for you so that you can see how the text will unfold, and as we work through the passages, we will compare the opening and closing arguments.

Objectives of This Study

I titled this study of Isaiah 40-66 "God's Highway Project" because that is how the journey from exile to kingdom is described in the opening verses of Isaiah 40. But as we will see, it really isn't a physical journey so much as a journey from brokenness to restoration. Isaiah 40 opens with God's imperative command to the prophet to comfort His people, and the subsequent chapters illustrate His methods and overall process for restoring broken people and healing a broken community.

Thus, Israel becomes a case study for us to examine how God works. From His model we will take the following applications:

- Understanding how God prepares His people spiritually, mentally, and emotionally for the oppression and exile looming on their horizon. That can apply to us as we wrestle with an eroding culture and its skewed values, knowing that the End Times is on our own horizon.
- Understanding what strategies God uses in bringing people out of a current experience of oppression, and in what capacity we ourselves are called to model or participate in the process.
- Understanding what specific issues arise during the experience of oppression. These include the reactions to abuse, oppression, or other victimization, and become stumbling blocks to being comforted, healed, and restored in relationships with others and

with God. They can also become secondary forms of oppression that remain even after the original circumstances are lifted.

We are picking up the historical narrative at the lowest point in Israel's exile experience. She is the victim of all kinds of physical abuse and suffering the emotional and psychological backlash of it. But she is also guilty of bringing her suffering upon herself because of her sin and unfaithfulness to God. Even in the depths of her oppression, she is rebellious and wrestling with God. When God begins to deal with her, He must address the sin and rebellion issues as part of the process.

While this is the case with Israel, this may not be the case in our own personal contexts. We (or the person we are trying to comfort) may not have brought our suffering upon ourselves because of sin. Sometimes we are innocent victims of other people's sin. However, sin can enter into the dynamic for us in how we react to the abuse or oppressive circumstances. The oppressor's sin is never overlooked, but neither is the victim's reaction to it. So, as we work through the text, we are going to discuss Israel's specific case first, and then tailor the principles of God's model to our own context.

How to Use This Study

We will be working through Isaiah 40-66 one chapter at a time, with a few exceptions. At the opening of each lesson, I will note the verses we will be covering. You need to read the verses on your own before beginning. You may read them in any Bible translation you prefer, but I will be using the New King James Version.

Once the overall chapter or selection is read, we will begin to work through the verses in chunks and discuss what is being pictured in the text, focusing on Israel's specific case and what God is modeling as He works with her. We will then tailor the principles of God's model to our own context. As we work through the sections, I will incorporate questions to help you with observing the biblical text, but also to encourage you to see Isaiah's model relevant to our own modern culture. I offer my own answers to some of the questions but not all. I encourage you to pause at each question and answer them for yourselves in light of your own experiences or views.

Each lesson ends with a discussion of the overarching theme that emerges from the verses with some additional questions for application or further study. I hope you find this study helpful, first of all, in being comforted yourself. I admit that, even as a mature believer, I have struggled to find comfort in the Scripture, mostly because of how I was raised, and this study has helped me personally learn how to take comfort from God's Word. I also hope that this study equips you to comfort others and have a positive impact on a hurting world.

Happy studying!

LESSON 1

Preparing the Way

READ

Isaiah 40:1-5

DISCUSSION

These opening verses flesh out the overarching theme for the rest of the study and give us a framework to guide our observation of the text. In this lesson, we will dig into the dynamics of the process for comforting people.

Isaiah 40:1-2

The text opens with an imperative command from God. *"Comfort, comfort My people!"* The repetition of the word makes it extra emphatic. It seems like a straight-forward command. We all know what it means to comfort someone, right? Maybe.

   Q: How do you define comfort? What is comforting to you?

   Q: How do you give comfort to others?

As we get into this study, we may find that God's idea of comfort isn't what we might consider comforting, but it is meant for comfort and healing. Coming to terms with that is a challenge we will have to face.

Comfort is the overall intent of God's Highway Project. God then lays out the objectives of the project. He is going to save Israel in two ways:

   1. He will end her warfare
   2. He will pardon her iniquity

The first objective, ending warfare, speaks to the physical conflict between Israel and her antagonists. There must be an end to the physical fighting. If the nation of Israel is going to be preserved to inherit the LORD's promises in her future generations, then she needs to be rescued from the hands of her physical oppressors. That is being "saved" in the sense of being physically preserved. She cannot begin to heal and be restored until people quit swinging at her. So, there is a physical aspect to her redemption when God brings her out of Babylon.

The second objective, pardoning sin, addresses the spiritual conflict in Israel's relationship with God that must be resolved. The reason she was exiled in the first place is because of her sin and idolatry, so she needs to be "saved" in the sense of spiritual salvation and being granted a place in the future heavenly kingdom. When we talk about Israel being "saved" in future chapters, we should keep in mind that there are these two kinds of salvation being offered. One is a temporal, physical preservation, and the other is an eternal, spiritual salvation. God's people cannot experience true comfort until the conflict on both fronts is accomplished. These are God's objectives that, together, comfort Israel.

Ending the conflict is a hot topic in our modern culture, and not just between Israel and her antagonists. There is a lot of fighting going on right now all over the world—physical warfare, ideological warfare, and verbal warfare on social media. And not just in the world but within our nation, our communities, and even within the Christian community as well. Churches are dividing left and right. Don't you wish that all the fighting would end?

> **Q:** Pick one instance of conflict in our world today. What it would take to end the fight?
>
> **Q:** Is peaceful coexistence possible?

I would say it isn't because the external conflict is driven by a spiritually-based internal conflict.

> **Q:** What is the real source of the fighting? (Read Ephesians 6:12 and James 4:1-3.)

Physical conflict is driven by two factors that are in league with one another: spiritual warfare and the sin nature; thus, physical conflict is really an outworking of the spiritual conflict. Peaceful existence cannot happen until the physical fighting *and its source* have both been resolved. That is why God addresses both objectives.

Isaiah 40:3-5

God issued the opening commands, declaring His intent and objectives. Now His herald, *"the voice of one crying in the wilderness,"* issues the command to the prophet, *"Prepare the way!"* This command is repeated in Isaiah 62:10 and becomes the main theme encompassing Isaiah 40-66. (The other theme is the reward, but we will talk about that in Isaiah 62.)

Q: What does that mean, "prepare the way"? What is "the way"?

Here in Isaiah 40:3, the text says to prepare the way "for our God." There is the ancient practice of people repairing the roadway and clearing away any debris so that the path is clear before an arriving king. That is one possible way to fulfill this command. But when we get to the end of this study and see the command issued again in Isaiah 62:10, there it says to prepare the way "for the people." This same command is mentioned a third time in Isaiah 57:14 with the added instruction to remove the stumbling stones for the "people." So, who is traveling the road, God or the people?

Let's consider what "preparing the way" means in terms of Israel's return from exile. She is embarking on a literal, physical journey as she leaves Babylonia, but she is also embarking on a spiritual journey as she leaves a place of brokenness and separation from God to be restored in her kingdom and that relationship with Him. On the one hand, the LORD is offering the means of redemption to His people, but by the same token, the people must make that turning in their life and return to Him. So, it is a two-way street, and the prophet stands at the crossroad between them as an intercessor. The command to "prepare the way" is given initially to the prophet but, as we will see in future chapters, the LORD also commissions two "servants" to facilitate the task as well.

There is a future appearance of a messenger described as "the voice of one crying in the wilderness." Malachi prophesies of him (Malachi 3:1, 4:5-6). The gospel writers identify him.

Q: Who is the voice crying in the wilderness? (Luke 3:1-6)

Q: What was the purpose of his message?

Obviously, John was not tasked with preparing a physical roadway. Instead, his purpose was to deliver a spiritual message that would turn the hearts of the people and prepare them, spiritually, for the coming of the Lord Jesus Christ. That turning, or returning, is a key part of the picture.

"Preparing the way" describes the overall process by which the LORD brings His people out of their oppression and sets them on the road of return to peace and well-being. Part of the endeavor will involve removing stumbling stones blocking the way to recovery, as mentioned in Isaiah 57:14, but let's look at the full four-part process as it is defined here in Isaiah 40:4.

The voice in the wilderness describes preparing the way of the LORD as building a highway. The process isn't too hard to grasp. We have all seen highway crews building a road at some time or another. What are the basic tasks?

1. Lifting up the low spots ("every valley shall be exalted")
2. Tearing down the high spots ("every mountain brought low")
3. Straightening out the winding roads and sharp turns ("crooked places made straight")
4. Removing the rocks and debris and smooth off the road ("rough places smoothed")

Notice the reversal of condition described in each piece of imagery. These reversals reinforce the idea of return (Hebrew: *shuv*) which is tied to the Hebrew concept of repentance. *Shuv* describes going in one direction, then reversing course and going back the way you came, physically or spiritually speaking. The reversal of course brings about a radical change of condition. When Israel fell away from the LORD, her condition changed drastically as she went into exile and oppression. The only way to end the oppression and return to a peaceful condition is by returning to the LORD. Isaiah will reinforce that key theme of return by the heavy use of reversals in the imagery going forward.

So, these are the four basic steps for building a literal highway, but God isn't talking about a literal highway. That is just a metaphor for preparing the way for His people to return to Him. So, how do these four highway-building steps translate into comforting and restoring a people? Let's walk through each step and talk about them in a human context.

The lifting-up: Lifting up those in "the valleys"—low in spirit—is a bit of a no-brainer. How do you lift up a person who is struggling and in need of comfort?

The tearing-down: This seems like an unlikely step in the process. These people are already oppressed and in despair. Why would they need to be torn down further?

When people suffer long-term abuse or oppression, they build defensive walls mentally, emotionally, and even physically to cope with the hurt. A self-righteous attitude and a victim mentality often lurk behind those walls. These walls can prevent them from being comforted and healed, and the LORD may need to strip away false sources of empowerment and comfort in the victim's life before He can begin the healing process.

The straightening of crooked places: What does a "crooked place" describe in the human experience? How does crookedness manifest itself?

We have all heard of people who are crooks. The same imagery applies to crooked places. The Hebrew words for "crooked" describes twisted or perverted ways or something deceitful, sly, or fraudulent.

That is a simplistic definition, but I think it is more than that. In my mind, I think of a crooked place as being caught in a maze. You start down one path, only to hit a wall, and then you have to make a decision as to which way to turn. That decision brings you to another wall or, worse, a dead end, and then you have to retrace your steps and try another way. Every decision you make leads you deeper into the maze until you are disoriented, lost, and completely frustrated. That describes being in a crooked place and how we get into it. It has to do a lot with how we make decisions, and pursuing sinful paths that lead us off of God's way, resulting in compromised lifestyles, bad coping habits, and skewed perceptions and/or values. Once we get off the path, everything gets twisted. Straightening our crooked places requires realigning with God's values and vision, turning from sin, and returning to the straight highway.

The smoothing of rough-going: This is where the command to remove the stumbling blocks comes into play. What are stumbling blocks? Stumbling blocks can be reactions to abuse or oppression that add to the oppression. They can even perpetuate oppression even after the oppressor is out of the picture. They keep a person from moving forward in life and prevent healing, reconciliation, and restoration of relationships. They also keep a person from being able to accept comfort when it is offered. Some examples of stumbling blocks are fear, despair, self-pity, anger, and shame, but we will find more in the coming chapters.

This is God's highway project. As we work through Isaiah 40–66, we will be looking at the LORD's model in how He lifts up, what things He tears down or challenges, how He remedies crooked places, what stumbling blocks He addresses, and how He goes about the process in general. We will consider how He achieves His goals of ending the fight and dealing with sin and compare those to the world's way of pursuing an end to oppression. And then we will take some strategies from His model over how to experience comfort for ourselves and offer comfort to other broken people.

Questions for further exploration:

- We know that John the Baptist was the "voice crying in the wilderness." How did his ministry illustrate these steps in God's Highway Project? Read Luke 3:7-18.

- Stumbling blocks are a particular topic in both the Old and New Testaments. Read through the following verses and think about how stumbling blocks come about: Isaiah 8:14-15, Ezekiel 3:20, Romans 9:32-33, Romans 14:13, 1 Corinthians 8:9, and 1 John 2:9-11.

LESSON 2

The Comfort of Empowerment

READ

Isaiah 40:6-31

DISCUSSION

Empowerment is a huge topic in our culture today. In an effort to level the playing field for marginalized or victimized people, we have adopted an almost universal message that "we" support them, encourage them, and will seek to make special allowance for them. That message is blasted across social media, and it is part of marketing messages for everything from little girls' shirts to major social movements. The all-inclusive "we" makes it sound as if all of society embraces this messaging and goal, lending a sense of gravitas and power to the movement. Let's see what God has to say about it.

Isaiah 40:6-8

God opened Isaiah 40 with the resounding command, *"Comfort My people!"* The voice crying in the wilderness then forwarded the message to the prophet, saying, *"Cry out!"* to which the prophet responds, *"What shall I cry?"* The voice in the wilderness replies, "Tell them they are going to die."

> *"... All flesh is grass, and all its loveliness is like the flower of the field. The grass withers, the flower fades, because the breath of the LORD blows upon it; Surely the people are grass. The grass withers, the flower fades, but the word of our God stands forever."* – Isaiah 40:6-8

Is that comforting, being told you are going to die?

No, of course not! This seems like a counter-intuitive message when comforting someone who is struggling, but let's consider it for a moment.

> **Q:** What does it mean to be like grass?
>
> **Q:** To what does God contrast flesh's fleeting condition?
>
> **Q:** This is supposed to be comforting, but there is little comfort in being told that you are frail and going to die. Why would it be necessary for God to establish this contrast between "all flesh" and His word as a first step?
>
> **Q:** When we comfort someone, why is it important to remember that we, too, are grass?

I'll share my answer to the last question and pose a fictitious scenario for an example. (This is not anyone's particular story but scraps of experiences I have gleaned from others.) Let's say I work with a woman who is depressed to the point of despair. I see her crying in the breakroom one day and ask her what is wrong, thinking I might have a word of comfort for her. Then she tells me her story. Her husband is talking about leaving her. They have marriage problems that are being aggravated by huge financial debts that they incurred some years before when the husband lost his previous job due to his anger issues. He is struggling to make ends meet by working two part-time jobs, and he is taking his stress out on her verbally and physically. She is facing the fear of being cut off from her home and children, and that she will not have the means of supporting herself if he should divorce her. Her current job is only a part-time position with few benefits. The woman is hurting physically and emotionally, hopelessly caught in a crooked place, and desperately looking for a way out.

I listen to this, and I am overwhelmed. I think about trying to support myself on my own paycheck if my own husband left me and immediately sympathize with her fear. Clearly the problems between her and her husband need intervention, but I am not a marriage counselor, nor do I have any means of relieving their financial debts or her husband's stress. I am in no position to promise her any physical support should her husband leave her. She will need financial help, personal counseling, and long-term physical and emotional support to which I cannot commit because my own resources are limited. (What I don't know is that she has turned to alcohol as a means of coping with her situation and her addiction has added to the strain with her husband.)

As I listen to her story, I quickly come to the realization that I am powerless to do anything to remedy her situation or relieve her despair. I can't tell her everything will be all right, because it won't. Any comfort I can give her will be fleeting at best and sadly insufficient. And yet her plight moves me deeply, and I sympathize with her to the extent that I myself now feel frustrated and hopeless.

That powerless feeling is God telling me that I am grass.

We have all felt powerless at some point in life. We may even feel it now with all the chaos besetting our country, our communities, or our families. Before we can even begin to minister to others who are feeling powerless, we should assess how we ourselves respond to powerlessness.

> **Q:** So, how do you personally respond to feeling powerless?
>
> **Q:** Where do you seek support and comfort?

When that feeling of powerlessness hits, it is almost a knee-jerk reaction to immediately seek the next higher power to deal with the oppression. What higher powers do we seek to help ourselves or our struggling person escape the oppression? Let's spin out some what-ifs and consider where we might turn for help in these cases.

> **What if** we feel we need physical strength to fight back against an abuser, like a bully on a playground or home invaders, for instance?
>
> Maybe we take lessons from a self-defense expert. Maybe we arm ourselves with a weapon. Maybe we empower ourselves with group support, like a neighborhood watch.
>
> **What if** the problem is in our inter-personal relationships?
>
> Maybe we seek self-help books, psychologists, doctors, marriage counselors, or financial or spiritual advisors to help us with other problems.
>
> **What if** the problem requires intervention from someone with more legal authority?

Maybe we appeal to our justice system or social media (social media has become a platform for social justice in this generation). Maybe we join advocacy groups and promote awareness of the problem on a public platform.

> **Q:** The sight of protesters holding up signs and demonstrating in the streets (more or less peacefully) has become a common sight in this age. Has heightened awareness and public protest solved the problem, or has it created more oppression?

What if the problem is bigger and community or state authorities aren't effective?

Maybe we expect national leaders to relieve us of oppression and secure victim's rights at a governmental level, and so we elect leadership based on the promises they make to marginalized or victimized people groups. (As we move toward socialism, there is an increasing demand on government to support all the people's needs and be the "savior.")

> **Q:** Is the government the solution to oppression, or does it create more oppression?

What if we face a national threat?

Nations turn to nations for help with wars. Israel has historically sought allies not unlike the United States for help, but what happens when a generation of leaders turns ambivalent or even antagonistic toward her? Allies didn't help her much with Babylonia.

It is not a bad thing to look to these sources for help. But you have to understand that, ultimately, they are all grass. They may help in one instance but not another. Their help may be fleeting and insufficient to deal with the problem. They may not be able to help at all.

What if these human-based power sources are still too weak or unreliable? What other power sources are out there?

In Israel's day, the world's power source lay in the imagined power of its idols, and Israel joined in that idolatry. They took God's creation, recreated it into what they wanted God to be, and then invested their created image with imagined power. But there is an alternative to idolatry and the occult, right? There is God.

This is the big question:

Q: What do we want God to be in our circumstances?

Isaiah 40:9-11

After spending three appropriately short verses on the mortality and fleetingness of man, the message then continues for twenty-six verses on the eternality and incomparable power of God. Israel is commanded to get up to the mountains and lift up her voice to proclaim the good tidings, beginning with the roar, "Behold your God!"

Q: In verses 10-11, what comfort is in the grand picture that God paints of Himself?

Verse 10 contains one of our opening inclusio themes: *"Behold, His reward is with Him, and His work before Him."* It will be easier to understand the role of the reward when we get to the end of the journey, so I will save the discussion of it for a future chapter. It is, in essence, God's way of providing justice and closure for the abused and abuser alike.

Isaiah 40:12-17

God now makes a series of rhetorical "who" questions.

Q: What qualities of Himself does God highlight with these questions?

Q: What value do "the nations" possess that God matches against Himself?

Q: What is God challenging with these rhetorical questions?

Having established who He is, God then begins to tear down all the power sources that Israel has set up for herself apart from Him. (These go back to our previous what-ifs.) He says, behold the nations. Your allies are powerless. Your government and justice system are worthless. Your leaders are powerless. They are all grass. (Lebanon is known for its mighty cedars which are used figuratively in Scripture as a metaphor for mighty leaders. In God's eyes, even these are grass.)

Stop for a moment and picture in your mind's eye our world today. Think of all the nations that are raging and battling one another, all the resources being diverted from one country to another in support of alliances, all the protests raging on college campuses and in our communities over claims of injustice. Fighting, fighting, fighting, everywhere—and all in pursuit of power. Now look at them from God's eyes. Do they hold any power?

Isaiah 40:18-26

God then asks, *"To whom then will you liken Me?"* and begins to address the power that Israel has sought from a spiritual realm. He tells Israel that her idols are grass, the same as her princes and judges. He blows on them and, poof, they are gone.

> **Q:** If idols, as defined here in Isaiah, refer to sources of power on which people rely for strength or prosperity, then what things does our current culture "idolize" as their source(s) of power?

Isaiah 40:27-31

And what is Israel's response in verse 27 to this glorious picture of her incomparable God? She appeals to an unknown audience in her social media channels, "God doesn't see my plight. I have been victimized! I have a just claim, but He has passed over it." Perhaps that is her rationale for seeking other power sources besides Him.

> **Q:** Do we feel like this in the midst of struggles, that the LORD doesn't see us? That He isn't doing anything on our behalf?

> **Q:** Who are some of the "unheard" victims in our communities today, as our current culture defines them?

Victims can become the target for the world's "empowerment" messaging. God fires back with His own empowerment message with more rhetorical questions. Have you not known? Have you not heard? How can you say this, knowing what you know about Me? Notice that He is challenging Israel to step away from the emotional response and take a rational view (by the way, this is an important first step in comforting someone—breaking them away from purely emotional responses).

When you feel powerless because the greater authority isn't addressing your claim, there is the desire to seek another means of empowerment. We are comparing God and the world in this chapter. Even the secular world will agree that to end oppression, you need power. It is all about the power. Empowerment has become a catch word in our modern culture.

    Q: How does God empower His people?

The fact is that God's people really don't have to do anything to get that power except believe that He has the power to save them, and then wait for Him. But do they believe He has the power? That is the crux of the problem for Israel, initially. For those of you who are parents, consider your own children. When they come running to you in tears because of a bully on the playground or they have fallen and skinned their knee, the fact that they run to you first and not someone else is an acknowledgment of their belief that you have the power and authority to fix the problem. God's children aren't running to Him. He has to fight just to get them to acknowledge that He has the ability to save them. For the next eight chapters, He will build a case for His power and His superior ability to save them.

Now, let's dig deeper into this lesson's theme.

GOD'S HIGHWAY PROJECT

The Comfort of Empowerment

    Q: God opens with a declaration of His omnipotence (power) and omniscience (wisdom, far-sightedness), but mostly His power. Why His power and not His love? Wouldn't love be more comforting?

    Q: Does the fact that God doesn't lead with love when comforting people challenge a perception we have of Him? What do we want Him to be in our circumstances: a God of power or a God of love?

    Q: What is the world's response when we present Him as a God of power?

    Q: In verse 9, God commands His people to get up to the mountains and lift their voice with strength to declare the good news.

Knowing that we are grass and only God can truly effect change, when we begin to minister to a person who is suffering or caught in a crooked place in life, what is the "empowering" message we need to communicate to them?

God's sovereignty and power are the focus for Part 1. We will see how He makes the case for His ability to save His people in the next seven chapters.

PART 1

NARRATIVE STRUCTURE

Part 1 covers Isaiah 40–48, but the first chapter is broken out as an introductory chapter. At the end of Isaiah 40, Israel brings a charge against God for not hearing her plight. Beginning in Isaiah 41, God responds by calling everyone, victim and oppressor alike, to the heavenly courtroom to hear their arguments. The opening and closing arguments of the chiastic structure span Isaiah 41-48, and mirror around the central figure of Cyrus, who is commissioned in Isaiah 45.

Chiastic Structure of Part 1 (Isaiah 41-48)

Opening Arguments

1a: Deliverance promised (41:1–42:25)

2a: Israel called as God's faithful witness (43:1-13)

3a: The judgment of Babylon promised (43:14-15)

4a: Do not remember the former things; a new thing (43:16-21)

5a: The burden of serving God; the effort of making idols (43:22-44:22)

6a: God as national savior for Israel (44:24-28)

    7: The commissioning of Cyrus (45:1-17)

Closing Arguments

6b: God as universal savior for the world (45:18-25)

5b: The burden of serving idols (46:1-8)

4b: Remember the former things; a new thing (46:9-13)

3b: The judgment of Babylon rendered (47:1-15)

2b: Israel rebuked as a treacherous witness (48:1-11)

1b: Deliverance accomplished (48:12-22)

LESSON 3

The Power of Fear

READ

Isaiah 41:1-20

DISCUSSION

Israel is in physical bondage to her Babylonian oppressors, but in Isaiah 41, God will address another, less tangible oppressor in her experience, and that is fear. Fear is more emotion than substance and yet no less powerful. Fear is a tool that oppressors use to gain and keep power, but fear has power in its own right and can be an oppressor even after the physical oppressor is overcome. Fear is the first stumbling block, and it can only be overcome by an understanding of God's power and sovereignty over the lives of His people.

Isaiah 41:1-4

Isaiah 40 ended with Israel's charge against God for ignoring her just claim like a judge who refused to help a victim. In response, God now begins to build a case for Himself. He has not forgotten Israel. He has both the sovereignty and power to save her, and He has a plan, if she will only wait on Him. He has promised to empower her, and He begins by giving her a voice.

In Isaiah 41:1, God calls His courtroom to order with a rebuke to the noisy coastlands who are drowning out the testimony of the victim. Let the victim be heard!

The victim's cry for a voice resounds in our culture today.

    Q: Why is being given a voice important to a victim?

> **Q:** Having one's plight go unacknowledged contributes to a victim's fear, but just because they are given a voice, does that relieve the fear?

As we will see with Israel, being given a voice can be a two-edged sword when the LORD calls everyone to the judgment seat and begins to examine her case.

God then tells both Israel and "the coastlands" His plan for the near future. In verses 2-4, He asks another series of rhetorical "who" questions as He announces the as-yet unnamed deliverer who He will raise up to deal with Babylon. The coastlands represent the outermost extremities of the nations under Babylonian rule—the totality of the empire from coast to coast. What He plans to do will rock the entire civilized world. We know from history that the deliverer mentioned in verses 2-3 would be Cyrus, King of Persia, who would conquer the Babylonian empire, set Israel free from her exile, and send her home to Jerusalem (at least as many Israelites as would choose to go). The announcement gives few details about this deliverer, but it does describe him as a *tsedek*, a righteous one, in verse 2, which is a discordant note. Most Bible translations don't include the word "righteous" in the verse, but it is the meaning of the original Hebrew word. It describes a man who is upright and on a straight path, and Cyrus does indeed plow a path straight through Babylonia with the LORD's help.

God then caps His grand prophecy with an "I AM" statement. "I, the LORD, am the first; and with the last I am He" (Isaiah 41:4b). He will make this statement two more times in Part 1 (Isaiah 44:6, 48:12) where He is making a case for His sovereignty and power.

Isaiah 41:5-7

The coastlands have a reaction to God's declaration: They fear. To combat their fear, they immediately turn to "empowering" one another with bold words and bolstering themselves with their idols. This is how the world comforts itself when it is afraid.

> **Q:** In our generation, we have seen what happens when something that is beyond human control or containment sparks a world-wide panic. (I speak of the COVID-19 outbreak.) What actions did the world take to combat the panic and fear?

> **Q:** To what idols (perceived sources of power) did the world turn for help and comfort?
>
> **Q:** Did the world's reaction relieve the oppression or create more oppression?
>
> **Q:** What other societal issues sprang up from trying to combat the threat according to the world's way? What was the ripple effect of isolation, for instance?

Isaiah 41:8-20

While all the coastlands are running around in a panic and appealing to their perceived power sources for comfort and a solution, God commands Israel, "Fear not." That imperative is repeated three times in this chapter (Isaiah 41:10, 13, 14), making it the theme for the passage.

> **Q:** Why would God tell Israel not to fear when He announces He is sending a deliverer? Isn't that a reason to rejoice?

We know first-hand just how easy it is to get caught up in an oppressor's panic. It is even more terrifying when the source of the panic has been occasioned by our God. God said that He would help His people if they would just wait for His solution to unfold.

Waiting. That is the hardest part. When it seems like nothing is happening, uncertainty creeps in and brings fear with it, and fear breeds a whole new host of problems.

> **Q:** How does God stem Israel's fear in verses 8-20? What promises does He make?

God begins by establishing who He is to Israel. She is His servant, His chosen one. He has not cast her away. She needs the reassurance of her relationship with Him because that relationship comes with promises of His strengthening, His help, His provision, and, perhaps sweetest of all, His vindication. He does not downplay Israel's powerlessness or her victimization. He answers it with His own power. Her enemies are nothing more than grass before Him, and He is going to cut them down.

Is there comfort in knowing that the abusive, overbearing person in your life, who seems so strong and holds such power over you, is just as fragile as you are? There can be, if we can see them through God's eyes. They may persecute us now, that persecution will end. There will come a day when they contend with our God, and their fury will be nothing compared to His fury. And when their day is over, they will lose a kingdom where we will gain one. But we have to endure the wait.

The waiting period is where the power of fear can grow.

The imagery in verses 17-20 should remind Israel of another time in their history when the LORD provided for them like this, namely, their exodus from Egypt. He spurs their memory of His faithfulness to them in the past and promises these things in the future so that they might *"see and know, and consider and understand together, that the hand of the LORD has done this..."* (41:20) Fear feeds on emotion. To battle the fear, God calls Israel to break away from the emotion and exercise reasoning instead. What do they know of God? What has He done for them in the past? Is He able to do it again in the future?

Isaiah 41:21-29

God lifts Israel up with this reassurance of His power, but how can she experience it when she has turned to her idols for power? In the second half of the passage, God calls her to the stand to present her case and her reasons for turning to her idols, and then brings His own charge against her. He tells Israel, I gave you a prophetic vision of how I intend to remedy your situation. Can your idols do the same? Can they tell you what will come? Give Me one example of how your idols predicted something and then it came to pass. Of course, they cannot.

Again, in verse 25, He repeats the prophecy of the coming deliverer. I will add it here in the New International Version which catches the gist better:

> *"I have stirred up one from the north, and he comes—one from the rising sun [that is, the east] who calls on my name. He treads on rulers as if they were mortar, as if he were a potter treading the clay."*
> – Isaiah 41:25 NIV

Prophecy is the ultimate test of godship. If these alternate sources of power cannot predict the future, they cannot control it. Where, then, is their power? Idolatry is futile.

And what does Israel say to God's charge against her? Nothing.

Now let's dig deeper into this lesson's theme.

GOD'S HIGHWAY PROJECT

The Power of Fear

Fear is the first reaction that God needs to address because it is a monstrous stumbling block to overcome, particularly when trying to comfort someone. First of all, it affects decision-making. It can drive a person to make bad decisions when trying to escape the abuse. It can also keep the person in an abusive relationship for fear of not having needful things like food, housing, a source of income, and medical help. It can keep victims from speaking up, and so the oppression continues. Fear is a tool that oppressors use to rule us.

Think about your own life.

> **Q:** Has fear ever kept you from speaking the truth or doing something that you know you should do?
>
> **Q:** Has fear ever caused you to do something you know you shouldn't do?
>
> **Q:** Has fear led you into a life of coping and compromise (a crooked place)? Coping doesn't relieve the oppression. It just perpetuates it.
>
> **Q:** What happens when a fearful person or group of people are also the ones in power? (For example, a child living with fearful parents, or citizens living in a nation run by fearful leaders.) What does life become under the leadership of fearful people?

I can speak to that with some experience. My mother (who is now with the LORD) was my oppressive person in life. I will temper my criticism of her and grant her some grace and forgiveness because I know something of her horrific childhood experience, but at the same time, I consider the legacy that her fear left in my life. Here is my story:

> *My mother had a very scarring and unstable childhood. When she was seven years old, her father died of cancer, leaving her and her sister*

with a mentally unstable mother who moved the family around from relative's house to relative's house. She suffered neglect at her mother's hand. Her mother often turned her out of the house and left her to fend for herself. She had to steal food at times to eat. Eventually, her mother gave her away to an adoptive couple. (Her mother only gave her away, not her sister.) Her adoptive parents were oppressive and abusive, and she didn't escape them until she married my father. But even then, they plagued her, and she actually came to the point of suicide one day, and it was only the fact that she had a little baby to care for that kept her from going through with it. It was at that point that she gave her life to Christ. This was her coming-of-age experience. It made her a very fearful person, and that fear ruled her all of her life.

Once she was married and master of her own family to a certain extent, she took back power over her life with a vengeance. She became a very strict, controlling person who clung to her husband and children with an iron grip. When she hit relationship obstacles in life, she would withdraw. Eventually she withdrew from social life altogether and lived vicariously through her children. But all her effort to control her world so that it would be safe and secure for her never relieved the fear, and she only ended up frustrating her family. She was a believer, a strong believer, and yet she failed to grasp this aspect of God's power. She put more faith in her own power and control over her world than she did in God, and it gave her no comfort.

This is my personal experience with a fearful person, and it helped me understand the ripple effects that fear creates. It affects all of our relationships, but most of all, it affects our witness for God.

Q: What are we saying about our God when we let fear rule us?

Fear doesn't just affect the individual person. It is socially contagious. It is hard not to be afraid when the entire world is running around in a panic and demanding that we act upon their fear.

Q: Think of our world today. What are some of the fears that have beset us culturally?

For the sake of discussion, let's use climate change as an example. I understand it is a divisive issue, and I will say up-front that I absolutely believe we should be good stewards of God's creation. That was part of Adam and Eve's original calling, and it is our responsibility as well. Part of the reason God sent Israel into exile is because she did not give the land its Sabbath rest so that it could renew itself. But in our current generation, fear has entered into our concern for our physical world to the point where, for instance, some people have decided not to have children because they fear we are destroying our earth.

Q: What are some other way this fear has begun to dictate how we now live?

Q: Have our efforts to stop climate change relieved our fear? Why or why not?

Q: How has our fear affected the next generation?

Q: How do we comfort a young person who is gripped by a fear of climate change?

This is where an understanding of God's sovereignty is vital. The earth is God's creation, not man's. As He demonstrated with Israel here in Isaiah, He acts on behalf of His creation when man abuses it. We also know from the book of Revelation that in the future He will also destroy His creation in response to an idolatrous generation. He is sovereign over His creation, and He displays His sovereignty through His handling of His creation.

When humans take the power of creatorship away from God and exalt themselves as creators of their environment, we cross a line, and we know we have crossed a line because fear has now entered the experience. Any time fear enters an experience, that is a red flag that something is wrong in the power dynamic because fear is an unspoken admission of powerlessness. People who feel powerless over something often react to that powerlessness by trying to take back control and assume a level of power or authority that they do not have. Fear can also come about when they have given idolatrous power and authority to something (or someone) that they shouldn't. This is just my opinion, but I think the fear of climate change has gripped the world largely because the world no longer acknowledges God as having sovereign power over His creation.

Fear Not

When all the world is afraid, that is when God's people cannot show fear. When we let the world's fear rule us, we deny the power of our God and His sovereignty over us. To the unbelieving world, we are saying our God isn't big enough, strong enough, resourceful enough, or even faithful enough to deal with our circumstances. When we fear, we take God's power from Him, and we lose the opportunity to show the unbelieving world His power in action. We lose our witness.

Fear is a stumbling block especially in battle, whether a physical battle or spiritual one. Did you know that, according to the Mosaic Law, fear is a reason to be exempted from battle? Deuteronomy 20:8 says:

> *"The officers shall speak further to the people, and say, 'What man is there who is fearful and fainthearted? Let him go and return to his house, lest the heart of his brethren faint like his heart.'"* – Deuteronomy 20:8

God doesn't want fearful people fighting for Him. Fearful people will bail in the middle of the fight, and they will take others with them because fear is contagious. God had a purpose for sending Israel into Babylonia, and He has a purpose for sending us into persecutions and trials—to refine us but also to use us as His witnesses. When we are in the midst of that battle, the natural fear reactions of fight or flight will kick in but without the control needed for a believer to accomplish God's objective in the circumstances. God needs His people to identify with His power and act with control according to His direction. We have to embrace the bigger picture of God working with us through these trials if we are going to prevail in the spiritual battle. Fear should never exempt a believer from the battle.

Let's bring this back to comforting fear in others.

> **Q:** When we are trying to comfort a fearful person, how do we do this, using God's model here with Israel? What do we need to communicate to them to help them combat their fear?

There is a **key verse** from the New Testament that I want us to remember as we deal with the stumbling block of fear.

"For God has not given us a spirit of fear, but of power and of love and of a sound mind." – 2 Timothy 1:7

The words of Isaiah go hand in hand with this verse. Isaiah 40-48 fleshes out the power aspect in dealing with fear. Isaiah 49-57 will flesh out the love aspect. But through all these chapters there will be the resounding challenge to see, hear, know, understand, and believe so that our decisions will be made from a sound mind, not fueled by fleeting emotion. Remember God's original comparison of what is fleeting and what is eternal. Human emotion is also like grass. It grows and fades from moment to moment and season to season. We will keep this verse in mind as we continue through this study.

LESSON 4

The False Comfort of Partiality

READ

Isaiah 42:1-25

DISCUSSION

Isaiah 42 focuses on a comfort for which all victims of abuse and oppression cry out, and that is justice. But justice can be defined very differently depending on the eyes through which it is viewed. Justice should be blind in the sense of being impartial, and it is when it is administered according to God's truth. But the scales of judgment can lose their sense of balance when they deviate from truth and begin to judge from the eyes of the victim. Then another kind of blindness sets in, the blindness of partiality.

Isaiah 42:1-9

Isaiah 41 concluded with a scathing rebuke to Israel concerning the futility of idolatry: *"Indeed [Hebrew: hen], they are worthless..."* The Hebrew word, *hen*, can also be translated as behold, see, or look. Isaiah 42 now opens with the same word, *hen* or behold, only this time we are told to look at a new figure who is a contrast to the idols of the previous chapter. The LORD now announces the coming of another deliverer known only as the Servant (Note: this is not Cyrus this time).

The Servant's character and purpose are described in much more detail than Cyrus. He has the Spirit of God upon Him, and His overarching task is to bring justice and light to the Gentiles—and, seemingly, only the Gentiles. They are curiously singled out. If we filter that statement through the eyes of the victim, Israel, it would seem that this deliverer is coming to give her oppressors a serious comeuppance, and yet His manner and actions have none of the forcefulness that a conqueror would display. Quite the opposite. It is a bit of a conundrum.

We know from the gospel accounts that the Servant figure will be realized as Jesus Christ (Matthew 12:15-21, Luke 2:25-32), but here, in Isaiah, Israel only has a picture without a name put to it. And in many respects, the "Servant" describes herself—maybe not the real her, but the ideal her. We saw her called this in the last chapter, and it is repeated throughout Isaiah. The tasks listed here are some of the same tasks with which she was originally commissioned. From her beginning, God called her out of all the nations to be the keeper and administrator of His Law and the intercessor for the people. So, she sees herself in this role. You might question me about that premise, but look at Paul's words in Romans 2, which we will get to in a moment. This is her historical view of herself. As noted in my Tanahk (Jewish Study Bible), Jewish scholars who have rejected Jesus say that this "Servant" is referring to corporate Israel. They imagine that this Servant is the embodiment of Israel—her ideal form (which He is in a way). So, when the LORD calls the "Servant" to be the light to the Gentiles, or when He says, *"I have called you in righteousness and will give you as a covenant to the people"* (42:6), it is tempting for Israel to cast herself into that self-righteous role.

These are the task of the Servant in verses 1-7. He will bring forth justice to the Gentiles. He will bring forth justice with firmness, faithfulness, and truth with the goal of establishing peace, security, and stability (that is the full meaning behind the Hebrew phrasing in verse 3). And He will not be discouraged. He can do this because He is invested with the authority of God Himself and is the embodiment of God's covenant to the people. He will be the light—a light to the Gentiles, the one who opens blind eyes and sets prisoners free from the bondage of their darkness.

> **Q:** What does it mean to be a light to someone?
>
> **Q:** The Servant will come specifically as a light to the Gentiles—the oppressors. Why single out the Gentiles?
>
> **Q:** Who has blind eyes—Israel or the Gentiles?
>
> **Q:** Who are the prisoners sitting in darkness—Israel or the Gentiles?

If we were to look at the Servant's tasking from captive Israel's perspective, I imagine she would see herself as the literal prisoner, but not necessarily the blind, since the light is for the Gentiles and not herself. In spite of her current circumstances, she still considers herself the "enlightened" one because of her historical calling. There is comfort for her in that identity. Regardless of how badly off she is, she is still superior to the Gentiles. You can categorize people by how you perceive them in comparison to yourself.

> **Q:** Just because a person is victimized, does that mean they see the issue clearly? Why or why not?

Can oppressors be in bondage with their victims? Certainly. Consider also that bondage is not just physical but spiritual as well. Oppressors may not be the ones in physical bondage, but they can be in bondage in a spiritual sense. Israel's blindness is also spiritually sourced. Being sunk in idolatry, she sees nothing clearly, least of all her own condition.

So, we have now introduced the spiritual side of the Servant's work. This isn't just about releasing Israel from physical bondage. It is about releasing her from her blindness to her condition and realigning everyone, Jew and Gentile, equally under God's law.

The Servant's task is to establish justice in the earth. Thinks about that for a moment. Think about the scope of that task, just within our own country. Here in the United States, we might not live under the brutality of an oppressive third-world regime or country beset by open warfare, but our justice system, for all of its sophistication, is broken. We see evidence of it on the news every day. Our societal values have so shifted that they have tipped the scales of justice unequally. Some people are victimized continually while other offenders are allowed to run rampant with impunity. Social movements have risen in response to unaddressed offenses, but freedom of speech is a right given to some but not others. In recent years, illegal immigrants have been given equal if not more rights than citizens (I speak during the upheaval of 2025 in the U.S.); and corruption, fraud, trafficking, violent protests, and all manner of crimes are rampant. The justice system turns a blind eye to this and often shackles those who have the ability to do something about it. We are systemically broken. We are in a crooked place.

Straightening crooked places is one of the tasks of God's Highway Project. So, what would it take to reestablish justice? I guess that depends on your definition of justice and on what you are basing it.

> **Q:** Is justice accomplished simply by lifting up the victims and treading down oppressors, or does that just tip the scales in the other direction?
>
> **Q:** How is equity different from equality?
>
> **Q:** What is needed to reestablish a balanced justice system?

You cannot have balanced justice without a set of values for a guide. You need a universal law, as mentioned in verse 4. Establishing that law would require a person with sufficient authority to enforce the law and remove the corrupted officials who refuse to administer the law rightly. Above all, it would require impartiality and the treatment of all people equally and all crimes with consistency and fair values.

The fact that the justice seems only for the Gentiles lays a foundation for some prejudice and self-righteousness here. As Israel sees it, this applies to them, not her. This kind of justice pits victim against oppressor with each side seeking to tip the scales in their favor. It doesn't end the fighting, which is God's overall objective, but rather promotes vengeance and punitive actions. It doesn't bring peace or security or stability. It doesn't heal anything for the victim. It can, in fact, turn the abused into the abusers by empowering them. I will come back to this in minute, but first let's finish the chapter.

The LORD has put this picture of His superior Servant and the sufficiency of His work up against the picture of Israel's futile idols whose work is worthless. Here, in verses 8-9, the LORD wraps up the comparison with the summary statement about His own Godship in His ability to predict the future. He points to the former things, which are the events in history that bear witness of His works and provide proof of His Godship. And now the new things—the prophecies—will be fulfilled in the future.

Isaiah 42:10-12

Surprisingly, the coming of this Servant is a reason for the Gentiles to sing. In verses 10-12, we see the anthem of praise begin at the ends of the earth, in the sea and all that is in it, then the coastlands, the desert wilderness (we are working our way inland), up to the tops of the mountains. The earth is filled with praise at the coming of the Servant and heralds His coming like the coming of a king. It is quite the opposite reaction from the fear expressed back in Isaiah 41:5-7.

Isaiah 42:13-17

Having summoned His Servant, the LORD embarks on His highway project with zeal. He paints two pictures of Himself: The mighty man of war and a woman in labor. So, here is a riddle for you . . .

> **Q:** How is a woman in labor like a mighty man of war? (Any woman who has borne children will probably chuckle at the battle analogy.) It's a bloody effort for both woman and warrior, but to what end?

The LORD begins His work by clearing the path of everything. He lays low the mountains and hills. He clears the vegetation. He dries up the waters so there is dry ground. And then He leads out the blind.

Back in verses 6-7, the Gentiles were the blind ones. Who is the blind now in verse 16? Israel. Israel is the one who the LORD is leading by the hand in paths that she has not known. Israel is the one who needs the darkness made light for her. Those who had once been the enlightened law-givers are the ones who need their crooked places (literally, their perverse ways) straightened. Isn't that a slap alongside the head! God singled out the oppressors as being the blind ones in need of law and light, but now it is the victim herself whom God judges as being equally destitute. That's the thing about God's law. It is impartial. Both sides are judged and both are found lacking.

Verse 17 says that the ones who trusted in idols are turned back and ashamed. The Hebrew word for "turned back" doesn't mean repent in this case. It means to be driven back or to draw back in heart. They recoil at this judgment. They don't want to hear it.

Isaiah 42:18-25

God expands on Israel's prejudicial self-righteousness with a sharp rebuke. He calls her very bluntly the deaf and the blind. She has become as unresponsive to Him as the Gentiles at whose hand she suffers, and as a result, she is blind to her own condition. We can run across a similar mentality when comforting someone. In a victim's mind, the blame for their situation is very often laid solely on the oppressor. It is the other person's fault. God corrects Israel's thinking in verses 23-25.

Q: Who gave her over to the Babylonians, and why?

Israel was supposed to be the law-keeper who established His justice, but she is as much the backslider as the Gentiles. She has no reason to think herself better than the Gentiles. If she herself is blind and cannot break her own bondage, she is incapable of being a light and lawgiver to the Gentiles around her. This puts to rest the notion that corporate Israel is the Servant in verses 1-7. The apostle Paul rebukes the Jews in his day with this same observation in Romans 2:17-24.

The Servant, who we know is Jesus Christ, is the individual who the LORD will raise up in the future to establish His law and His justice, but He will come to save all nations, Israel and the Gentiles together. And the fact that He will come not just to right things for Israel but for all the nations is cause to sing, at least from the nations' perspective. Previously, in verses 10-12, the Gentiles' reaction to the LORD shedding light on their condition was to sing and rejoice and embrace the coming Servant. Israel's reaction is a stark contrast. In verse 17, she recoils and is ashamed. In verse 25, she does not take the lesson to heart. She doesn't do any self-assessment.

Isn't it curious that while the coastlands—the Gentile world—rejoices at the Servant's law and justice, Israel herself recoils from it? She shuts her ears and eyes. She wants God to lift her up and show her partiality, which He will do but not without judging her own actions as well.

GOD'S HIGHWAY PROJECT

This chapter brings together three entwined themes: light (which is figurative of enlightenment), justice, and partiality. The light is the source of enlightenment upon which judgment and justice depend. Partiality masquerades as an enlightened point of view when, in fact, it darkens the light, skews judgment and justice, and undermines the comfort that the cleansing light was meant to bring.

We began this study with the comparison between the fleetingness and instability of flesh compared to the enduring qualities of God's word (His light), so let's consider the contrasting sources of light first.

Light and Enlightenment: The World vs. God

The establishment of justice begins with a foundation on a central, universal truth—the light which allows for clear sight, discernment, and right judgment. God's Servant and His word are true sources of light and enlightenment, but the world, Israel included, has historically sought its comfort in human sources of enlightenment apart from God.

In Isaiah's day, the Torah (Mosaic Law) was supposed to be the preeminent source of enlightenment for Israel, but she corrupted the administration of that justice. Her administrators believed that they were the superior "enlightened" ruling class that wielded the laws as they saw fit and could dictate their version of social norms even when they failed to uphold God's rules and values. And the community followed them blindly and fearfully. As a result of having closed her eyes to God's "enlightenment," the nation of Israel found herself among the deaf and blind prisoners sitting in darkness.

The pursuit of enlightenment has long spurred the intellectual and philosophical movements on the Gentile side as well. History has seen the philosophy schools of early Greece, the Renaissance, and the "Age of Enlightenment" in Europe in the 17th and 18th centuries. During the Age of Enlightenment, the ideas of tolerance, the superiority of science, and the separation of church and state got their foothold. These movements embraced knowledge, reason, and truth (apart from God) as the power by which humans improve their own condition. In our own modern generation, we are seeing the pursuit of a new form of "enlightened" or "woke" thinking that is less about logic, reason, or even factual truth, and more about adopting a set of social values that weigh justice in favor of marginalized people and the victim's "just claim." And justice is no longer something for just the courts to decide. Social media platforms increasingly serve as both judge and jury for social justice issues.

> **Q:** How have these things created a kind of blindness and deafness in our society?

The False Comfort of Partiality

The reason God has put Israel in prison is because she has perverted His justice and allowed herself to be blinded by bribery and partiality. The LORD commanded His people not to show partiality; and when they do, there are consequences. Here are a few verses:

> *"You shall not show partiality to a poor man in his dispute."* – Exodus 23:3

> *"You shall not show partiality in judgment; you shall hear the small as well as the great; you shall not be afraid in any man's presence, for the judgment is God's . . ."* – Deuteronomy 1:17

> *"You shall not pervert justice; you shall not show partiality, nor take a bribe, for a bribe blinds the eyes of the wise and twists the words of the righteous."* – Deuteronomy 16:19

> *"Therefore I also have made you [Israel] contemptible and base before all the people, because you have not kept My ways but have shown partiality in the law."* – Malachi 2:9

What was true of Israel is true of us today. Justice should be blind, and yet we live in a culture where the blind eye of partiality and preferential treatment are becoming a common-place oppression. We have become very victim-centric in our worldview.

Equal opportunity quotas and DEI requirements have driven public and employment policies in the past. Partiality like this can drive who gets a job, who gets a college degree, who gets a loan, or who gets into public or governmental offices. It is not an issue of who is most qualified or merits the position but what marginalized people they represent. The "woke" culture sounds enlightened, and yet it is oppressive and punitive by nature. Its effort to provide equity for the marginalized has lifted up a particular cross-section of the citizenry while turning a blind eye and deaf ear to others, even to the point of skewing the justice system. Like Israel, we are becoming blind and deaf prisoners of the system.

Partiality is a form of oppression. It proposes to comfort victims by tipping the scales in their favor and thus empowering them over their oppressors. That only skews social values, which then impair our judgment and create a crooked place in which we are caught, and yet, like

Israel, we fail to stop and consider how we got into our crooked place. To break this kind of oppression, the Servant who is coming to establish justice in the world must show no partiality when meting out that justice, which will seem exceedingly harsh in a culture that caters to victims. He is going to turn the world on end with His form of justice.

Being Light-bearers in Oppressive Times

Israel was called to be God's light-bearer, but by Isaiah's day, she was anything but that. Her leaders and judges were oppressive to their own people in dispensing justice and yet she maintained this skewed perception of herself as the "enlightened one." God tore down that mountain. In truth, she was deaf and blind and caught in a crooked place by her own fault (42:16). The oppressive situation in which she found herself was less about what the Babylonians had done to her and more about what she had done to God.

Q: What has our current culture done to God?

We are called to be light-bearers in this world, but holding this line can be a struggle. Paul exhorts us:

> *". . . work out your own salvation with fear and trembling; for it is God who works in you both to will and to do for His good pleasure. Do all things without complaining and disputing, that you may become blameless and harmless, children of God without fault in the midst of a crooked and perverse generation, among whom you shine as lights in the world, holding fast the word of life . . ."* – Philippians 2:12-16

The Servant, Christ, has given us a commission to be His light-bearers in our crooked and perverse generation. So, how do we work out our salvation as the His light-bearers? (Working out our salvation does not mean that we do these things to gain salvation, but as a response to the commission being given to us.) So, let's work it out . . .

In Romans 2:17-24, Paul draws from Isaiah's imagery in Isaiah 42 when he rebukes the Jews for lifting themselves up as lights to the degenerate world and yet practicing all the things they self-righteously condemn. So, how about some self-reflection as a first step?

> **Q:** God's goals are to comfort and end conflict. Are you provoking fights in your family or community of friends by showing partiality or favoritism?
>
> **Q:** Do you always side with the one you perceive is the victim and turn a deaf ear to the other without listening to both sides equally?

In 2 Corinthians 6:14, Paul exhorts us not to be unequally yoked with unbelievers, saying, *"... what communion has light with darkness?"* There are a lot of people professing to be "enlightened" in our world, and yet they are willfully blind to the LORD and in darkness. And yet they come to us, demanding we join them in their fight against injustice.

> **Q:** In regard to these people, what does Paul mean when he says not to be unequally yoked?

In Ephesians 5:8-17, Paul talks about the need for light-bearers to know what is acceptable to the LORD and walk in that righteousness and truth.

> **Q:** What are God's "woke" values for treating people?

Paul goes on to say in Ephesians 5:8-17 that we are not to have fellowship with "unfruitful works of darkness," but rather expose (convict, refute) them. Part of the job of a light-bearer is to expose injustice, but also to be circumspect about how we do it because we live in evil days. In our current culture, we are caught in the pendulum swing between a broken justice system on side and an equally extreme and unjust reaction to it on the other.

> **Q:** How do we strike a godly balance between the two sides?

It is good to sympathize with victims, even advocate on their behalf, but the one thing we cannot do is let ourselves be sucked into that victim identity—that view of ourselves or others as perpetual victims of injustice. Like Israel, it is less about what the oppressors have done to them as what they have done to God. That statement might not go over so well today, but perhaps that is the light we need to shed on their situation. We cannot join them in that victim mentality because it will ultimately undermine an identity with God and keep us from aligning with His view of justice and values.

> **Q:** Showing partiality does not bring comfort. What does?

LESSON 5

The Comfort of Validation

READ
Isaiah 43:1-21

DISCUSSION

The need for validation is something that drives everyone. It is necessary for our well-being and feeling of acceptance. It reaffirms our sense of being valued. It is often offered as a reward for good behavior—at least, behavior that is social-sanctioned or behavior that an oppressor or abuser deems as acceptable. Thus, the need for validation can be leveraged by oppressors to keep the victim under their thumb, but first it requires a warping of the victim's view of themselves and their values. That is one of the "crooked places" that God has to straighten out. To do that, He has to provide a new source from which a victim finds validation, how they perceive their personal value, and what is deemed acceptable. The world's values contrast sharply to God's values in this, and half the battle in comforting a person is getting them to see themselves as being of value in God's eyes, as we will see with Israel today.

In the last chapter (Isaiah 42) God brought a charge against His people for their blindness and deafness—their failure to respond to Him and to be obedient to their calling. It was a sharp tear-down that confronted Israel with her own condition. She has no reason to puff herself up as God's chosen, "enlightened" people when she has walked away from that relationship. Now, Chapter 43 begins with "But . . ." What does that suggest?

Isaiah 43:1-7

This section is bookended in the repeated phrase, *"I formed you,"* but we will see that phrase crop up again the next chapter (Isaiah 44:2, 21, 24). The fact that God is Israel's Creator is a vital point in the case He is making in these chapters. There is also the imperative command to "fear not" which is repeated twice in this chapter and twice in the next chapter (Isaiah 44:2, 8). So, we have this pairing of themes: "God is your Creator. Fear not."

> **Q:** Why is it important to remind Israel that they are formed by Him (and not just Israel, but everyone called by God's name)?
>
> **Q:** For what are they formed?
>
> **Q:** After the rebuke of the previous chapter, God now switches the tone of His words in this passage. How does God comfort Israel's fear now?

Having declared His power to redeem Israel in previous chapters, God now comforts Israel's fear with the assurance of His love. He is able to redeem her because she is His. He has claimed her for Himself and He will protect her. He has ransomed her before when she was in Egypt. He has sacrificed men to redeem her life (speaking of the death of the firstborn sons of Egypt). She is precious to him, He loves her, and He will bring her descendants back when this is done. He promises this.

Let's pause for a moment in our observation of the text and dig deeper into our theme of validation.

GOD'S HIGHWAY PROJECT

The Comfort of Validation

People who are struggling and broken need validation that they are loved. The LORD has rebuked Israel for her unresponsiveness to Him, her disobedience, and her faithlessness in pursuing other idols, and yet He assures her that He still loves her.

> **Q:** On what is God's validation of Israel based—on the merit of what she has done or because He has chosen to value her?
>
> **Q:** How is that a comfort, not just to Israel, but to us in regard to our own redemption?

Being "liked" or trending on social media has become a potent and destructive form of validation for our young people that puts them under the world's sway, just as Israel was under the world's sway. God combats Israel's need for validation by calling her back to an identity with Him.

> **Q:** An eroded sense of identity and loss of purpose was preventing Israel from seeing God as a comfort and source of validation. How has the same problem been perpetuated in our own culture?
>
> **Q:** How do we combat the need for online validation in our youth?

The things that God proposes to do for Israel here are specific to Israel's experience in coming out of exile. There is a pattern to it that was first established when they came out of Egypt and was replayed as they came out of Babylonia. It was replayed in more recent history after the Holocaust when Israel became a nation again, and it will replay at least one more time in the End Times, when He brings her out of future Babylon's grip again.

What we take from this is not necessarily the literal promises God gave to Israel, but an understanding of God's glory as it is revealed in how He deals with Israel. When His deaf and blind servants fail to give Him glory of their own accord, He establishes His glory and Godhead in spite of them. His glory is revealed by what He has allowed to be done to them and what He will do to restore them. But the work is on His end, not theirs. Israel is presented in a very passive role throughout these passages.

Fear vs. Power, Love, and a Sound Mind

Here in Isaiah 43:5, God returns to the subject of fear, and now we see another way in which He tackles that stumbling block. He has already reassured Israel of His power over her circumstances and ability to save her. He now reassures her of His love and desire to save her. This tracks with Paul's reasoning in Second Timothy:

> "For God has not given us a spirit of fear, but of _power_ and of _love_ and of a _sound mind_." – 2 Timothy 1:7

We haven't talked yet about the aspect of a sound mind, but it has been running in the background in these chapters.

Q: What does it mean to have a sound mind?

Q: Some translations render the Greek phrase as self-discipline or sound judgment. The Amplified Bible adds that it speaks to abilities that result in a calm, well-balanced mind and self-control. Given these definitions, how do power, love, and a sound mind work together to counteract Israel's fear here in Isaiah?

God had a purpose for sending Israel into Babylon, and He has a purpose for sending us into persecutions and trials—to refine us but also to use us as His witnesses. When we are in the midst of that battle, we need a way to control the fear so that we accomplish God's objective in our circumstances. A sound mind, bolstered by the dual assurance of His power and love, empowers us to speak up as His witnesses, as Paul goes on to say in 2 Timothy 1:7-10. He begins with the key verse on dealing with fear, but then develops the thought farther:

"... Therefore do not be ashamed of the testimony of our Lord, nor of me His prisoner, but share with me in the sufferings for the gospel according to the power of God, who has saved us and called us with a holy calling, not according to our works, but according to His own purpose and grace which was given to us in Christ Jesus before time began, but has now been revealed by the appearing of our Savior Jesus Christ, who has abolished death and brought life and immortality to light through the gospel," – 2 Timothy 1:8-10

Now let's return to Isaiah 43 and see how the command to be a witness enters the dynamic.

DISCUSSION

Isaiah 43:8-21

"Bring out the witnesses!" God roars in His courtroom, then turns to Israel. "You are My witnesses."

Q: Why are witnesses important in building a court case?

Q: Verses 10-12 are bookended with the phrase, *"You are My witnesses,"* speaking to Israel. Of what is she bearing witness?

God commands Israel to tell the world what He has done for her, how He saved her even before any of these other so-called gods existed. He proclaimed what would happen, when there was no foreign god among her, and it was done. That alone is proof that He is God, and He alone can save. (That is my paraphrase.) Notice, there is a strong emphasis on God's role as Israel's Savior.

> **Q:** What steps does God take to save Israel? What is His plan?

Remember, back in Isaiah 40:2, God laid out His objectives for saving Israel by ending her conflicts on all fronts. Salvation or redemption for Israel is a two-fold picture. He saves her in the physical sense by bringing her out of Babylon and returning her to her land, thus preserving her lineage as a people. He also has a plan to save her spiritually by removing the sin issue and bringing the spiritual warfare to an end.

> **Q:** Here He speaks of bringing down Babylon, which will be accomplished by Cyrus of Persia. Which kind of salvation is He going to accomplish as His first step—physical preservation or spiritual salvation?

> **Q:** In the previous chapter (Isaiah 42), God introduced the second, unnamed Servant who would bring forth justice to the Gentiles. Why is it necessary to task a second Servant? What salvation is the Servant going to accomplish that is different than Cyrus?

> **Q:** Consider the order in which God is working. When comforting or counseling a victim, why start with removing them from their circumstances before tackling the sin issue?

Having made a case with what He has done to save Israel in the past, the LORD then turns to a declaration of what He will do in the future. He describes His take-down of Babylon much like His take-down of Egypt, then says, "Now, quit dwelling on the past and cast your vision toward the future. I am doing a new thing"—new, because it hasn't happened yet, but Israel will know it when it happens because it will follow the pattern of the former thing. It will be a sign to her when He builds a road through the wilderness to bring her back to Him as surely as the parting of that sea.

These promises are very specific to captive Israel in her Babylonian exile. These are not for us. But we can grasp the principle of God's strategy. By commanding Israel to remember what He has done for her in the past and what He has promised to do in the future, He is appealing to her rational thought, that she might know, believe, and understand—that she will be sound of mind and, thus, bring her fear under control. We are called to do the same thing and for the same reason, to help us mentally through difficult times.

> **Q:** What are some former things that you remember about God's work in your life that have given you comfort in a time of difficulty or uncertainty?
>
> **Q:** What promises do you rely on for comfort now?

GOD'S HIGHWAY PROJECT

Being a Witness

Being a witness is an act of validation. It is the act of confirming something is true or correct. It can also be an affirmation that a person— their ideas, feelings, and actions—is acceptable and worthy. God has validated Israel as His own chosen people. Now He asks for validation in return in their willingness to bear witness of His mighty works and Godship, and that He has spoken truthfully of past and future things.

We, like Israel, are called to be God's witness in upholding the truth of His Word, and also Christ's witness when we tell the story of what He has done for us on the cross as our Savior and will do when He returns. When we bear witness of Him, we are validating Him. Did you ever stop to think that He wants our validation as much as we need His?

Questions for Self-Reflection:

> **Q:** How do you get your validation in life?
>
> **Q:** How can a pursuit of validation be a stumbling block for a person caught in or coming out of an oppressive or abusive situation?
>
> **Q:** Have you been able to use your witness of the "former things" God has done in your life to comfort another hurting person?

LESSON 6

The Promise of Prosperity

READ

Isaiah 43:22–44:22

DISCUSSION

In these past few chapters (Isaiah 40–43), God has been making a case for His ability to save Israel. He has laid out the fullness of His power, His past record of delivering her (from Egypt), and made a great avowal of love to her. He urges her to be of sound mind and bear witness of Him, that He is who He says He is. A sound mind, bolstered by this understanding of His power and love, was meant to help her battle her fear as she endures her exile.

In addition to this, He reminds her of all the blessings that He promised she would receive if she only returned to Him, as outlined in the Mosaic Covenant. If she obeyed His Laws, He would give her a world of well-being, security, and abundant life as well as the means of prospering for generations to come. If she disobeyed, then she would have the opposite experience. She would fall victim to the curses (Deuteronomy 28) and those curses would not be lifted until she returned to Him as He promised in Deuteronomy 30:1-10.

The problem is that Israel wanted the prosperity without having to obey all those rules, and she pursued idolatry as a means to that end. As a result, God sent her into exile, just as He promised. Now He is locked in this struggle with her, trying to make her see not just the futility of it but the sheer foolishness of it. We are now picking up in Isaiah 43:22 with the comparison of God's assured blessing in a future kingdom to the world's illusion of prosperity in this life. Which is more able to comfort and deliver Israel from her misery?

Just as He did with Chapters 41 and 42, God ends Chapter 43 with a rebuke. In Isaiah 41, He rebuked Israel for the futility of her reliance on idols. In Isaiah 42, He rebuked her for not walking in His ways and being obedient to His Law—the very Law that He gave her the last time He made a road for her out of her captivity. God is her Savior, not just because He delivers her out of her oppressive circumstances, but because He is the only one who can relieve the oppression caused by her sin (which, in Israel's case, just happens to be the reason why she is in her physical circumstances). Now, He takes her to task over the sheer folly of idolatry.

Isaiah 43:22-28

Israel sees God's provision for her salvation through the sacrificial system as being burdensome. She is weary of it, weary of Him, and has gone to other gods. He takes it personally. Notice the emphasis on the repeated word "Me" in His charges against her in these verses.

God points out that she wasn't the one being wearied and burdened. She was wearying *Him* and burdening *Him* by not dealing with her sin. Seeing that this was the path she is determined to take, He let her go—forced her to go, really. He sent her away. But now Israel's sin has brought her into truly burdensome oppression, and she wails over being victimized and that God has overlooked her just claim (Isaiah 40:27).

Have you ever watched someone's life implode like this? Having turned a deaf ear to all advice and warnings, they rejected the relationship with God, if they even had one, and started down a worldly path in pursuit of—whatever. As the consequences of their decisions begin to unfold, they then try various methods of coping, but their life only gets deeper and deeper into that crooked place with each poor decision. Finally, when they find themselves so entrenched that they are unable to cope any more, they begin to wail that they have been wronged somehow and show up again on your doorstep, appealing to you for sympathy and support. Isn't it wearying? Can you empathize with God here?

> **Q:** What should our response be to people like this who come to us seeking comfort and support, knowing what we know of how they got into their problems? (There is a fine line between being supportive and enabling more bad behavior, isn't there?)

This is how God responds when Israel does this to Him. God says to her, "You and I need to have a discussion." (That's how my mother always began these conversations.) Then He goes on, and I paraphrase: "State your case. Let's examine the facts and see how you justify your claim. Your first father (Adam) sinned and was cursed (and now, not one of you is without sin). Your advocates who might have interceded on your behalf have only added to the transgressions. The sacrifices that you scorned were the only things that would have acquitted you in My eyes, and you refused to perform them. You didn't do what would have brought you the blessing and honor, so now you will reap the curse and reproach."

> **Q:** Why would God be so brutal about this? Wasn't He supposed to be comforting Israel?

Back in Isaiah 40:8, God stated that His word endures forever. Those blessings for obedience and curses for disobedience are all part of God's word to Israel. Once spoken, they were written in stone, and He cannot go back on His word. If He did, then the promises that He is making for her future now would be valueless. The promises made in Deuteronomy to send her into exile for disobedience are as much a witness to His past track record of mighty works as the exodus from Egypt was. He warned her of the consequences in all their gory detail, and now He has to follow through, for His own honor. But even in the breaking, there is hope.

Isaiah 44:1-5

Following those laws about the blessings and curses is God's promise to take Israel back if she will return to Him (Deuteronomy 30:1-7). This is the whole reason why He is making a way for that now. Isaiah 44 opens with a hopeful *"Yet hear now . . ."* Israel has reason to fear the oppressor, but even more reason to fear being left in that oppression by her angry God. Again, God holds out the promise of His blessing, if she will only return to Him. He repeats the command, "fear not," and gives her this promise in verse 3:

> *"For I will pour water on him who is thirsty, and floods on the dry ground; I will pour My Spirit on your descendants, and My blessing on your offspring"* – Isaiah 44:3

Water has been a recurring motif in these passages, and the provision of water in the wilderness is a signature act that the LORD performs as He delivers Israel from bondage. He did it first during her exodus from Egypt. Back then, the *physical* deliverance and provision of water were paired with the *spiritual* provision of the Law for dealing with her sin.

> **Q:** In verse 3, we see the same promise for physical provision, but what new spiritual provision is the LORD promising this time?

> **Q:** How is the giving of the Spirit a comfort?

In the King James Version, the Holy Spirit is called a Comforter. Jesus speaks of Him in the Gospel of John:

> *"And I will pray the Father, and he shall give you another Comforter, that he may abide with you for ever . . . But the Comforter, which is the Holy Ghost, whom the Father will send in my name, he shall teach you all things, and bring all things to your remembrance, whatsoever I have said unto you."* – John 14:16, 26 KJV

> *"But when the Comforter is come, whom I will send unto you from the Father, even the Spirit of truth, which proceedeth from the Father, he shall testify of me:"* – John 15:26 KJV

In other Bible versions, that Greek word for comforter (*paraklētos*) is translated as Helper or Advocate. It describes one who pleads another's cause before a judge or acts as an intercessor. Jesus said that this Spirit would come after His ascension and lead His followers into a deeper understanding of the truth of the Word of God. He would also give them divine strength to enable them to persevere under trials and persecutions on behalf of the kingdom. But, most importantly, He would be an "indwelling" Spirit.

> **Q:** Why does the indwelling aspect make a difference?

This goes along with what God promised in Deuteronomy 30, that when Israel returned, He would circumcise His people's hearts, not their flesh. There would be an internal change in the heart rather than a mere external altering of the flesh.

> **Q:** God deliberately pairs the picture of pouring out water, which is easy to understand, with the pouring out of the Spirit, which is

harder to understand. How is the pouring out of the Spirit like the pouring out of water or giving of rain? (Hint: what does it produce?)

Israel's response to this promise of abundant life in verse 5 is to renew her identity with God.

> **Q:** Do these promises of blessing and abundant life mean that God has overlooked Israel's transgressions?

No, they don't. But clearly the Law was not a sufficient agent to deal with Israel's sin issue since it relied on her own volition and initiative in performing it. That is why God must provide a way to satisfy the Law Himself so that she can return to Him and still have hope of future blessings. Only He can blot her transgressions and He does it for His own sake, as He previously pointed out in Isaiah 43:25.

Isaiah 44:6-8

These verses give us a summary statement of who God is. He has proved the enduring quality of His word in sending Israel into exile for her disobedience as He said He would, and He will be good to His word in making a way for her return. And all those blessings and promises of prosperity are on the horizon if Israel will only return.

Isaiah 44:9-11

God then levels the challenge at those who still choose idols. Compare Him and the blessing He offers with His rivals! Previously, He rebuked Israel for the futility of her idolatry. Now He reveals the foolishness of it, beginning with its unprofitableness.

> **Q:** Israel has opted for a worldly pursuit of profit and prosperity. How does the world determine what is profitable?

The definition of "profit" in the Hebrew is rooted in the idea of rising above or ascending. These idolized things are meant to lift a person up or help them get ahead in the world, and that is what makes them valuable. They are valuable based on man's values and the standards by which man ranks himself against other men.

The first thing God points out is that these people spend a lot of money pursuing these idols and get no profit in return. They have a figurine of wood or metal molded to their liking and then put it on the shelf. How many things do we have sitting around on our desks, shelves, bookcases, etc.? They may be pleasant to the eye, have encouraging messages inscribed on them, or have memories attached to them that are comforting to us. But that is all they have to offer in the way of comfort. They don't help when we are facing a difficult boss or an angry family member. They can't cure cancer or solve our financial problems. (A pursuit of such pricey "collectibles" may be adding to our financial problems.)

Isaiah 44:12-20

Despite there being no profit in these idols, the people spend an inordinate amount of time and effort pursuing them. In verses 12-17, we see the blacksmith hammering away as he fashions the idol, but what is his end condition? He toils until his strength fails, and he is still hungry and thirsty. The craftsman spends even more time. He plants the tree and harvests the wood. He selects a particularly fine piece of wood and uses part of it to fashion his idol. The rest of the log he throws on the fire. Which offers more comfort: the warmth of the fire and the roasted meat, or the unburnt portion that he worships? That is the utter absurdity of idolatry, and God gives those who pursue it over to the lie. He closes their eyes and hearts and lets them persist in their blindness and stupidity.

In the Law, God continually reminds Israel that He is the one who gives them the ability to prosper and profit from their efforts. Her idols offer only the illusion of such help. The pursuit of power, salvation, and prosperity through idolatry is the lie that takes a person off of God's highway and can blind them with the false promise of deliverance. The LORD sums it up in verse 20, *"A deceived heart has turned him aside and he cannot deliver his soul, nor say, 'Is there not a lie in my right hand?'"*

Isaiah 44:21-22

God has repeatedly made the point that He formed Israel, which He reiterates here. He is her Creator. And yet Israel, who is herself a created thing, has now created gods of her own to rival Him, which is part of the absurdity of idolatry. The power to deliver and redeem is only in the hand of the Creator, not created man or man's created things. If those idols had created Israel, then they would have power to redeem her, but they didn't and they don't. She was the one who created those things and then attributed power to them that she herself did not have. The idols could do no more for her than she could do for herself. God commands Israel, "Remember this truth!"

What can God the Creator do for Israel that her created idols cannot do? He blots out her transgressions and thus provides a release from the curse. That phrase, *"I have blotted out your transgressions,"* brings the argument back to His opening statement in Isaiah 43:25, which was Israel's point of departure from Him. He now implores her, *"Return to Me, for I have redeemed you."*

GOD'S HIGHWAY PROJECT

The Promise of Prosperity

God challenges Israel (and us) to consider what is profitable and worth pursuing, and where we look for comfort. Is it found in the future, eternal blessing that He offers according to His definition and His provision, or is it in the fleeting blessing we achieve by our own works, according to our own or the world's definition.

> **Q:** What does our world make into idols—things that help people get ahead, raise their status among their peers, or lift them up?

> **Q:** There are profitable things in life that are not bad in themselves. At what point can profitable things become idols? (Read 1 Timothy 6:10, 17-19.)

Idols have no power, and yet, there are people who believe they do have power; and this isn't just a problem for ancient Israel. Once in my varied career, I worked for a picture-framing shop, and I remember the day a young man brought in a bit of wood that was supposedly a piece of the Cross. Yes, the Cross. He was almost frantic over parting with it, even to have it framed, and demanded I treat it with the utmost reverence because it was a holy thing (and he had paid an exorbitant sum for it). I looked at him in disbelief. It was a piece of wood. It could have come off of a fence post. At that moment, I felt like the craftsman in this passage, being asked to take a useless piece of wood that was clearly an idol in this young man's life, and, in essence, build a shrine for it. And I had to do it, though my soul rebelled against it, because he was the client and this was the business. It was a souring experience. I would like to have known what comfort the young man thought he would get as a return for all the money he had spent (the frame itself was not cheap) but, of course, I could not ask.

>**Q:** What do you think this young man believed he would benefit from his relic?

God's way is the only true way to a lasting experience of prosperity and security, but presenting this motivation to a struggling person can have both an upside and downside.

>**Q:** When you are dealing with someone who is struggling, why is it important to cast that vision of a future blessing to come if they return to (or come to) a relationship with Christ?

>**Q:** What is the danger of building up a person's hope of prosperity in this world or this life?

I worked for a time in the communications department at Prison Fellowship Ministries, and I remember the warning that was given to volunteers who ministered in the prisons. Volunteers were told not to promise inmates that a relationship with Christ would make the consequences of their sins disappear. It wouldn't necessarily get them out of prison any sooner. It wouldn't guarantee that their addictions would magically disappear. It wouldn't mean that the broken relationships would be healed and reconciled or that they would have it easy from here on. The immediate release that they were being given was a spiritual release, and with the Spirit's help, the physical bondage and brokenness might be overcome with time. So, it was important to cast the vision of a future prosperity, but to be realistic about what abundant life looks like from God's eyes and when the full experience of that might be realized.

>**Q:** Even within the Christian community, there are prosperity cults that promise the experience of abundant life. What is their idea of prosperity and how do you get it?

In regard to Israel's response in Isaiah 44:5 where she returns to her association with God after He promises the blessing, we should pause and consider how difficult it is to change the mindset of a person who has walked away from God and begun to cling to a personal or worldly source of empowerment to relieve his or her oppression.

> **Q:** In your experience, does the rational argument (or even pointing out the foolishness of their actions) work? Why or why not?

> **Q:** How do you convince them of God's power and love so that they will let go of their identity with their idol and embrace that identity with God? Can you convince them, or is this something the LORD has to do?

When we are comforting a struggling person, are there times when a little bit of tough love and a rather blunt stating of the obvious are necessary to break them out of their self-pity and wrong pursuits? I think so. However, remember where this chapter began. This rebuke comes on the heels of God's earlier avowal of love and validation. This has been a pattern with Him through the last several chapters. On one hand, He offers the reassurances of His ability and desire to reclaim His people. They are precious to Him and He loves them. On the other hand, He doesn't shy away from addressing the sin, which is a stumbling block and source of conflict between Himself and Israel. These are the lifting-up and tearing-down steps in His highway project.

> **Q:** When comforting a struggling person, why is it important not to overlook the sin factor in their actions (or reactions) and not focus just on the oppressor's sins? Why is it important to be impartial about that?

> **Q:** Why is it important to balance rebuke with comfort and validation?

LESSON 7

The Comfort of an Ever-present God

READ
Isaiah 44:23-28

DISCUSSION

So far, in Isaiah 40–44, God has made a case for His power (omnipotence) and His wisdom and far-sightedness (omniscience). Now, Isaiah 44 ends with a grand poetic statement of His omnipresence—His enduring, transcendent presence among His people, Israel. He points out that He has been with her in the past, from her beginning; He is working in her now; and He will deliver her in the future with a coming deliverer.

Isaiah 44:23

The narrative section opens in Isaiah 43:23 with an imperative command: "Sing!" This marks the end of the previous series of rebukes for Israel's idolatry and unfaithfulness and transitions into the next narrative picture, that of a coming king. The "sing" commands always accompany pictures of the savior-kings, almost like princely heralds. In Isaiah 42, the description of the Servant was followed by a "sing" command. Here in Isaiah 44, it precedes the picture of God as the universal Savior-King, and His agent, Cyrus of Persia, who is also a savior-king in his tasking. The command to sing will show up again in Isaiah 48, 49, 52, and 54 associated with the Sin-bearing Servant. So, there is a pattern to them.

Isaiah 44:24-28

A poetic structure sets these verses apart from the rest of the text. There are three sets of "who" statements describing a progression. The LORD is building toward something. Let's consider the progression.

Verse 24 begins with a grand "Thus, says the LORD," followed by a description of His relationship to Israel. He is her Redeemer. He is her Creator who formed her from the womb. He makes the initial statement, "I am the LORD," and follows it with three simple "who" statements that describe Him from the beginning:

1. "Who makes all things,"
2. "Who stretches out the heavens all alone,"
3. "Who spreads abroad the earth by Myself;"

These three simple statements are followed by three more complex sentences in verses 25-26a that describe His work in the present (that is, Isaiah's day):

1. "Who frustrates the signs of the babblers, and drives diviners mad;"
2. "Who turns wise men backward, and makes their knowledge foolishness;"
3. "Who confirms the word of His servant, and performs the counsel of His messengers;"

I will come back to this picture of God in the present, dealing with babblers, diviners, because I think these have a striking parallel in our current culture, but first let's look at the final verses. The final set of three "who" statements in verses 26b-28 are the most complex, bringing the poem to the grand announcement of the coming of King Cyrus. Cyrus is called by name for a particular task in the future.

1. "Who says to Jerusalem, 'You shall be inhabited,' to the cities of Judah, 'You shall be built,' and I will raise up her waste places;"
2. "Who says to the deep, 'Be dry! and I will dry up your rivers';"
3. "Who says of Cyrus, 'He is My shepherd, and he shall perform all My pleasure, saying to Jerusalem, "You shall be built," and to the temple, "Your foundation shall be laid."'"

Thus, we have a picture of God in His transcendent role. In addition to being all-powerful and all-seeing, He is an ever-present God which He reveals through His work with Israel.

Q: What comfort does an ever-present God offer?

God's creatorship has already been discussed thoroughly in the past chapter, so let's look more closely at His work in Israel's present. It says in verse 25 that He frustrates the babblers, the diviners, and the wise. These are the experts and "influencers" who went head to head with prophets like Isaiah, and presumed to act as intercessors between spiritual and human realm. They were given to speaking many words with little content, and yet, they were the ones who had the people's attention—the most "followers." They were considered the authorities and trusted sources of information, but their credibility was based on their own self-promotion and the power that the people gave them, not on God's truth. Even so, they were able to sway people's opinions, behaviors, and lifestyles with their empty messaging, false product endorsements, and visionary views. This made God angry, so He messed with these forecasters and experts, just to show His power. They are a sharp contrast to God's own servants and messengers, whose word He validates and brings to pass.

So, this was Israel's present culture in Isaiah's day and also in the days of her exile when she was at the mercy of foreign masters. She was bombarded with the messaging of the babblers, authorities, and experts, who were at odds with God's messengers.

Israel's present condition leads into God's declaration of her future. Notice the details of His prophetic words in the last set of verses. They specifically foretell the cities of Judah and Jerusalem being rebuilt. God speaks of "the deep" and its rivers being made dry—those are figurative references to the Gentile empire of Babylon and its reversal of condition which He will accomplish through Cyrus. And yet they aren't only figurative. In regard to the rivers drying up, this statement was fulfilled in a very literal way. The Medo-Persian army entered heavily-fortified Babylon by diverting the Euphrates River which ran through the city, effectively drying it up so that the invading army could pass under the city's massive walls.

Cyrus is now specifically named and specifically tasked with facilitating the rebuilding of Jerusalem and laying the Temple's foundation, both of which were accomplished as a result of his decree. God lays out the future in glorious detail, something which no other god can do.

Isaiah's words are specific to Israel, but they aren't without parallels in our own day and culture.

GOD'S HIGHWAY PROJECT

Dealing with the Babblers, the Diviners, and the Wise

Our world today, like Israel's, is full of babblers. They are the talking heads on the news stations and social media that blast out their forecasts 24/7. They are the social influencers who try to mold our future for us with dire warnings of what will happen if we don't embrace their worldview and lifestyles. (Have you ever noticed how often they use fear tactics in their messaging? That is the tool of an oppressor.) In the prophet Jeremiah's day, they were the leadership that cried "Peace, peace!" when there was no peace—kind of like community leaders who declare that a mob overrunning a city, looting buildings, and burning cars, is a mostly "peaceful" protest. How much comfort and healing does a community get from that kind of messaging? Jeremiah remarked that it "healed the hurt" of God's people very little (Jeremiah 6:14, 8:11). And yet these people have declared themselves the enlightened and wise among us.

God laughs at their efforts. He drives the forecasters mad, and turns back the "wise"—those expert advisors who send us down one course in life only to be confronted with a lack of success. When they reach the conclusion that what they had prescribed wasn't the way to go, they scratch their heads, change their messaging, and go winging off on another, more popular idea. Their credibility is based on how many people listen to them—their power base—and their knowledge lacks true understanding, discernment, and wisdom.

This is the scary thing, though. If you hear a particular message often enough and to the exclusion of all else, you begin to buy it, even if it is a lie. Israel bought the lie, and look where it landed her.

> **Q:** How do we know what is truth and what is a lie? How do we sort out God's servants and messengers from the world's babblers and so-called experts?
>
> **Q:** There are many New Testament verses that remind us that there are wolves at work, even within God's flock. How do we recognize them?

The very first promise that God made in Isaiah 40 was that His word would endure forever. It has been and will be ever-present throughout the ages of man, despite our current culture's effort to eradicate it. That gives it stability and a proven track record, more than all the trending fads and talking heads in social media. It is for His own glory and faithfulness to His word that He frustrates the efforts of babblers and experts and gives them over to the lie.

Just as He frustrated the influencers in Israel's day, He will frustrate the influencers of our own day who reject the truth for a lie, and when we see that happening, it will be a sign to us that a shake-up is coming, as Paul says:

> *"Let no one deceive you by any means; for that Day will not come unless the falling away comes first, and the man of sin is revealed, the son of perdition, who opposes and exalts himself above all that is called God or that is worshiped, so that he sits as God in the temple of God, showing himself that he is God . . . The coming of the lawless one is according to the working of Satan, with all power, signs, and lying wonders, and with all unrighteous deception among those who perish, because they did not receive the love of the truth, that they might be saved. And for this reason God will send them strong delusion, that they should believe the lie, that they all may be condemned who did not believe the truth but had pleasure in unrighteousness."* – 2 Thessalonians 2:3-4, 9-12

> **Q:** The LORD is speaking here of the beginning of the End Times, when an ungodly, one-world government under one lawless ruler will appear on the scene. It will rock our age much like the coming of Cyrus rocked Babylon's age. Where do we find comfort when all this begins to happen? (Hint: Read 2 Thessalonians 2:15-17.)

We find comfort in knowing what the Word of God says about these events, His love for us, and also the promise He gives to us that, according to His grace, we are not destined for the wrath to come, as Paul writes in his earlier letter to the Thessalonians:

> *"For you yourselves know perfectly that the day of the Lord so comes as a thief in the night. For when they say, 'Peace and safety!' then sudden destruction comes upon them, as labor pains upon a pregnant woman. And they shall not escape. But you, brethren, are not in darkness, so that this Day should overtake you as a thief. You are all sons of light and*

sons of the day. We are not of the night nor of darkness. Therefore let us not sleep, as others do, but let us watch and be sober... putting on the breastplate of faith and love, and as a helmet the hope of salvation. For God did not appoint us to wrath, but to obtain salvation through our Lord Jesus Christ, who died for us, that whether we wake or sleep, we should live together with Him. Therefore comfort each other and edify one another, just as you also are doing." –1 Thessalonians 5:2-6, 8-11

> **Q:** Speaking to parents, we may have this comfort for ourselves, but where is our comfort when, despite our best efforts, our children succumb to the social pressure of the world's influencers and fall for their lies?

Spoiler alert: God is going to comfort these concerns in Isaiah 49 and 54.

Elevating God

God's highway project described here is specific to Israel's near future as He prepares her to come out of exile, and yet we see His transcendent character on display. He is God—past, present, and future—which He reveals through His work with Israel. He is all-powerful, all-knowing, and ever-present—the beginning and the end—and not just in Israel's life but in ours.

We have been applying the lessons in these chapters from the aspect of comforting broken and struggling people. In as much as we are called to lift them up, a great part of the comfort we offer comes from elevating God in their eyes. This is the elevated view that God gives of Himself to Israel when she is at her lowest. The challenge for us is to take this view of Him and make it relevant to our struggling person, because this isn't just for Israel. These aspects of His character are universal and never-changing.

How do we do this? How do we make this view of God relatable to a person who is despairing and disillusioned with life, who has perhaps finally woken up to the reality of their situation and the lies they've been told, and has hit rock bottom? We can point to God's work with Israel as one proof, but our struggling person might not find that relatable, so we will need to point them to other evidence. If they are believers who have walked away from God, as Israel did, perhaps they have their own personal examples from the past of which we can remind them, as God does with Israel. But what if they are unbelievers without any background with God? To what evidence can we point? There is our own lives. It might be good if we spent a little time preparing ourselves mentally for that eventual conversation.

Personal Preparation

    Q: Begin by asking yourself, do I believe this picture of God myself? Do I believe that God has had a hand in all the things that have happened to me in life, good and bad? (If you don't believe it yourself, you won't be able to convince others.)

    Q: Why do I believe it?

    Q: Can I point to any specific examples where God has worked in my own life? (Not everyone will have a grand testimonial to share, but it doesn't have to be grand. Maybe you have prayed for something or simply asked God a question, and it was answered in a way that could only have come from God.)

    Q: What if you don't have that experience yet? How do you get it?

    You could always ask God to give you the experience you need for the sake of witnessing. That is a specific prayer. You might even ask for it in front of your struggling person.

    Q: Do you have enough faith in the Lord to sit down with your struggling person and pray a specific prayer?

    Q: Do you think God would honor that request?

If you can find a way to draw your struggling person into your walk of faith with you, it can be a very, very powerful thing, but it will only happen if you yourself believe in the power and love of God and are willing to bear witness of it.

LESSON 8

The Glory of the Savior King

READ
Isaiah 45:1-25

DISCUSSION

Rejoice! A messiah is coming! The LORD is calling a savior who will release Israel from her bondage! The LORD's commissioning of Cyrus, King of Persia, is the high point of Part 1's chiastic structure in which God makes an argument for His supremacy and sovereignty in the face of the idols that Israel has set up as His rivals. Cyrus is the irrefutable proof. Idols cannot call a future man by name to do their bidding as God does with Cyrus.

On the surface, Isaiah 45 seems to focus on the figure of Cyrus, but we will see that Cyrus is only an agent and a small part of the much bigger picture. The overarching theme is that God is the only Savior, and not just of Israel but the whole earth.

Isaiah 45:1-13

In the opening verses, God addresses Cyrus personally. Notice that there are no imperative commands to Israel in this section. The deliverance that God grants Israel through Cyrus is by grace and grace alone.

In the opening verse, God calls Cyrus "His anointed one," which is the Hebrew word *mashiach*, from which we get the word *messiah*. The title of "anointed one" is reserved for Israel's high priests and kings, those who are the designated "deliverers" for God's people. We talked about the concept of salvation or deliverance in Isaiah 40. There is a purely physical side to saving someone, and then there is the spiritual side as well. The tasking of all "anointed ones" or messiah figures is to set people free—to end the fighting on one or both fronts. God's anointed kings set His people free when they vanquish Israel's physical enemies. God's anointed priests set the people free spiritually in facilitating the pardoning sin.

Cyrus is a Gentile king, and he is the only Gentile ever given the title "anointed" in Scripture. This is an unprecedented statement that God makes here in Isaiah 45:1. His use of that word challenges Israel's understanding of what role a messiah plays in the grand scheme of things.

Cyrus, as a messianic figure, is commissioned with two tasks: 1) releasing Israel from the hands of oppressive Babylon, and 2) spreading God's fame. He will subdue the nations, break the power of their kings, and liberate the captives. To this end, God gives Cyrus a meteoric success that is beyond explanation, which then accomplishes the second objective: that both Cyrus and Israel would know that God is who He says He is (45:3-4). Cyrus's success is definitely not due to Cyrus's own prowess. The LORD makes it very clear that He goes before Cyrus to clear the way for His people. Cyrus is merely His human agent.

Ezra records Cyrus's decree that liberates Israel, and we see in Cyrus's words a repeating of the tasking that the LORD gives him here in Isaiah:

> *"Thus says Cyrus king of Persia: All the kingdoms of the earth the LORD God of heaven has given me. And He has commanded me to build Him a house at Jerusalem which is in Judah. Who is among you of all His people? May his God be with him, and let him go up to Jerusalem which is in Judah, and build the house of the LORD God of Israel (He is God), which is in Jerusalem. And whoever is left in any place where he dwells, let the men of his place help him with silver and gold, with goods and livestock, besides the freewill offerings for the house of God which is in Jerusalem."* – Ezra 1:2-4

And so, Cyrus makes this grand proclamation extolling the LORD, and yet the LORD remarks repeatedly in verses 4-5 that Cyrus has not known Him. Why would the LORD say that?

We know from historical accounts that Cyrus is pantheistic. He acknowledges and tolerates all the gods of the people he conquers, so he has no problem acknowledging the God of Israel or even decreeing a temple be built for Him, but that doesn't mean that he has a personal relationship with Israel's God. That does not matter in God's eyes, though. If His own people will not give Him glory, He will use someone like Cyrus to spread His fame. Cyrus is just an agent for accomplishing the tasks.

In verses 7-8, God returns to speaking of Himself as the Creator. He creates light and peace. He also creates darkness and calamity. "Calamity" is the word *ra* in the Hebrew, which can be translated as evil, distress, misery, or injury. There might be a bit of a challenge for us to grasp this part of God's character.

> **Q:** In what sense is God the Creator of evil or calamity?
>
> **Q:** Why would He do this to His people?
>
> **Q:** Why would He do this in our lives? (Why do bad things happen to good people? That is a question a struggling person will ask, and you should prepare for it.)

There are a number of answers to that, but let's just consider Israel's case and how she came to be a captive in Babylonia. When God's people became hopelessly corrupt and violent, He raised up even more brutal Babylonia to deal with them. We read that prophecy in Habakkuk 1. That was God, in a sense, creating calamity. Habakkuk saw that vision of Babylonia overtaking Israel and was so appalled that he questioned God:

> *"You are of purer eyes than to behold evil, and cannot look on wickedness. Why do You look on those who deal treacherously, and hold Your tongue when the wicked devours a person more righteous than he?"*
> – Habakkuk 1:13

In other words, how can You even look at those lawless Babylonians, let alone use them against righteous Israel? See, there it is. That sense of self-righteousness that says, we may be bad, but they are worse. They are the ones who need the law thrown at them, not us. God has to tear down that notion of self-righteous entitlement, and for Israel, it took a nation bigger and more wicked carrying her off into exile before she submitted to the LORD's sovereignty. Like Habakkuk, Isaiah similarly saw the vision of Babylonia overtaking Israel. But now that the end of the Babylonian exile is in sight, God uses Cyrus of Persia to create some more calamity, this time against Babylonia. God has His uses for calamity and "evil." When He sets out to free His people and reestablish them in their kingdom, entire nations have to rise and fall in the process. For individual citizens living through their nation's demise, life is appalling and brutal, and the righteous suffer with the wicked.

Then, in verse 9, the LORD abruptly switches the focus of His address. He is no longer talking to Cyrus, but to a third party who has apparently raised an objection to His commissioning of Cyrus. We assume that the audience is Israel, and while Isaiah doesn't record the complaint outright, we can infer from God's response that Israel doesn't like His plan or His choice of messiah.

> **Q:** Why would Israel have a problem with God raising up this deliverer for her?

God's rebuke is rather blistering. He reminds her that He is the sovereign Creator. Just as He has created her, He will create a deliverer for her. He will use whatever human agent that He chooses and will direct his ways. How is she in any position to strive with Him over this? Verse 11 loses some of the sarcasm in the New King James Version. The New International Version catches the gist of the words better:

> *"This is what the LORD says—the Holy One of Israel, and its Maker: 'Concerning things to come, do you question me about my children, or give me orders about the work of my hands?'"* – Isaiah 45:11 NIV

In verse 13, the LORD goes on to say that Cyrus will let the exiles go free "without price or reward," meaning Cyrus would not exact a price from Israel to buy her way out of bondage. The salvation and redemption she is being granted is free and by the grace of the LORD. That is not to say that Cyrus will not get a reward, but his reward comes from the LORD.

GOD'S HIGHWAY PROJECT

Preparing for Calamity

There is a lot of calamity in our current world and even more looming on our horizon. I believe that the events foretold in the book of Revelation are literal events and that there will be a time of horrific upheaval on a world-wide scale as a one-world government is established before Christ comes to establish His own kingdom. But the LORD has a purpose in letting the calamity run its course, and in the end, He will bring a kingdom of righteousness and peace out of it. As kingdoms begin to rise and fall in the grand sweep of those events, there will be a disruption of all the supports that give us a sense of security and well-being—economic support, medical support, food and housing needs, justice, and policing needs.

One of the applications of this study is to understand how God prepares His people for what is looming on their horizon.

> **Q:** How do we prepare ourselves, mentally and spiritually, for what might end up as the demise of our nation as we have known it? How do we overcome the fear of an uncertain future?

> **Q:** National concerns aside, have you ever questioned God's reasoning or purpose in bringing some calamity into your own personal life? Did you challenge Him over why it had to work out the way it did?

DISCUSSION

The commissioning of Cyrus was the pinnacle argument in the chiastic structure for Part 1. Cyrus is the key piece of evidence that God uses to build His case for His Godship and Creatorship, demonstrating not just His omnipotence and omniscience, but omnipresence in Israel's affairs. We now move into the closing arguments of the chiastic structure. God is going to make a series of final points which revisit earlier statements. Much of the narrative will sound redundant, having already been stated in past chapters. What we are looking for is how the closing arguments resolve the issue. God Highway Project has been focusing on the promised reversal of Israel's condition—valleys lifted up, mountains brought low, etc. The closing arguments will resolve the issue either by presenting a reversal of conditions, or by adding a twist to the dynamic.

Isaiah 45:14-17

The LORD switches back to addressing Cyrus in verse 14 where He declares that all exalted kings would come and bow to him; but more than that, these kings would confess that Cyrus's success was from the LORD Himself. This is part of Cyrus's purpose, to spread God's fame.

Cyrus himself would know that God was the God of Israel, and Israel would know God was God over her. Now even the Gentile nations bow to that understanding. In response, there arises a righteous third party, perhaps the prophet himself, who praises God as Israel's Savior on one hand and rebukes idolaters on the other hand. The thrust of his message emphasizes that the LORD will bring about an everlasting salvation for Israel, and she need not be ashamed or disgraced to call Him LORD.

So, here are the opening and closing arguments:

Opening Argument: (Isaiah 45:1-8) God's commissioning of Cyrus to which there is an objection from a third party. God answers that objection with a rebuke (Isaiah 45:9-13)

Closing Argument: (Isaiah 45:14) God's rewarding of Cyrus. That is the resolution. We also see a reversal in the kind of response God gets. There is no objection this time, only praise (45:15-17).

But the praise for God's everlasting salvation, mentioned in verse 17, raises a question.

Q: Is Cyrus the messiah through whom God accomplishes an everlasting salvation?

We know from history that Cyrus is not. He conquered Babylonia and sent Israel back to her land with everything she needed to begin again, but his own empire didn't last, nor did Israel remain free of physical bondage from later Gentile nations. In Jesus's day, she is under Roman rule. Then, in 70 A.D., the Romans expelled her from her land again, and even today, she has yet to fully regain sovereignty over the land that God promised her, namely Jerusalem. And we know that she will not fully come into her kingdom again until the Messiah (the Messianic Davidic king) comes. So, Cyrus is a messiah, but he is not "the" Messiah. He shares the same title and has some tasking in common with the Messiah to come, and he even drives Israel's expectations of what a messianic figure should look like.

Q: When the greater Messiah appears in the future (in His first advent), Israel has a similar objection to Him as she did to Cyrus. Why did she object to Him?

Q: When He comes in His second advent, what will be her response?

I find it interesting how the pattern with Cyrus repeats with Christ.

In Chapter 45, the LORD begins to build this picture of a messiah with Cyrus, but His plan isn't just to save Israel but to save the world through Israel's future Messiah. But the coming of that future Messiah is contingent on Israel being preserved as a people. Cyrus's deliverance is the means to that end. Starting here in verse 17, the near picture of national deliverance through a messiah king begins to telescope out to a distant picture of universal deliverance through a greater Messianic King.

Isaiah 45:18-25

Opening Argument: (Isaiah 44:24-28) God's declaration of His transcendent (past, present, and future) work in the nation of Israel

Closing Argument: (Isaiah 45:18-25) God's declaration of His transcendent work to save not just the nation of Israel, but all the world through Israel

God's summation parallels the pattern of His opening declaration, but the scope of His salvation now expands to become universal. In Isaiah 45:19, He once again speaks of Israel in her present day (Isaiah's day), similar to what He said in Isaiah 44:25-26. He makes the comparison between Himself and the idolaters who cannot save. He does not speak in secret like the diviners and soothsayers who turn to dark places for wisdom. He speaks plainly. He speaks righteously (Hebrew: *tsedek*), in the sense of laying a straight path which is morally and legally just. Following that path leads to the experience of being justified or set free. God also speaks what is right (Hebrew: *meshar*), referring to uprightness (vertically) or straightness (horizontally) in the sense of making something smooth or level. Figuratively, it speaks of judging with equality and impartiality, making sure the scale is level when meting out justice. When the scales are balanced, there is peace. He is making crooked paths straight and rough places smooth. This is God fully engaged in His highway project.

Having presented Himself as God past and present, He then presents Himself as God of the future in verse 22. This picture differs from the opening picture. In the opening picture (Isaiah 44:26-28), Cyrus is the deliverer on the near-horizon and the salvation he brings is for the nation of Israel specifically. But now that Cyrus has been commissioned and his task completed, the LORD reveals an even greater salvation plan with this shocking statement in verses 22-23:

> *"Look to Me, and be saved, all you ends of the earth! For I am God, and there is no other. I have sworn by Myself; the word has gone out of My mouth in righteousness, and shall not return, that to Me every knee shall bow, every tongue shall take an oath."* – Isaiah 45:22-23

The salvation God describes now isn't just national salvation for Israel, although the nation corporately will be justified in the end (45:25). This salvation is a universal offering of salvation to all the earth, Jews and Gentiles alike. He is not just the God of Israel but the God of all creation, although He works through Israel to accomplish that salvation. But this salvation is not a salvation that Cyrus will facilitate. Just because this salvation picture comes after Cyrus does not mean it is speaking of Cyrus as the ultimate messiah. Cyrus's work is limited to the near-future release of Israel and only in the physical sense. This later passage is casting the vision now to a more distant future and the next coming deliverer—the Sin-bearing Servant who is God Himself. We see the same phrasing from Isaiah 45:23 in Philippians 2, where Paul says,

> *"Therefore God also has highly exalted Him and given Him the name which is above every name, that at the name of Jesus every knee should bow, of those in heaven, and of those on earth, and of those under the earth, and that every tongue should confess that Jesus Christ is Lord, to the glory of God the Father."* – Philippians 2:9-11

Cyrus the messiah may do this in a limited sense by conquering Babylonia, but Christ the Messiah will bring all the world into subjection when He returns as the future Messiah to set up His kingdom. This is the expansion of the picture in the closing arguments.

GOD'S HIGHWAY PROJECT

The Stumbling Stone of Conscience

It is the LORD's desire to end conflict and establish peace, not just in the world but between the world and Himself. This is why He extends salvation to all, Jew and Gentile alike. But consider the ramifications of mixing of two radically different cultures. His desire is to create universal peace by reconciling them into one, new identity, but instead, a new spate of objections and fighting breaks out. To resolve the conflict, Paul and the apostles must address a particular stumbling stone—the stumbling stone of conscience. Paul specifically references this passage in Isaiah, quoting Isaiah 45:23 when he addresses the issues plaguing the church in Rome (Romans 14:11).

> **Q:** What conflict beset the Roman church? (Romans 14:1-21)

Paul addressed the Jews and Gentiles in the Roman church who were fighting each other because they had conflicting consciences over lifestyle choices. The Gentiles argued that they had been set free from the bondage of the Law and had complete liberty to do what they wanted, particularly in regard to what they ate or what days they observed as holy; to the opposite extreme, the Jews argued for restraint by observing the letter of the Law. But both sides went too far in their stances. The Gentiles wanted a complete lack of restraint, and the Jews, too much restraint. Paul seeks to end the fighting by rebuking both sides, saying,

> *"But why do you judge your brother? Or why do you show contempt for your brother? For we shall all stand before the judgment seat of Christ. For it is written: 'As I live, says the LORD, every knee shall bow to Me, and every tongue shall confess to God.'"* – Romans 14:10-11

Not only does Paul quote Isaiah 45:23, he brings the context of Isaiah 45 into the argument. Earlier in Isaiah 45, Israel raised an objection to God's use of a Gentile king, Cyrus, who He anoints for His purpose. That title, messiah, was only ever reserved for Israel's priests and kings. No Gentile was worthy of that title. God levels a scathing rebuke at Israel in response, saying in essence, who are you to judge Me and My decisions? If I say this Gentile is righteous, then in My eyes he is righteous. This is the exact point that Paul now makes in Romans, and he speaks equally to both camps. Who are you to judge God's determination of who is righteous? That is for God to decide. Paul goes on to say,

> *"So then each of us shall give account of himself to God. Therefore let us not judge one another anymore, but rather resolve this, not to put a stumbling block or a cause to fall in our brother's way."* – Romans 14:12-13

So, we are back to the task of removing stumbling blocks of oppression, the only difference being that this time the oppression is something the church has created within itself (not unlike the oppression of the Pharisees and Sadducees in Jesus's day). Sadly, some of the worst oppression can be found within the church body, and that is to our shame.

God desires peace and fellowship among those whom He has set free, but liberty can be a heady thing, and it can renew a self-serving attitude of power and entitlement that impedes fellowship. By the same token, enforcing a life of severe restraint under rules concerned only with the fleeting side of life creates a false sense of moral superiority, and those rules become the means by which we take one another's measure. This also wrecks fellowship. A balance must be struck over how much liberty to allow and how much restraint to demand, and that balance is struck in living a life foremost in conscience to God, to whom we must give account, but also by examining our motives for demanding more liberty or restraint.

Q: What effect are our attitudes and actions having on our fellowship?

Q: Are we feeding our sense of entitlement or self-righteousness and creating a toxic environment that drives people away from God and a relationship with Christ?

Q: Are there legitimate reasons for curbing our own liberty for another's sake? For example, if a person is struggling with alcoholism, should alcohol be served at a meal that they are attending? That is an obvious case of placing a stumbling block in front of a person, but you get the idea. Sometimes there are legitimate reasons to accommodate a weaker member or even a stronger conscience over something, or at least make allowances for it so as not to create conflict.

Our churches today may or may not suffer division over Jewish versus Gentile consciences the way that the Roman church did, but we are certainly a culture of diverse lifestyle choices, and consciences over those choices can cause conflict among our members. Part of God's Highway Project is to remove stumbling blocks, and Paul has identified this kind of conflict over conscience as a stumbling block.

> **Q:** If we can, how do we remove these kind of stumbling blocks? (Read Romans 15.)

> **Q:** There is tremendous pressure in our culture to embrace inclusivity. Is there a line we draw when it comes to accommodating lifestyle choices? If so, on what do we base that division?

We have two roles that must be balanced in this effort. One is to prepare the way. We are called to play a part in comforting people and facilitating their return to the LORD. But on the other hand, we are God's representatives to a fallen world, and we are called to live lives that glorify Him. Like Cyrus, we have a purpose to spread God's fame throughout the world. Whatever we do, we cannot in any way lower God's reputation in the world's eyes or undermine His role as Creator and King.

Throughout Isaiah 45, God's Creatorship has been emphasized over and over again, and this is one aspect of His Godship that is hotly contested by the inclusivity agenda. For a man or woman to suddenly decide that they don't like the gender with which they were born is a direct affront to the God who made them. There are certain lifestyles with which the LORD takes issue because they corrupt the order and purpose which He designed mankind. People who are caught in the wash of identity confusion that this world has generated or engaged in these alternative lifestyles are certainly in a broken place. If they are going to find peace and well-being, they need to identify with their Creator and return to Him. To that end, they need someone who is willing to come alongside them and lovingly explain to them what is the path to a relationship with God. The path begins with an understanding of God in His sovereignty as their Creator, the purpose for which He has made them, and then what an on-going relationship with Him looks like. They may not want to hear this and may reject our effort to draw them back to God's Highway, no matter how lovingly or humbly we present it. They will most certainly reject it if we do not present it in love. We as Christians can tank the effort completely if we don't approach it with a humble and loving attitude. But in our effort to love them, we cannot overlook the sinful behavior. God has modeled this for us repeatedly. On one hand He will address Israel's sinful behavior very bluntly, but He always balances it with assurances of love. And He usually does it in that order. "What you are doing offends me, but I love you." So, often we reverse those statements. "I love you, but . . ." Does the order of those statements make a difference? I think it does.

We can prepare and present the way of return, but it often fails because at some point, the person in that broken place must come to the acknowledgment that what they are doing or how they are living does not please or glorify their Creator. If they are going to find peace and well-being that He offers, it will require a realignment on their part with His vision and values. If they choose to reject the relationship, there is little we can do about it. It is a matter between them and God.

Unfortunately, we as believers often fail to balance the love of the person with the address of the behavior that is breaking their relationship with God. Our hardened stance can become the stumbling stone that hinders their return to God or derails it completely.

That being said, there are some lines for inclusivity that the LORD draws for those within the congregational body of believers. We find an instance of this in 1 Corinthians 5, where Paul addresses adultery within a congregation that has not been addressed. He says,

> *"I wrote to you in my epistle not to keep company with sexually immoral people. Yet I certainly did not mean with the sexually immoral people of this world, or with the covetous, or extortioners, or idolaters, since then you would need to go out of the world. But now I have written to you not to keep company with anyone named a brother, who is sexually immoral, or covetous, or an idolater, or a reviler, or a drunkard, or an extortioner—not even to eat with such a person. For what have I to do with judging those also who are outside? Do you not judge those who are inside? But those who are outside God judges. Therefore 'put away from yourselves the evil person.'"* – 1 Corinthians 5:9-13

We do not judge those who are unbelievers. It is the LORD's task of convicting them of their lifestyle. But believers who know the path that they are to walk and yet are engaged in flagrant, unrepentant, sinful lifestyles face judgment for this, even to the point of being exiled from the congregational body for a time. Here in Isaiah, God uses a temporary exile to bring Israel to an acknowledgment of their sin and spur the desire to return to Him. Paul advises a similar exile experience until the believer's behavior is corrected. But the exile must not be permanent, lest the sinning member despair. The door must always be left open in the hope of their return, as Paul explains in 2 Corinthians 2,

> *"This punishment which was inflicted by the majority is sufficient for such a man, so that, on the contrary, you ought rather to forgive and comfort him, lest perhaps such a one be swallowed up with too much sorrow. Therefore I urge you to reaffirm your love to him."*
> – 2 Corinthians 2:6-8

As much as our heart aches for these believers who are often dear to us as family or friends, there is a level of inclusivity that we cannot, in good conscience to God, accommodate or validate because of the damage it does to His reputation in the eyes of the world. We offer the reassurance of love and acceptance, but the behavior must be dealt with for the sake of the congregation's witness before the world.

There is a second line that we draw in how far we as believers go in asserting our freedom in Christ. Just because we have the liberty to do something, doesn't mean we *should* do it. Paul gives us an example of this in 1 Corinthians 10.

> *"'I have the right to do anything,' you say—but not everything is beneficial. 'I have the right to do anything'—but not everything is constructive. No one should seek their own good, but the good of others... If an unbeliever invites you to a meal and you want to go, eat whatever is put before you without raising questions of conscience. But if someone says to you, 'This has been offered in sacrifice,' then do not eat it, both for the sake of the one who told you and for the sake of conscience. I am referring to the other person's conscience, not yours. For why is my freedom being judged by another's conscience?... So whether you eat or drink or whatever you*

do, do it all for the glory of God. Do not cause anyone to stumble, whether Jews, Greeks or the church of God—even as I try to please everyone in every way. For I am not seeking my own good but the good of many, so that they may be saved." – 1 Corinthians 10:23-24, 27-29, 31-33 NIV

What we do, we do for the sake of others, not ourselves. Being helpful and edifying is for other people's benefit, and we should consider whether our actions require more liberty or more restraint as we endeavor to comfort them and lead them to Christ. But we must also keep God's glory in mind. Because of Christ, we have the freedom to sit down to the table with unbelievers and share the gospel. That is a freedom which Israel did not have under Mosaic Law. But even as we sit down with them, we have to be mindful of the messaging our actions present in regard to God's reputation. If what they give us to eat or otherwise join them in something that is glorifying to an idol in their life, then we cannot do that with them. We know that an idol is nothing, but in their eyes, it has a power that rivals God. Thus, we refrain, for the sake of their conviction, not ours. They may ask us why we can't join them, which then gives us the opportunity to teach them about our God and Savior, but that opportunity only comes when we draw that line.

Inasmuch as we can, we live at peace with all men. We know that we all are sinners with faults, and so we do not judge ourselves as better than a person caught in a crooked place because of ungodly lifestyle choices. We do not shun them for it. Instead, we come alongside them, sit down with them at lunch, talk with them, and look for teaching moments when we can present the true way to comfort and well-being. But there are a few lines we cannot cross. One is not dealing with sin in the congregational body. Believers should know the way to walk uprightly before God. Theirs is not a sin done in ignorance. If the sin is not dealt with, it infects the whole congregational body; therefore it must be addressed with a firm hand and the reassurance of acceptance back into the body once the behavior has been corrected. A time of exile has its benefits. Isaiah and Paul agree on that.

LESSON 9

The Comfort of Laying Down Burdens

READ

Isaiah 46:1-13

DISCUSSION

In Isaiah 46, God returns to the previous argument on the burdensome effort of serving idols versus serving Himself. Since we are now in the closing arguments for Part 1, the text might feel redundant because it will contain much of the same phrasing and topics as the opening arguments. The exercise is to find the differences and consider whether they resolve the issue, present a reversal of it, or expand the picture. In the chiastic structure, these opening and closing arguments are paired:

Opening Argument: (Isaiah 43:22-44:22) The effort of serving God versus the effort of making idols

Closing Argument: (Isaiah 46:1-8) Idols that must then be carried versus God who carries His people

Isaiah 46:1-8

Back in Isaiah 43, God took Israel to task for being weary of serving Him with sacrifices when in fact He was the one being wearied by her sin. He then went on to point out the extreme amounts of time and effort she put into fashioning her idols. In reality, she didn't mind putting some effort toward her own salvation. She just didn't want to do it His way. He also pointed out that His way came with a blessing, but what profit did she gain from her idolatry? None. So, her complaint as well as her actions were utterly foolish and self-defeating. Now He returns to this theme with another rebuke for Israel over her idolatry and points specifically to the Babylonian deities, Bel and Nebo, as perfect examples of just how burdensome idolatry can become.

Bel and Nebo were the supreme gods of Babylon and symbols of that nation's pride in their power and wisdom. Their idols were lavishly bedecked with gold and silver and paraded through the cities of Babylonia on celebration days. And yet, for all their pride and pomp, these Babylonian gods are humbled and made to stoop and bow when God gives them into the hand of Cyrus.

God points to the weary beasts (animal and human alike) staggering under the heavy load of the Babylonians' pride. Those idols had no power. They could not create themselves. They had to be carried everywhere, and wherever they were set down, there they stayed. They only created more of a burden on the people instead of relieving it. The irony of the people's plight is that they would have had some relief if they had simply put down that idol and walked away. But they don't. They blindly put their shoulder to the task of carrying their "saviors" and groan like weary beasts.

Unlike Bel and Nebo, God is one who carries His people. In fact, He considers it His duty as Israel's Creator to bear the burden of His creation; and not just for a season but continuously, from birth to old age, and He is more than willing to deliver them from those who would lay such a burden on them. (I think this is part of the reason why He forbade the people from making any image of Him. He did not want to be perceived as a god who had to be carried about. That is belittling to Him.) "To whom will you liken Me?" God asks. How comforting would it be to be carried instead of having to bear that burden? Is there even a comparison?

The main point in this contrast is that when a person turns from a dependence on God's strength and power, they must then shoulder that heavy burden themselves or place it on another person to bear, and that burden often adds to the burden of the oppressive circumstances and makes things worse. Israel once turned away from God, claiming that the sacrificial service He demanded for her redemption was too wearying and burdensome. Instead, she now sacrifices her own well-being by carrying these burdensome idols that cannot save her. The irony is rich.

Q: Why don't the people lay down that burden and return to Him?

Those idols were symbolic of Babylonia's pride and offered the illusion of power and empowerment. Maybe Israel doesn't want His help because she thinks she can handle it herself. That smacks of pride, doesn't it? Maybe she has believed the lie that she can empower herself. Maybe there is a fear of letting go of the tangible illusion to cling to an intangible God. Maybe there is shame or despair or self-pity driving her (these are all stumbling blocks, by the way). In our culture, we may not carry physical idols, but we still idolize and cling to people or things that offer the illusion of comfort, power, or self-empowerment, often because they validate us as victims.

God commands Israel to listen to Him in verse 3 and then to remember in verse 8. Remember this comparison, *you transgressors*. There is sin at the heart of Israel's refusal to lay down her burdens and rely on God.

Isaiah 46:9-13

This next set of verses opens with the repeated command to remember in verse 9 and ends with the repeated command to listen in verse 12. The repeated commands and the reversal of their order signals a chiastic structure. God is making a closing argument to the issue of idolatry.

Opening Argument: (Isaiah 43:16-21) Do not remember the former things; behold, a new thing (a reference to Cyrus)

Closing Argument: (Isaiah 46:9-13) Remember the former things; there is no God like Me (final reference to Cyrus in verse 11)

God says, *"Remember the former things of old…"* in verse 9. To paraphrase His words: "Remember when I brought you out of Egypt, and I went head-to-head with Pharoah's gods? Remember how Pharoah's wise men and sorcerers were able to mimic Moses and Aaron in turning water to blood and bringing frogs out of the Nile? Those magicians only added to the people's plight but could not relieve it. I, as the one true God, was able to deliver you when they could not. It is no different now. I am God and there is no other." He repeats that twice for emphasis, then goes on to speak of future things. "These Babylonian gods are no different from Egypt's gods. I have already determined their end and have set the wheels in motion to accomplish it by sending Cyrus." (Cyrus is the "bird of prey" referenced in verse 11.)

He goes on to say, *"Listen to Me, you stubborn-hearted . . ."* in verse 12. There is a stubbornness in Israel's refusal to acknowledge what God has done for her in the past and His ability to relieve her burden even now. God revisits this issue of carrying burdens, only He puts a twist on it. Not only will He carry Israel through this trial, but He will also carry His salvation "to" her. Notice the interplay of "near" and "far" in verses 12-13:

> *"Listen to Me, you stubborn-hearted, who are far from righteousness: I bring My righteousness near, it shall not be far off; My salvation shall not linger. And I will place salvation in Zion, for Israel My glory."*
> – Isaiah 46:12-13

Israel is far from God spiritually and far from her land physically. As God builds His highway, He is the one who closes the gap between Himself and Israel by providing a solution to the spiritual distance, even as He delivers her back to her land physically, and He promises that this salvation is not far off. It will not delay.

GOD'S HIGHWAY PROJECT

The Comfort of Laying Down Burdens

In the final verses, God belabors Israel's stubbornness. Before He can begin to offer healing and help, His people need to acknowledge that they need His help and desire it. She needs to be willing to lay down that burden, but it requires some humility on her part.

We have been approaching this study from the aspect of helping a struggling person in oppressive circumstances, and it is not hard to recognize that this is really the first step in the process. Part of what is keeping them in their oppression is their pride, their belief in their own empowerment, and their stubborn insistence on shouldering the burden themselves. You really can't do anything until they acknowledge that they need help, and this usually doesn't happen until they have exhausted themselves and all other avenues of support, relief, and comfort. And God lets them go through that breaking-down process. In truth, He cannot intervene until they have bowed to this reality because the glory for that intervention needs to be all His. He does not share His glory.

In Matthew 11:20-24, Jesus delivers a similar rebuke to the stubbornly impenitent cities of Chorazin and Bethsaida who did not repent when they saw the mighty works that were done in them (kind of like God rebuking Israel for not having remembered the former things). Jesus then holds out the invitation:

> *"Come to Me, all you who labor and are heavy laden, and I will give you rest. Take My yoke upon you and learn from Me, for I am gentle and lowly in heart, and you will find rest for your souls. For My yoke is easy and My burden is light."* – Matthew 11:28-30

> **Q:** We know the nature of Israel's burden in Isaiah, but how does this translate into Israel's experience in Jesus's day? Who are the heavy laden of whom He is speaking?

When Israel leaves her Babylonian exile, idolatry is one thing to which she does not return once she is back in her land. She no longer has the burden of carrying idols, and yet the service she renders to God becomes burdensome once again, thanks to the Pharisees and Sadducees who bring her back into a form of bondage with their "traditions." In Mark 7:9-13, Jesus rebukes these leaders for laying the burden of their man-made traditions on the people and thus making the Word of God of no effect. In Matthew 23, He rebukes them for their hypocrisy in imposing burdensome practices on the people that they themselves do not practice and pronounces woes on them. Jesus warns about idolizing such men, currying their favor, or following their example.

That was Jesus's day, and it spoke to the specific burden being levied by an oppressive and prideful authority in conflict with God. Jesus offered His followers the comfort of having that burden lifted when they acknowledged Him as Lord and master.

> **Q:** How do His words extend now to us in regard to shouldering a burden placed on us by oppressive authority or even burdensome religious practices?

> **Q:** How can leadership become idolized?

Isaiah 46: The Comfort of Laying Down Burdens

There are some religious sects and cults that bring their followers into a form of bondage by demanding that they lift up their leadership to a position of power that rivals God's place in the believer's life. Congregations can idolize their pastors or leadership, or a church leader can demand to be idolized by keeping an iron grip on his congregation and not allowing any teachings except those that parrot his own beliefs, even when those beliefs are not in line with biblical instruction. This is how many cults form, when its leader is given power over the lives of congregants to the extent that they dictate who may or may not be admitted to membership or even associated with it. The apostle John addressed an instance of this in his third apostolic letter in regard to Diotrephes, who put people out of the church for receiving the apostles (3 John 1:9-10). Paul addresses the issue of sectarianism in the Corinthian church (1 Corinthians 1:10-17). The Corinthians were squabbling over which leader they held as authority: Paul, Apollos, Cephas, or Christ.

> **Q:** Religious leadership can create oppression. How can religious practices become a form of bondage as well?

Some religious sects demand a tremendous number of rites that a believer has to perform to have a relationship with God or even salvation. Those who dispense those rites assume power over their people—power that they should never have—and their followers give them that power out of fear that they will lose their place in heaven. Any time fear enters the equation, it is because power is being given to someone or something that rivals God. If part of your person's struggle springs from the bondage of a church whose leadership has adopted these kinds of oppressive, controlling practices and inserted themselves into the relationship between God and the believers, it is important to address the fear of leaving that church. Those burdens can be hard to lay down because of the fear over losing their salvation. I think this is why God draws attention to the "near" and "far" aspects of His salvation here in Isaiah.

> **Q:** Who approaches whom in regard to righteousness? Does man approach God, or does God approach man?

> **Q:** Though we are not Israel, do we have the same experience of being far from God and yet brought near?

Paul writes about this extensively in His letter to the Ephesians:

> *"For by grace you have been saved through faith, and that not of yourselves; it is the gift of God, not of works, lest anyone should boast. For we are His workmanship, created in Christ Jesus for good works, which God prepared beforehand that we should walk in them ... But now in Christ Jesus you who once were far off have been brought near by the blood of Christ. For He Himself is our peace ... And He came and preached peace to you who were afar off and to those who were near. For through Him we both have access by one Spirit to the Father."*
> – Ephesians 2:8-18

We have peace and access to God the Father through Christ and the Spirit alone. No other intermediary is mentioned there, and those who insert themselves into that relationship or demand that we perform any kind of rites or works to secure our salvation do so to their own peril. This should be a comfort to us, and a comfort we can give our struggling person.

> **Q:** Apart from religious practices, do we also have cultural or even family "traditions" that are burdensome or cause anxiety?

This is just my opinion, but I think of gift-giving at Christmas. God never intended for a memorial of His Son's birth to become the grand end-of-year event driving a capitalist economy.

Those are some examples which apply the specific principle of Jesus's words in Matthew 11. The oppression of church authority or men's traditions may not be the issue with which you (or your struggling person) are grappling. Maybe your heavy burden takes another form. Maybe it is something as simple as not wanting to humble yourself to accept God's grace and forgiveness for some sin.

> **Q:** Is there a heavy burden that you are bearing in your life that is keeping you in bondage?

> **Q:** Is this a burden that God asks you to bear, or is it one that He offers to carry for you?

> **Q:** What do you need to do to put down that burden?

Bearing One Another's Burdens

Step 1 is the struggler being willing to lay down the burden and begin to work through the process of healing. Step 2 involves the transfer of that burden to another who can carry it, namely God, but what part do we as His human agents play? In Galatians 6, Paul speaks of bearing one another's burdens in regard to helping a person who is struggling with sin (as Israel is here in Isaiah).

> *"Brethren, if a man is overtaken in any trespass, you who are spiritual restore such a one in a spirit of gentleness, considering yourself lest you also be tempted. Bear one another's burdens, and so fulfill the law of Christ."* – Galatians 6:1-2

Q: What does Paul mean when he says bear one another's burdens and so fulfill the law of Christ?

Q: What attitude do we need to have when we begin to help a struggling person with sin in their life?

I would like to offer a warning with this idea of bearing others' burdens, or perhaps remind you of something God said at the beginning of this study. All flesh is like the grass, but the Word of God endures forever.

Q: How can carrying another's burden bring you into bondage?

Q: How can bearing that burden for them become your "Bel" and "Nebo"—a testament to pride?

LESSON 10

The Comfort of Vengeance

READ

Isaiah 47:1-15

DISCUSSION

Is vengeance comforting? That is an uncomfortable question to answer. Our righteous Christian side will say no, absolutely not, but our carnal side might beg to differ. If there is no comfort in it, why do so many people seek it? Because it is empowering. But which is more empowering and ultimately satisfying: when we take that vengeance for ourselves or let God avenge us?

It should be no surprise that the topic of vengeance crops up within Part 1's discussion of power and empowerment. In previous chapters, God has promised Israel that He will deliver her from exile, but it is not enough that He simply takes her out of Babylonia's hands. Here in Isaiah 47, He grants her the vindication of witnessing His humiliation of the seemingly invincible oppressor who has tormented her. Babylon, the capital city of the Babylonian empire and seat of her strength, is personified as a haughty young woman of tremendous wealth and prestige who suddenly experiences a horrific reversal of fortune and loses everything at the hand of an angry God.

In the chiastic structure of Isaiah 41-48, these opening and closing arguments are paired:

Opening Argument: (Isaiah 43:14-15) Babylon's judgment promised
Closing Argument: (Isaiah 47:1-15) Babylon's judgment rendered

Isaiah 47:1-7

The LORD's rebuke begins in verses 1-2 with a series of imperative commands to Babylon.

> "Come down and sit in the dust ... Sit on the ground ... Take the millstone and grind ... Remove your veil ... Take off the skirt ... Uncover the thigh ... Pass through the rivers."

His words are brutal and debasing as He drags the "tender and delicate" tyrant off her throne. She was anything but tender to His people, so He strips off that veil of hypocrisy and uncovers her to her shame.

"Sit in silence ... Go into darkness." In her hubris, Babylon has called herself the Lady of Kingdoms, but the LORD reminds her of how she came to that exalted place:

> "I was angry with My people; I have profaned My inheritance, and given them into your hand. You showed them no mercy; on the elderly you laid your yoke very heavily. And you said, 'I shall be a lady forever,' so that you did not take these things to heart, nor remember the latter end of them." – Isaiah 47:6-7

God gave Israel to Babylon for a time because He was angry with Israel and needed to deal with His people, but Babylon was only ever His tool. After witnessing the fury that the LORD meted out to His own wayward people, one would think that Babylon might have taken a lesson from that and been more circumspect in handling Israel, but she wasn't. She took her role as God's agent too far and was merciless to His precious people, and it is for her hubris and lack of mercy that she now suffers punishment.

Isaiah 47:8-11

Babylon's first failing is that she did not take Israel's example to heart. That was her first failing. God then addresses the lies that she has told herself. She thinks she is secure in her position, but she is not. She thinks she is untouchable and invincible, but she is not. She thinks that she will endure and her legacy will live on, but it will not. God says death and grief will come upon her in one day, and then He tells her why.

- She has relied on her "sorceries" and "enchantments," a power based in occult sources which will prove to be only illusions.

- She has trusted in her wickedness, saying to herself, "no one sees me."
- Her worldly wisdom and knowledge have warped her.
- She has become haughty and entitled.

Q: What parts of Babylon's profile do we see in our own culture today?

God says evil will come upon Babylon in one day and from an unknown source. We know from the book of Daniel that Babylon was taken in one night, the very night when Belshazzar saw the writing on the wall which Daniel translated for him. That night, the kingdom fell into the hands of Medo-Persia (Daniel 5). God is true to His word.

Isaiah 47:12-15

The passage ends with the LORD's scoffing challenge to Lady Babylon to consult her famed soothsayers and magicians, who will not be able to deliver her. They just add more fuel to the raging inferno of God's anger, and all of her merchants and traffickers will abandon her.

There is a mixing of near and distant prophecies in this passage. The end of Old Testament Babylon will resemble the fall of a future Babylon in the End Times, as recorded in Revelation 18. Here are some excerpts:

> *"And he cried mightily with a loud voice, saying, 'Babylon the great is fallen'... And I heard another voice from heaven saying, 'Come out of her, my people, lest you share in her sins, and lest you receive of her plagues... In the measure that she glorified herself and lived luxuriously, in the same measure give her torment and sorrow; for she says in her heart, "I sit as queen, and am no widow, and will not see sorrow." Therefore her plagues will come in one day—death and mourning and famine. And she will be utterly burned with fire, for strong is the Lord God who judges her.'"* – Revelation 18:2-8

> *"The kings of the earth who committed fornication and lived luxuriously with her will weep and lament for her, when they see the smoke of her burning, standing at a distance for fear of her torment, saying, 'Alas, alas, that great city Babylon, that mighty city! For in one hour your judgment has come.'... The merchants of these things, who became rich by her, will stand at a distance for fear of her torment, weeping and wailing,"* –Revelation 18:9-11, 15

> **Q:** Knowing the abuse and oppression Israel suffered at the hands of Babylon past (and Babylon future), is the LORD's vengeance sufficient to comfort her?
>
> **Q:** There is one thing that we don't see in all of this passage and that is Israel's participation in God's vengeance. Why is that important?

Israel's lack of participation here is a sharp contrast to the statement God made back in Isaiah 41:15-16, where He promised her that she herself will take part in tearing down "the mountains and hills"—the exalted ones who have oppressed her—as part of His vindication.

> *"Behold, I will make you into a new threshing sledge with sharp teeth; You shall thresh the mountains and beat them small, and make the hills like chaff. You shall winnow them, the wind shall carry them away, and the whirlwind shall scatter them; You shall rejoice in the LORD, and glory in the Holy One of Israel." – Isaiah 41:15-16*

God said that, and yet, we see here in this chapter that Israel has no part in the LORD's vengeance against Babylon. God takes vengeance on His people's behalf, while Israel stands by as a witness. In fact, as He has told her in the past, vengeance is His and His alone (Deuteronomy 32:35). So, how do we reconcile these two statements?

> **Q:** How does Israel play a part in her own vengeance without actually playing a part?
>
> **Q:** John the Baptist's message in Matthew 3:7-12 (cf. Luke 3:7-17) parallels the same imagery of threshing, winnowing, and removing chaff that is used in Isaiah 41:15-16, but whose task is it, according to John the Baptist? Is it the nation of Israel's task to take vengeance or the task of the One who represents her before God, who is Himself equal parts Israel and God?

GOD'S HIGHWAY PROJECT

We have been talking about the four steps in God's Highway Project. Step 1 was lifting up those in the valleys. Step 2 was bringing the mountains and hills low. Taking vengeance is a way of lifting one person up by taking another down, and when man does it, it is often done under the guise of justice, but it is not justice.

> **Q:** How is vengeance different from justice?

They differ in their motives. Justice settles conflicts with equality to both sides. A law is made. A punishment is set. When a person transgresses that law, they know exactly what the punishment will be, and they accept the punishment for it. But once fair retribution and recompense is made, that is the end of the matter. Both sides walk away from each other as equals once again. Justice is meant to accomplish God's main objectives: To end the fighting and reconcile the sin.

> **Q:** When we take vengeance for ourselves, is our goal to end the fighting and pardon the sin?

No, it isn't. Human vengeance has a different motive. Vengeance is a way of glorifying oneself by inflicting punishment or retribution for an injury or wrong—particularly an injury to one's reputation. It's an act of domination by which you take back what is due to you, as you see it, plus a little more for good measure and to ram home the message of who is greater. It isn't about reestablishing equality. It is about self-glorification, and it moves beyond beneficial punishment into destructive humiliation. That act of humiliation will create a stumbling block for both the perpetrator and victim, which we will discuss in Isaiah 54.

There is serious comfort in vengeance, and the world whole-heartedly endorses that means of empowerment. Today, we live in a culture that has become hypersensitive to victims of social injustice, and we see the threshing sledges with their sharp, raking teeth at work across all venues of social media—and not just from actual victims but from those who identify with them and support them. These sharp teeth thresh their antagonists into physical, mental, emotional, and even spiritual ruin. And people "like" it.

> **Q:** Do you know anyone who is so consumed by a desire for vengeance (or simply to lift themselves up) that they take every opportunity to rake over their opponent with sharp teeth and tear them down?
>
> **Q:** What comfort does the vengeful person get from it?

> **Q:** Does it bring healing to our community when self-empowered victims turn to tearing down their oppressors beyond repair?
>
> **Q:** Who gets the glory for the take-down?

Vengeance is a punishment best left to God. He is the only one who can do it thoroughly, justly, and with the beneficial outcome of ending the fight instead of prolonging it.

How Israel understands her role in regard to taking vengeance is supremely important because, as we will see in later chapters, there is a new kingdom coming, and God's people—these victimized people—will be ruling in it. That means they will have power and authority over people who were once their oppressors.

> **Q:** When people who have been abused or oppressed are given power and authority over their abusers, what do they often do with it?

Vengeance is not Israel's, or ours, to take. What remains for us, then, is how to react to our abusers until the LORD vindicates us.

> **Q:** Even as our world is becoming more hostile towards us on account of our faith, are we content to wait for the LORD's vindication?
>
> **Q:** When we have a grievance over some injustice done to us or another person, do we take up the role of a threshing sledge with sharp teeth in how we respond to that?
>
> **Q:** Is that tearing-down in line with God's goal to end the fighting?

Whatever tearing down happens as part of God's Highway Project, it must be kept in alignment with God's overall objectives to end fighting and pardon sin. When an oppressor's world begins to implode under the LORD's hand, it is tempting for the one who has suffered at their hand to take personal stabs at them, to gloat, or to heap more rebuke on them. Proverbs 24 offers wise instructions to the oppressor and the victim:

> *"Do not lie in wait, O wicked man, against the dwelling of the righteous; do not plunder his resting place; for a righteous man may fall seven times and rise again, but the wicked shall fall by calamity. Do not rejoice when your enemy falls, and do not let your heart be glad when he stumbles; lest the LORD see it, and it displease Him, and He turn away His wrath from him."* – Proverbs 24:15-18

Paul reminds us of the LORD's command not to avenge ourselves:

> *"Repay no one evil for evil. Have regard for good things in the sight of all men. If it is possible, as much as depends on you, live peaceably with all men. Beloved, do not avenge yourselves, but rather give place to wrath; for it is written, '"Vengeance is Mine, I will repay," says the Lord.' Therefore 'If your enemy is hungry, feed him; if he is thirsty, give him a drink; for in so doing you will heap coals of fire on his head.' Do not be overcome by evil, but overcome evil with good."* – Romans 12:17-21

Even as we examine Israel in our case study, we should not neglect the lesson of Babylon. At times, we unknowingly become God's tool for dealing with another person, for better or worse, but how we acquit ourselves in our part of that process will be judged. Self-assessment and introspection is vital when we step into that role.

> **Q:** When we see negative consequences playing out in someone else's life, as we see with Israel, do we take that to heart? Do we consider, and then adjust our own path?

There are rewards for the works we do in life, good and bad, and we should not labor under the assumption that the reward God determines for our works is necessarily a good and pleasant thing. Job reminds us that *"those who plow iniquity and sow trouble will reap the same."* (Job 4:8)

David wrote,

> *"Therefore the LORD has recompensed me according to my righteousness, according to the cleanness of my hands in His sight. With the merciful You will show Yourself merciful; with a blameless man You will show Yourself blameless; with the pure You will show Yourself pure; and with the devious You will show Yourself shrewd. For You will save the humble people, but will bring down haughty looks."* – Psalm 18:24-27

It is wise to take a lesson from Babylon when we are tempted to lift ourselves up above others and boast of our own security in God's favor. While our salvation is secure in Christ because of God's grace, our works will be evaluated in the end as well, apart from that salvation, and we will be recompensed, for better or worse, for how we have acquitted ourselves in the course of this life, particularly toward God's people.

So far in this study, I have been ending lessons at the end of chapters, but in this case, I am going to incorporate part of the next chapter with this one in order to compare the picture of Babylonia's reigning daughter with Israel's reigning daughter.

READ

Isaiah 48:1-11

DISCUSSION

In the wake of His humiliation of Babylon in Isaiah 47, God turns a blistering rebuke on Israel. Just because He has avenged her doesn't mean that she is above reproach in His eyes. Back in Isaiah 43, He had charged her with bearing witness of His mighty works. Now He rebukes her for having failed in that calling. We see again the impartiality of His judgment of both the Gentiles and Jews. In the chiastic structure of Isaiah 41-48, these opening and closing arguments are paired:

Opening Argument: (Isaiah 43:9-13) God calls Israel to be His witness.
Closing Argument: (Isaiah 48:1-11) God rebukes Israel for her failure to be His witness.

Isaiah 48:1-11

God opens with a sarcastic description of the people of Judah. Just as Babylon was the reigning "daughter" of Babylon, so Judah is the reigning "daughter" of Israel, being preeminent among the tribes and associated with the capital city, Jerusalem. Thus, between Isaiah 47 and 48, we have this comparison of two haughty, entitled "daughters." Judah rests on her reputation and entitlement. She swears by the name of the LORD and bandies His name about—but not in truth or righteousness. She says she trusts in the LORD, but there is little evidence of that. Instead, she has stubbornly persisted in her idolatry and is no better than Babylon.

God brings this charge against His own people, that they have not borne witness of Him or given Him glory for His mighty works among them. For the last eight chapters, God has been harping on the fact that He has declared the former things and brought them to pass, and now has pronounced new things which He will bring to pass as a witness to the world of His Godship and that He is who He says He is. But now, in the closing argument, He reveals another reason for making these predictions—to safeguard His glory against His own people's treachery. God declares that He did the former things before there were any gods in Israel, so that she could not say that her idols ordained these events (48:5). Now He is declaring the new things, so that she can't dismiss Him by saying that these things are nothing new or that she already knew they would happen (48:7). These things aren't just the natural outworking of cause and effect, or a case of "what goes around comes around" or karma or fate or however you wish to dismiss it. This is God doing something deliberately and with forethought.

Clearly God is angry with His people. He has made them glorious for His own glory, but they have become complacent and dismissive of Him and His work. They give His glory to idols or take credit themselves, and He cannot bear it.

God brings judgment on Babylon and Israel alike. When we look at Babylon's end in the previous chapter (Isaiah 47), we see that Babylon wears herself out appealing to her astrologers and stargazers, and in the end, the pieces of wood that she called her gods are nothing more than tinder for a fire, and not even a comforting one. Babylon is given over to her destruction for her idolatry, and nothing saves her. But God deals differently with Israel. In verse 10, He sends her into a "furnace of affliction" and lets her wear herself out crying to idols, but she doesn't suffer a complete destruction. Instead, it becomes a refining process.

Q: Why does He deal with Israel differently?

In verse 11, the LORD repeats the phrase *"Lema'ani, lema'ani"*—for My own sake, for My own sake—for emphasis. He has invested Himself in His people, and He is as tied to them as they are to Him. But Israel needs to understand that He alone is sovereign over their lives, and that what He gives, He can take away. Even so, He will give again to those who are faithful to Him as they endure the furnace of affliction. Once that furnace has done its refining work, the faithful remnant of Judah will return to claim their inheritance in the land of Israel.

The Furnace of Affliction

We, as Church age believers, are not Israel. That is an important distinction to make. And yet, we are named among God's people because of the blood covenant forged through Christ's death on the cross. As a result, we walk in Israel's footsteps and are made to endure seasons in the furnace of affliction.

> **Q:** When you think of a person caught in a furnace of affliction, what do you picture them going through?
>
> **Q:** Perhaps you yourself have spent a season in the furnace of affliction. What form did your furnace take?

We have all spent time in the furnace, but perhaps not for the same reason as Israel.

> **Q:** We know why God put Israel through that experience. Why does He put us through that experience?

Can we become complacent and dismissive of His work in our lives? Yes, we can. Can we fail to be a faithful witness for Him? Yes, we can. When life is manageable, we can live day to day with nothing really good or bad happening and never once bear witness of our glorious God to the world. If we only give Him glory when we have reached the ends of our own resources, are we surprised when He makes our lives an ongoing trial by fire? It is to His glory that we go through these trials and accept His refining of us.

> **Q:** Are the fiery trials that we face meant for punishment or purification? What is the difference?
>
> **Q:** We have been filtering these passages through the task of comforting people who are in the furnace of affliction. Where is comfort found in the ordeal? (Hint: Read 2 Corinthians 4:7-11, James 1:2-4.)
>
> **Q:** Is there comfort in knowing that it is only a refining process and not a complete destruction for us as God's people?

LESSON 11

The Comfort of God's Sovereignty

READ

Isaiah 48:12-22

DISCUSSION

As I prepare this study in 2025, the current U.S. president and his administration are now in full swing, pursuing the goals of peace, well-being, and security for the nation as they see it, and causing no little upheaval in the process. The outworking of the president's agenda has been uplifting and hopeful for some but horrifying for others, and the outcry of those who oppose his agenda is unrelenting. I find myself aching for an end to the barrage of angry words and protests, and wonder what it would take to bring us national peace, because it seems like every citizen has their own idea of what that looks like. How do we achieve national peace in our country today? How do we define peace? Is it something we even want anymore? These are the thoughts that came to me as I delved into the final verses in Isaiah 48.

Isaiah 48 concludes Part 1 of God's Highway Project, focusing on the theme of God's power and sovereignty over His people as He works toward His goal of peace. God has been building His argument for His ability to deliver Israel and restore her peace, well-being, and safety, and He has answered His opposition with strength. Now He wraps up His case with some bittersweet closing statements that mingle lament for what has been lost and rejoicing over release and national peace to come.

In the chiastic structure, we have these opening and closing arguments:

Opening Argument: Redemption promised (Isaiah 41:1-42:25)
Closing Argument: Redemption accomplished (Isaiah 48:12-22)

Isaiah 48:12-16

The content of these verses is a repetition of much of what we have heard before. The challenge is to identify who is speaking. This is vitally important because, as we go into the next chapter, we will see God conversing with an unnamed Servant identified only as "Me." Just as Cyrus was the focal point in Part 1, "Me" will become the focal point of Part 2, and He is introduced here at the end of Isaiah 48 in preparation for Part 2.

I should warn you that commentators have a field day with the pronouns in verses 12-16, and depending on the theological stance they espouse, they will splinter and splice the text to cast "I," "Me," and "him" into various characters. But it was never meant to be splintered and spliced the way some have done it. The interpretation of these pronouns must be consistent with the syntax of the sentence, the overall verse, and the greater contexts of Part 1 and Part 2. So, before you turn to any commentaries for a deeper understanding of these verses, I'd like you to work through the text with me and see what conclusions we draw from a simple observation. Afterward, I will comment on the cutting and splicing that various commentators have done, and why I disagree with them.

Let's begin with verse 12.

> "Listen to Me, O Jacob, and Israel, My called: I am He, I am the First, I am also the Last." – Isaiah 48:12

Q: Who is speaking here?

This is God speaking in the first person ("I"). He made this same statement back in the opening argument in Isaiah 41:4 and again 44:6:

> "Who has performed and done it, calling the generations from the beginning? '*I, the LORD, am the first; and with the last I am He.*'"
> – Isaiah 41:4 (emphasis added)

> "Thus says the LORD, the King of Israel, and his Redeemer, the LORD of hosts: '*I am the First and I am the Last*; besides Me there is no God.'"
> – Isaiah 44:6 (emphasis added)

Q: What does God mean when He says He is the First and the Last?

In all three instances, this statement is made in the greater context of God proving His Godship over His rivals, the idols, by His former actions and future prophecies. In Isaiah 41:1-4, God revealed His calling of Cyrus to deal with Babylon and ended with this statement of Himself. We know from what we have read in past chapters that God's ability to call Cyrus is proof of His Godship in contrast to Israel's idols. He did the former things—the miracles in Egypt at Israel's beginning—and He prophesies of this new deliverer coming in the future. Thus, He is the first and last in regard to Israel's generations, from beginning to end. He is her transcendent God. The context is the same in Isaiah 44:6, and now in Isaiah 48:12. Thus, the repeated statement here in Isaiah 48:12 is the closing bookend to that argument. Next verse . . .

> *"Indeed My hand has laid the foundation of the earth, and My right hand has stretched out the heavens; When I call to them, they stand up together."* – Isaiah 48:13

> **Q:** Who is speaking here?

Again, this is God speaking in the first person ("I"). He made this same statement back in the opening argument in Isaiah 42:5 as a preamble to His commissioning of the Servant (not Cyrus).

> *"Thus says God the LORD, <u>Who created the heavens and stretched them out, Who spread forth the earth and that which comes from it,</u> Who gives breath to the people on it, and spirit to those who walk on it: 'I, the LORD, have called You in righteousness, and will hold Your hand; I will keep You and give You as a covenant to the people, as a light to the Gentiles, to open blind eyes, to bring out prisoners from the prison, those who sit in darkness from the prison house.'"* – Isaiah 42:5-7 (emphasis added)

Thus, in addition to being the first and last in Israel's history, God is first in the sense of being the Creator of the universe. Next verse . . .

> *"All of you, assemble yourselves, and hear! Who among them has declared these things? The LORD loves him; he shall do His pleasure on Babylon, and His arm shall be against the Chaldeans."* – Isaiah 48:14

> **Q:** Who is speaking here?

Note that a different speaker seems to be speaking all of a sudden. If the LORD was still speaking, it would be phrased in the first-person point-of-view. Thus, the sentence would read,

"I, the LORD, love him."

But that is not what the verse says. It says,

"The LORD loves him."

The phrasing has switched to a third-person point-of-view, as if an outside observer is calling to the greater assembly and making this observation. We have seen these sudden switch of speakers in the past where a third party inserts a comment or question, which the LORD then answers, but it isn't clear here who the third party is. We might assume it is the prophet himself calling to the greater assembly.

Q: Look carefully at the pronouns in the verse. Who is "him" and "he"?

We tend to identify pronouns by whether our Bible version capitalizes the word or not. Lowercase "he" indicates a human being; capitalized "He" refers to one of the Godhead. But we need to be careful about relying on capitalization for interpretation because there is no capitalization in the original Hebrew text. Capitalization is something that translators have added for our benefit, based on their understanding of the text, and capitalization rules are not consistent across all Bible translations. So, instead of relying on the capitalization of pronouns for our interpretation, let's consider the content of the verse. Clearly, it is speaking of someone, a human agent, who will deal with the Babylonians according to the LORD's pleasure. We know that human agent is Cyrus, the servant-king featured in Part 1, whose work is being wrapped up. According to this verse, he is also one whom the LORD loves. That seems like an odd statement to throw in there, considering that Cyrus is a pagan Gentile who doesn't know God. Perhaps for this reason, some Christian Bible commentators have clipped the phrase, "God loves him," out of its context and interpreted it as God loving Christ (the Servant), not Cyrus. But that is inconsistent with the text.

Q: Why would God love Cyrus?

Q: What does that tell us about God?

In the next verse, the speaker switches back to speaking in the first person.

> *"I, even I, have spoken; Yes, I have called him, I have brought him, and his way will prosper."* – Isaiah 48:15

We are still on the topic of Cyrus. The "him" here in verse 15 connects with the "him" in verse 14. But the speaker has changed. We know this because the prophet or third party cannot claim to be the one who called Cyrus or made his way prosper. That was the LORD's doing. Another clue that the LORD is speaking now is the use of the phrase, *"I, even I."* That phrase is used repeatedly in the book of Isaiah when the LORD is speaking of Himself to His people (Isaiah 43:11, 43:25, 51:12). The LORD is merely confirming the third party's statement.

Again, some commentators erroneously plug Christ into these verses:

> *". . . The LORD loves him [Christ]; he [the LORD] shall do his pleasure on Babylon and his arm will be against the Chaldeans. I, even I, have spoken; yes, I have called him [Christ], I have brought him, and his way will prosper."*

If these verses are talking about Christ, why throw a random reference to the Chaldeans into the middle? This doesn't make sense. Interpreting the text through such snipping and splicing of phrases is a poor handling of the text, and I disagree with commentators who do this. I think they are reading their own doctrinal stance into the pronoun "him." "Him" is clearly referring to Cyrus. Thus,

> *". . . The LORD loves him [Cyrus]; he [Cyrus] shall do His [the LORD's] pleasure on Babylon and His arm will be against the Chaldeans. I, even I [the LORD], have spoken; Yes, I have called him [Cyrus], I have brought him, and his way will prosper."*

This is the closing statement on the topic of Cyrus, and the last reference to him in the text. His character is notably absent in Isaiah 49-66.

And now we come to the final verse in this selection, which hits us with a whammy.

> *"Come near to Me, hear this: I have not spoken in secret from the beginning; from the time that it was, I was there. And now the Lord GOD and His Spirit have sent Me."* – Isaiah 48:16

Isaiah 48: The Comfort of God's Sovereignty

Let's walk through this phrase by phrase:

- *"Come near to Me..."* The pronoun "Me" suggests that God is still speaking from the previous verse.
- *"I have not spoken in secret..."* That is a repetition of what God said back in Isaiah 45:16 when He was commissioning Cyrus. This is still God speaking.
- *"From the beginning..."* This is another way of saying, "I am the First," which hearkens back to that earlier identification of God as Creator in verses 12-13. God has repeatedly declared Himself "from the beginning" throughout Isaiah. When He uses that phrase, we understand that He is "from the beginning" in the sense of being the Creator, but He is also from Israel's beginning, as attested by the mighty works He did for her in former times.
- *"From the time that it was, I was there..."* That speaks again to God's transcendent omnipresence.
- *"And now the Lord GOD and His Spirit have [has] sent Me."*

Ba-boom! There is the whammy. Notice, there are three persons mentioned in this verse: the Lord GOD, His Spirit, and "Me." It is not the LORD speaking but "Me." This raises some questions.

> **Q:** If "Me" is not the LORD, then who is speaking in this verse?

He isn't named, but He has been sent. Thus, He is a Servant much like Cyrus, except He isn't Cyrus. Cyrus has not spoken once throughout the text. Notice the "now" in the phrase—*now* the Godhead has sent "Me." Cyrus's work is done, and now this new Servant steps to the forefront to begin His tasking.

> **Q:** Has this Servant been speaking throughout the whole verse? If so, then the Servant is making some pretty hefty claims. What aspects of God's person or character is He attributing to Himself?

> **Q:** Is the Servant speaking only in verse 16, or has He been speaking in the previous verses as well?

The claims that "Me" makes in verse 16 are reiterations of verses 12-13. I would argue He has been speaking as far back as verse 12. But that opens up some new revelations.

When "Me" says, *"I, even I have spoken; yes, I have called him,"* He is claiming to be the one who called Cyrus. He is a Servant like Cyrus, and yet He eclipses Cyrus in authority, as if Cyrus were merely a prince acting at His direction.

When He says, *"My hand has laid out the foundations of the earth, and My right hand has stretched out the heavens,"* He is claiming to have been with God at the time of Creation and actively participating in that task.

When He says, *"I am He, I am the First, I am also the Last,"* He is claiming equality with the Godhead.

> **Q:** Is the Servant God Himself or is He a human agent? Can He be both?

Such a question would have been preposterous and unthinkable to ask in Isaiah's day. Jewish scholars attempt to explain it by saying the Servant is merely a human agent, or perhaps the prophet sent with a divine message, and thus, speaks for God. But from where we stand in history, knowing what we know about Jesus Christ, we recognize the triune nature of the Godhead and the hypostatic union of God and man revealed in these verses. The Servant, "Me," is Jesus Christ. Christ Himself declares in Revelation 22:13, *"I am the Alpha and the Omega, the Beginning and the End, the First and the Last."*

All this time, it seemed that the LORD God was speaking. All of the statements in 48:12-16 are nothing more than what had been said by Him before. The only difference now is the revelation of a new speaker, and that twist throws a whole new light on the closing argument. Where God was speaking, now "Me" is speaking. From now on, we will see a curious mingling of these two voices, which seem to speak as one at times but then, separately, or in conversation with one another. This is the glorious power of God, that with a simple, understated comment inserted into a closing argument, He can upend everything you thought you knew about Him.

Before we move on, I want to pause and gather together the picture of "Me" that has been presented so far. Remember, the chiastic structure has paired Isaiah 48 with Isaiah 42 for comparison, and between the two, we have a compound picture of this new character coming on the scene. He is at the same time a servant and king, man and God.

Servant, King, Man, God

Isaiah 42 opened with the picture of a man—a human deliverer simply referred to as the Servant. The LORD declared that He would raise up this deliverer, invest Him with the Holy Spirit, and task Him with no small feat of reestablishing the law and justice in the earth. The Servant would embody the covenant between God and His people. He would be a light to the Gentiles and would release prisoners from prison. He is cast as a humble Servant under the LORD's authority, and yet He is no common servant. He is also a king.

The opening arguments in Isaiah 42 fully establish the Servant-king as a man. The closing arguments in Isaiah 48 fully establish Him as God. This accords with the description of Him given in Isaiah 9:6-7, which says,

> *"For a Child will be born to us, a Son will be given to us; and the government will rest on His shoulders; and His name will be called Wonderful Counselor, Mighty God, Eternal Father, Prince of Peace. There will be no end to the increase of His government or of peace on the throne of David and over his kingdom, to establish it and to uphold it with justice and righteousness from then on and forevermore. The zeal of the LORD of armies will accomplish this."* – Isaiah 9:6-7 NASB20

His titles as Mighty God and Eternal Father have now been established at the end of Part 1. As we move into Part 2, His roles as Wonderful Counselor and Prince of Peace will take center stage. Thus, we will see the totality of His kingly character fleshed out.

When we come to the New Testament, we are given this same composite view of Jesus Christ in the gospel accounts. Matthew presents Him as the king; Mark, the servant. Luke presents Him as a man; John, as God. In the book of Revelation, Christ identifies Himself with many phrases from Isaiah for the specific purpose of driving us back to this Old Testament picture.

Now, let's finish off Chapter 48. In the final verses, the LORD Himself is speaking (or perhaps it is "Me" speaking).

Isaiah 48:17-19

The chapter ends on the theme of peace and what makes for peace, and it is a comment that ties back to the theme of fear in Isaiah 41.

In the opening argument, God belabored the futility of idolatry and set up the comparison between the idolatrous nations who feared because they relied on their idols and Israel who did not fear—or at least, faithful Israel did not fear. Those of Israel who persisted in idolatry still had much to fear. In Isaiah 42, He rebuked her again for her disobedience to His commandments, which brought on her the promised curses from Deuteronomy.

Now, in Isaiah 48:17-19, God makes a similar comparison between those who have peace and those who don't. Israel has yet to experience peace because she has forsaken the commandments and followed the path of the fearful, idolatrous nations. The rebukes in Isaiah 41 and 42 become a lament in Isaiah 48:17-19 over what has not been accomplished and why. "Oh, that you had heeded My commandments!" the LORD cries. Obeying the commandments would have spared Israel this ordeal and brought her a blessing of peace, but the blessing has been lost. Peace can only be achieved by adherence to God's Word and, we should note, in the absence of fear.

This lament in Isaiah 48:18 finds a parallel in the book of Luke 19:42-44, where Jesus raised a similar lament over Jerusalem for her blindness and disobedience. The New International Version catches the gist of lament best:

> *"As he approached Jerusalem and saw the city, he wept over it and said, 'If you, even you, had only known on this day what would bring you peace—but now it is hidden from your eyes. The days will come upon you when your enemies will build an embankment against you and encircle you and hem you in on every side. They will dash you to the ground, you and the children within your walls. They will not leave one stone on another, because you did not recognize the time of God's coming to you.'"* – Luke 19:41-44 NIV

> **Q:** What cost Israel her peace this time?

> **Q:** Of what future event is Jesus speaking?

Isaiah 48:20-21

Now, in verses 20-21, the ordeal seems to have ended. Israel's deliverance by the hand of Cyrus, as promised in Isaiah 41, is now declared accomplished in Isaiah 48:20 as the LORD issues the command, "Go forth from Babylon!" with a voice of singing. Isaiah 48:20 is full of imperative commands. Go! Flee! Declare! Proclaim! Utter to the ends of the earth! All the verbs in this section are in perfect tense indicating that they have been completed. Even though these events are literally in the future at the time Isaiah speaks them, they are as good as accomplished. Thus, lament is turned to rejoicing and sorrow to gladness. This grand reversal is typical of Isaiah's narrative style.

Isaiah 48:21 then switches to a third-party speaker, who responds to the LORD's commands with a song of praise; but note, it is not over His future deliverance but of His past deliverance.

> "And they did not thirst when He led them through the deserts; He caused the waters to flow from the rock for them; He also split the rock, and the waters gushed out." – Isaiah 48:21
>
> **Q:** Why would the speaker choose to remind Israel of this episode in her past instead of focusing on the future deliverance?

The water theme in this verse connects to the idea of peace being like a river in verse 18. But what was the source of that flowing water? The rock that was split. Funny, that of all God's provisions on that Exodus journey, the rock is the one mentioned here. Paul tells us in 1 Corinthians 10:4 that the rock was Christ. Thus, it reinforces the identity of the speaker "Me" in verses 12-16 as being Christ. Christ was part of God's former works; He is also part of God's future works. Christ was the one who was struck so that the literal living water might sustain Israel in the desert; He will be struck again to provide living water that brings spiritual peace to all men. Once again, the veiled image of Christ is presented in the text.

Isaiah 48:22

Isaiah 48:22 ends the chapter with a final comment that there is no peace for the wicked, which closes the thought begun in verse 18. Peace, or *shalom*, is the reward for obedience.

Isaiah 48:22 is important to note, because this same verse is repeated in Isaiah 57:21. Thus, these verses create bookends (an inclusio) for Chapters 49-57 with the theme of peace and what makes for peace, which will be the focus of Part 2.

A blessing of peace now comes out of this experience in the furnace of affliction. Peace is a new theme going forward, but what makes for peace?

> **Q:** What does peace encompass?

The Hebrew word for peace is *shalom*, and it means completeness, soundness, health, and welfare. It includes the experiences of safety, prosperity, tranquility, and contentment, and a reconciliation of relationships between people, but also a harmony with God.

> **Q:** What has to happen for a community or nation to enter into such an experience?

According to God's words here in Isaiah, Israel would have peace in obeying His commandments. This implies that the nation needs to be re-established under the Laws that would bring not just social justice but a means of spiritual redemption as well (at least until such time as a more permanent sacrifice presented itself through the next Messiah's work). Cyrus was unable to achieve either of these with lasting effect. Even though he released Israel from her physical oppression and let her go back to her land, it did not bring her peace as a nation.

Peace is not an easy thing to achieve. So far, the LORD has addressed the initial question of where to seek power and empowerment, and the stumbling block of fear that is preventing Israel from experiencing comfort and peace. But there are other, deeper issues besides these that must be resolved before true peace can be achieved, issues like despair, shame, anger, silent withdrawal, and the need for closure. Part 2 will begin to address these.

GOD'S HIGHWAY PROJECT

The Comfort of God's Sovereignty (Part 1 Wrap-up)

The theme of Part 1 has focused on God's sovereignty. As God set out to comfort His people, He addressed the issues of power and empowerment first, presenting Himself as eternally superior to any other temporal sources of empowerment that His people might seek. Is God's power and sovereignty comforting? Some may say yes, and others, no.

> **Q:** When is God's sovereign power comforting?
>
> **Q:** When is it not comforting?

His power can be comforting when it works for us—when it lifts us up and validates us, when it vindicates and avenges us (Isaiah 41a, 42a, 43a, 44a, 45, 47, 48b). But it can be terrifying when it is wielded in judgment (Isaiah 41b, 42b, 43b, 44b, 48a) or is seemingly unfair because its judgment is impartial to victims (we discussed this in Isaiah 42).

God establishes His sovereignty and power first, then His love. When we are comforting people who are struggling, it might be tempting to focus on the love aspect of God's character.

> **Q:** Why is it essential to lay the foundational understanding of God's sovereignty first?
>
> **Q:** How do we build a case for God's power that will help a struggling person cling to Him (not us) as a comfort and help? What are some key things they need to know?

Now, let's walk through the highway-building steps:

The Lifting-Up and Tearing-Down Processes

The steps of taking down mountains and lifting up valleys are seen in the alternating pattern of strong rebuke and consolation. God doesn't offer one without the other.

> **Q:** Why must rebuke be tempered with love when ministering to a person who is caught in a "crooked place" or on a rough road in life?

> **Q:** What happens if there is only consolation and no rebuke for sin?
>
> **Q:** What happens if there is only rebuke and no consolation?
>
> **Q:** How can it affect the person's perception of a relationship with God when we don't follow God's model?

In the course of ministering to or counseling an oppressed or suffering person, we might need to address the sin in that person's life that is causing their brokenness. But if we follow God's model, the tearing-down must be paired with a lifting-up. Paul himself had to correct the Corinthian church over this after they came down on a man so hard that he was on the verge of despair (2 Corinthians 2:3-11). We see the same pattern modeled in Revelation 2-3. In Christ's address to the churches, He uses a balance of rebuke and consolation, except for the persecuted church of Smyrna to whom He gives consolation only. We need to strike the same balance with our own struggling person.

Straightening Crooked Places

This step of the process involves straightening out attitudes and behaviors that have become "crooked" (twisted or perverted, deceitful or sly). Crookedness can also manifest itself in being puffed up and self-righteous—having a distorted perspective. These are all things that empower oppression, and it takes some breaking to straighten them out.

God used Cyrus to break Babylonia's grip on her victim and remove suffering Israel from her oppressor's control.

> **Q:** Why is it a necessary first step to take a victim out of an oppressor's hands, even if it is just a stop-gap measure?
>
> **Q:** Does simply taking the victim out of oppressive circumstances solve the person's problems? Does it mean they are healed and restored physically, mentally, emotionally, or spiritually?
>
> **Q:** What else has to be addressed?

The oppressor isn't the only problem, although the victim would like to think they are; and part of straightening crooked places requires an impartial assessment of both parties and not overlooking the sin in the victim's life as well. That oppressive experience—that season in the furnace of affliction—may have had a purpose in correcting crookedness. Impartiality was an important element in the restoration process.

Smoothing Rough Places: Grappling with Stumbling Stones

Some examples of stumbling stones in these chapters were:

> **Stumbling stone #1: Truths about our condition that we don't want to acknowledge.** God began with the statement that all flesh is like grass. There can be an unwillingness to acknowledge our own powerlessness, limitations, weaknesses, or sin, which then becomes a stumbling stone to being healed or comforted. Christ is described in Isaiah as a stumbling stone to those who refuse to believe in Him (1 Peter 2:4-10, Isaiah 28:16, Isaiah 8:14).
>
> **Stumbling stone #2: Where we seek comfort.** Tangible things like idols (literal stones or figurative ones) or other physical sources can become false sources of comfort or salvation. Idolatry is definitely a stumbling stone over which God and Israel battle. When comforting a struggling person, you might find that there are temporal things or even people to which they are clinging that are keeping them in their oppressive circumstances, and it takes some breaking to get them to let go of those.
>
> **Stumbling stone #3: Emotional reactions to the abuse or oppression that add to and/or perpetuate oppression.** These can linger even after the actual oppressor is out of the picture. Fear was the major stumbling stone in Part 1 and is linked to the themes of power and justice. Other sub-topics under this theme include the desire for **validation, vindication,** and **vengeance**. These, too, can become stumbling stones if not pursued correctly.

The Stumbling Stone of Fear

Reverence for God's supreme power and sovereignty spurs a healthy kind of fear and conviction in us, but fear of our adversaries or circumstances can override a fear of God to the point where that fear becomes a stumbling block to our relationship with Him and our ability to be comforted and restored.

> **Q:** Is the knowledge of God's superior power all that is needed to overcome our fear of adversaries or oppressive circumstances?
>
> **Q:** What else do we need from God in terms of comfort?

Fear is the first and perhaps the greatest stumbling block that God addresses because it carries a power that rivals His own and can spawn other kinds of stumbling. There are nine imperative commands not to fear, seven of which fall in Chapters 41-44. Let's consider what we have learned about fear so far:

- **Fear stems from a feeling of powerlessness.** That powerlessness can spur the desire to take back the power by human means instead of relying on God's power. It can spur a despair that causes the victim to turn inward and shut down. This produces new stumbling stones such as self-pity, withdrawal, and isolation.

- **Fear drives decision-making in a way that can override sound reasoning.** For this reason, it is often a tactic that oppressors use to overpower and control us. A fearful person might seek relief from oppression in the wrong way, or they may refuse to leave an abuser for fear of being on their own. Fear can keep a person from speaking the truth (bearing witness) or doing something they know they should do. It can also make them do something they know they shouldn't do.

- **Fear is emotion-based.** Emotions are like the grass. They are fleeting things, and when emotions drive behavior and reasoning, they lead to crooked places. God calls Israel to use a sound mind instead of her emotions. He urges her to consider His past faithfulness and deliverance, that she might see, hear, know, understand, and believe He is who He says He is and that He is able to help her in her struggle. Israel is then called to bear witness of that belief. Our witness of God's deliverance and comfort is vital because it becomes a way of comforting other fearful, struggling people.

- **Fear can be guilt-based.** It can take a person into a dark place and imprison them there. A person might remain in the dark for fear of sin being brought to light. Thus, fear is tied to the stumbling block of shame, which God and the Servant will remedy in Part 2.

- **Fear is often a red-flag that something is wrong in the power dynamic**—that power has been given to something that doesn't or shouldn't have power over us. When this happens, fear results (as we discussed in Isaiah 41).

God's strategy for combating fear is summarized in 2 Timothy 1:7, which was our key New Testament verse.

> *"For God has not given us a spirit of fear, but of power and of love and of a sound mind."* – 2 Timothy 1:7

When we internalize an understanding of God's power and presence in our circumstances, the fear becomes manageable (2 Corinthians 4:7-10).

We all struggle with fear. Oppressed or abused people struggle with fear more than most. Their fear and the doubt it causes can infect us if we aren't well-grounded in God's power and love and His Word. So, how well-grounded are you? Answer these questions for yourself.

> **Q:** What do you believe about God's sovereignty and power?
>
> **Q:** What do you believe about His love and who you are to Him?
>
> **Q:** Has He been faithful to you in the past?
>
> **Q:** If you give a difficult situation to Him, do you believe He has the power to deal with the problem?
>
> **Q:** If He has the power to deal with it, do you *trust* Him to deal with it? Are you willing to let go of your other sources of empowerment and let Him control the situation?
>
> **Q:** Do you trust Him enough to be at peace with His handling of the situation, or are you still looking for validation, vindication, or vengeance?

PART 2

NARRATIVE STRUCTURE

Chiastic Structure of Part 2 (Isaiah 49-56)

Opening Arguments

- **1a:** The Servant is commissioned/seeks His reward from the LORD (49:1-4)
- **2a:** Salvation promised to the Gentiles through the Servant (49:5-13)
- **3a:** Problem: Israel despairs that the LORD has forsaken her (49:14)
- **4a:** God promises to bring Israel back to her kingdom (49:15-26)
- **5a:** The Servant endures shame to comfort Israel (50:1-11)
- **6a:** The eternality of God's righteousness/reward for the faithful (51:1-8)
- **7a:** Israel exhorts the Arm of the LORD to reveal Himself (51:9-11)
- **8a:** God's fury removed (Israel has drunk the cup) (51:12-23)
- **9a:** Awake, awake, purified Israel! (52:1-3)
- **10a:** Glorious God humbles Himself to become a servant (52:4-6)

11: Proclaim the good news! Salvation accomplished (52:7-9)

Closing Arguments

- **10b:** The Arm of the LORD laid bare (in strength and weakness) (52:10)
- **9b:** Depart, depart, purified Israel! (52:11-12)
- **8b:** The Servant glorified for His sacrifice (drank the cup for Israel) (52:13-15)
- **7b:** The Arm of the LORD is revealed (53:1-10)
- **6b:** The eternality of the Servant's righteousness and reward (53:11-12)
- **5b:** Israel's shame is removed after the Servant's death (54:1-10)
- **4b:** Israel and her children glorified in the kingdom (Isaiah 54:11-55:5)
- **3b:** Solution: Despair will be relieved when Israel returns to the LORD (55:6-13)
- **2b:** Salvation extended to the Gentiles (56:1-8)
- **1b:** Wicked servants "decommissioned" for rewarding themselves (56:9-12)

Note: Jewish commentaries conclude Part 2 at Isaiah 57, which ends with the same verse as Part 1 ended in Isaiah 48:

> "'There is no peace,' says the LORD, 'for the wicked.'" – Isaiah 48:22
>
> "'There is no peace,' says my God, 'for the wicked.'" – Isaiah 57:21

Thus, they say these verses are the marker verses separating Parts 1, 2, and 3.[1] I see the sections breaking a little different. I think the repeated verses certainly form an inclusio with the theme of peace that encompasses Chapters 49-57, but as I worked out the chiastic structure, I saw the chiasm break at a different place. Instead of peaking at the picture of the Sin-bearing Servant, the chiasm peaked at the command to proclaim the "good news." This command is where the theme of comforting struggling people is realized, and it is sandwiched between the picture of God pouring out the cup of wrath on His people and the Sin-bearing Servant who took the cup of God's wrath on their behalf. That is the "good news," that the cup has been taken from all of us.

For the purpose of this study, I will end Part 2 at Isaiah 56, partly because of the chiastic structure but also because the eschatological pictures unfolding in Part 3 begin with Isaiah 57. Jewish scholars who don't see Christ in the text won't recognize the significance of Isaiah 57 or the role it plays in the grand sweep of events pictured in Part 3, but I will explain it at the end, once we have finished the discussion of the theme.

---

[1] Adele Berlin and Marc Zvi Brettler, editors; Michael Fishbane, consulting editor. The Jewish Study Bible: Jewish Publication Society Tanakh Translation. Oxford; New York: Oxford University Press, 2004, pp 783-784, 882 (sidenote headed "Chs 49-57").

LESSON 12

The Stumbling Block of Despair

READ

Isaiah 49:1-13

DISCUSSION

As we move into Part 2 of God's Highway Project, there is a distinct change in the narrative tone. All mention of Cyrus and Babylonia, the former things and new things, are now gone. Now God begins to address Israel intimately, as a bridegroom dealing with a wayward bride, in an effort to reconcile the relationship between them. Rebuke is softened into exhortation as He extends grace and peace to her, and He lays before her the vision of a glorious kingdom and a reward for the faithful who return to Him—all of which is bound up in the saving work of the Servant. The Servant identified only as "Me" is a new voice that now mingles with God's voice as He addresses Israel.

There is a new set of stumbling blocks for Israel to overcome, the first of which is despair. Despair is something that the Servant Himself suffers, and in the opening verses of Isaiah 49, He models a particular strategy for combating it.

Isaiah 49:1-4

The chapter opens with an address from the Servant. You might think that the Servant is the personification of the nation of Israel because verse 3 says, *"And He said to me, 'You are My servant, O Israel, in whom I will be glorified.'"* But this is not the nation of Israel speaking, which will become evident in verse 5. The Servant who is speaking is from the bloodline of Israel and He represents Israel, but He is His own person.

The Servant opens with a proclamation to the coastlands, introducing Himself. This may seem a little odd. Why wouldn't He address Israel first? There is a reason for it. The author is structuring this opening passage of Part 2 in a particular way so that it creates a parallel picture with the opening passage in Part 1 (Isaiah 41). Both Part 1 and Part 2 open with an address to the coastlands, followed by the introduction of a deliverer.

Back in Isaiah 41, we discussed who the "coastlands" were. The coastlands represented the outermost reaches of the Babylonian empire in those days, and generally referred to the Gentile nations in their entirety, "from coast to coast." Isaiah 41 then went on to talk about the coming deliverer, Cyrus. Remember the forceful, exultant tone that the LORD took in announcing that king in Isaiah 41:2-4? He said,

> *"Who raised up one from the east? Who in righteousness called him to His feet? Who gave the nations before him, and made him rule over kings? Who gave them as the dust to his sword, as driven stubble to his bow? Who pursued them, and passed safely by the way that he had not gone with his feet? Who has performed and done it, calling the generations from the beginning? I, the LORD, am the first; and with the last I am He."* – Isaiah 41:2-4

The Servant now describes Himself with similar exultant statements in Isaiah 49.

> *"Listen, O coastlands, to Me, and take heed, you peoples from afar! The LORD has called Me from the womb; from the matrix of My mother He has made mention of My name. And He has made My mouth like a sharp sword; in the shadow of His hand He has hidden Me, and made Me a polished shaft; in His quiver He has hidden Me. And He said to me, 'You are My servant, O Israel, in whom I will be glorified.'"* – Isaiah 49:1-3

Like Cyrus in Part 1, the Servant now takes center stage as the conquering king in Part 2. He is glorious. He is confident and full of purpose as He embraces His mission. But then He follows His introduction with an oddly despairing comment in verse 4:

> *"Then I said, 'I have labored in vain, I have spent my strength for nothing and in vain.'"* – Isaiah 49:4a

This is a complete reversal of tone. Despite the gloriousness of His mission, the Servant suddenly sinks into doubt and despair. He says, *"I have labored in vain,"* meaning without purpose, and again, *"I have spent my strength in vain,"* meaning His effort has been like a vapor or breath—futile and fleeting.

Before we talk about the reason for the Servant's despair, let me ask you . . .

> **Q:** Have you ever felt like the Servant, that you have labored at something for no purpose and spent your strength on things that were futile or fleeting?

We might say that about our past lives before we became Christians, when we pursued the things of the world and the flesh. We might even say that of our current lives. Perhaps you have grappled with addiction and have despaired because of the seeming futility of your effort to break away. Perhaps you have grappled with a wayward spouse or child. Ever feel like you are wasting your breath?

The Servant remarks that He has been engaged in what seems like a vain pursuit. Let's consider our own unsatisfying pursuits. Sometimes, when we are engaged in pursuits that don't reap the reward that we think they should, it is good to begin with a reflection on the nature of our pursuit. Back in Isaiah 40, the LORD presented us with the contrast between what is fleeting and what is eternal. Anything that is sourced in God and His word is eternal in nature and reaps an eternal form of comfort and reward. Anything sourced in the flesh is fleeting and futile and offers little lasting comfort. If we are feeling a sense of fruitlessness, it might mean that we are pursuing the wrong thing, and that can be a reason to despair. But, like the Servant, we might be pursuing the right thing—some godly task—and still despair because we feel like our effort has been pointless. Have you ever had this experience? Maybe it was in the raising of the aforementioned children, who became rebellious and left the faith that you so diligently tried to instill in them. Maybe you despaired of reaching someone with the message of God's grace. Maybe you witnessed to them for years but to no avail. Despair happens, even when we are engaged in godly pursuits.

> **Q:** What earthly effort is causing the Servant to despair?

We know the Servant is Christ, and it is not hard to imagine Him expressing these very sentiments as He wept in the Garden of Gethsemane the night before His crucifixion. He had been sent to comfort His people, but all His words and healing works had seemed to do so little good. Everyone had deserted Him in this hour of trial. Not even His own disciples offered Him any comfort. What had He accomplished in this life?

> **Q:** Did He fail to accomplish His task as the conquering king mentioned in verses 1-3?

No, of course not. He was the conquering king, even as He hung, dying, on that cross. Is that what a conquering king was supposed to do? Where was His sword? Where was His army? Why didn't He conquer and claim His kingdom? There is the desire to compare Him with Cyrus, and in this He seems to fall short. This is the opening challenge to Israel's thinking: how do you define a conquering deliverer?

While Cyrus and the Servant both share that messianic role as conquering kings who release Israel from bondage physically, this Servant will do what Cyrus did not. He battles to release His people from spiritual bondage first. That death on the cross is where the narrative is heading a few chapters from now. On the eve of that spiritual battle, facing rejection from His own people and even death as a result of their treachery, it is not hard to imagine Him in despair, thinking His earthly effort to have been as fleeting as vapor and without purpose. But this is only His first battle. The second battle that He undertakes in His second advent will be as a conquering king who saves His people from their physical bondage as well, and that effort will have no call for despair. Having conquered in the spiritual battle, success in the physical battle is assured.

But from where He stands, as a mortal man looking toward that cross on the eve of that first great battle, His future is bleak, and it doesn't seem like it will accomplish anything.

> **Q:** What helps Him combat His despair?

He declares,

> "... *Yet surely my just reward* [Hebrew: *mishpat*] *is with the LORD, and my work* [*pe'ulla*] *is with my God.*" – Isaiah 49:4b

The phrase *"my just reward"* is the New King James Version translation of the Hebrew word, *mishpat. Mishpat* is better translated as judgment or justice, which ends with a recompense, for better or worse. Here in Isaiah 49:4, the Servant is expressing a desire for *mishpat,* that the LORD judge His case and render Him the justice due to Him. This is a terrifying request to make, especially when we consider how that judgment played out for Christ at the cross, and yet He makes this statement with confidence that the LORD will judge justly and the recompense He will receive will be worth the effort.

The Servant also says, *"My work is with my God."* The Hebrew word for "work" is *pe'ulla*, which refers to work which you do or perform for a wage, recompense, or reward. The Servant understands that His work is for the LORD, according to the will of the LORD, and as the LORD's worker, the LORD will give Him recompense or wages when the work is accomplished.

Thus, the Servant rests in the promise of a reward or recompense He will receive from the LORD for having done what was asked of Him, and that reward will be the outworking of the LORD's justice and judgment. Keep in mind, we are building toward that picture of the Servant's sacrifice in Isaiah 53.

Isaiah 49:5-13

The LORD now responds to the Servant with three proclamations introduced by the phrase, *"The LORD says . . ."* In the first, He expands the Servant's tasking. In the second, He promises the reward of a crown to the Servant. In the third, He describes the blessing that will flow to the people as a result of the Servant's work.

In verses 5-6, it is revealed that the Servant's tasking will not be to save Israel alone but to save the whole world, to the ends of the earth. Thus, the Servant becomes a universal Savior. The author is making another parallel, this time with God's statements in Isaiah 44-45 as He commissioned Cyrus. There God presented Himself first as the redeemer of Israel as a nation (Isaiah 44:22-28), but then He expanded the scope of that salvation and offered it to all the earth through Israel (Isaiah 45:22-23). Just as God is a universal God offering salvation to all, so the Servant (who is also God) is a universal Savior.

This expanded tasking is followed by a promise of rulership (49:7). The LORD increases the glory and reputation of the Servant by causing kings and princes to bow to Him who they once despised. We talked about a victim's needs for validation, vindication, and vengeance in Part 1, and this is what the LORD grants the Servant when He gives Him that crown. The very people who spat on Him will grovel at His feet.

In verses 8-12, the LORD explains the blessings that then flow from the Servant's work. The LORD's words here echo what was previously said about the Servant in Isaiah 42:1-9. The Servant will be a covenant to the people. He will restore not just Israel's heritage but the whole earth. The prisoners will be set free of bondage and brought into the light. They will not hunger or thirst or suffer exposure. God's Highway Project will be accomplished.

Before we go on with the rest of the chapter, let's dig deeper into this lesson's theme of despair, in regard to the Servant's experience, because He is modeling a strategy for us.

GOD'S HIGHWAY PROJECT

The Servant's Strategy for Combating Despair

The first and greatest reason for despair is when a person is facing death, whether from persecution or sickness or the consequences of a sinful lifestyle. The Servant identifies deeply with those facing a dark future because He, too, faced it. He grappled with the feeling that His life had been pointless and purposeless—nothing but a vapor—and the only thing that gave Him comfort was that vision of a future. That is a bit of a twist, isn't it, combating despair over death with a hope for the future? But that is exactly where Christ, the Servant, cast His mind. He chose to believe that the LORD would not forsake Him through the ordeal, that there was a purpose in it even if He Himself couldn't see it. He understood that He would have to submit to the LORD's justice in His case, but there would be an eternal reward for Him when it was over. This kind of comfort can only be had by faith—faith in the LORD's promises and trust that He will be good to His word, even unto death. Faith can be the hardest thing to ask of a despairing person because it demands that they let go of their earthly life—a life which is already lost to them—and embrace a life of which they have heard but not seen.

It didn't matter that a majority of God's people still rejected the comfort the Servant offered them or the salvation He purchased for them. The Servant's reward was not judged according to His earthly success in comforting people, only that He completed His task to the LORD's satisfaction, and His focus remained fixed on that future reward. Though He was hard-pressed and perplexed, He did not despair. Thus, He becomes our model.

As we will see with Israel, people under oppression and in despair will often reject a comforter's efforts for various reasons. But a lack of success is not a reflection on the comforter, and that is an important point to remember when we feel frustrated with our effort to comfort someone. If we look for a reward for that effort from the suffering person, we often will not get it. We should limit our sights to doing what the LORD has asked of us, as the Servant did, and let Him be the judge and rewarder of that effort.

As He grapples with despair, the Servant takes comfort in His belief in:

1. The faithfulness of the LORD
2. The justice of the LORD
3. The reward He would get from the LORD once His work was accomplished.

The reward that the LORD holds out for the Servant is two-fold:

1. A personal reward, which is the crown of kingship in the Servant's case. (It was the same reward offered to Cyrus who also was called to be God's servant.)
2. The reward of knowing that a blessing would come from His effort that would bless many people to come. This trial that He was facing would leave a legacy that would help other suffering people.

The Reward of a Crown

Kingship is the reward for both of God's faithful servant-kings. Cyrus was given rule over the Babylonian empire and more. Christ, the Servant, will come into a universal kingdom where He will reign for a thousand years (Revelation 20:1-6). Revelation 20:4 details how those who died for their faith will receive thrones and reign with Christ as priests and princes for that thousand years. Peter calls believers in Christ a royal priesthood (1 Peter 2:9).

> **Q:** Are these Scriptures saying that reward of royalty is something we, too, can hope to attain?

There is a great deal of opinion and debate as to whether or not the pursuit of the reward of a royal crown is even part of the program for us as believers. In my years as a Bible student and teacher, I have heard the following perspectives:

- **There is no promise of a reward for us.** Clearly that is not the case here in Isaiah, nor does that stance hold up in the New Testament teachings, either. A simple concordance search shows just how many times the topic of reward and crowns crops up in both Old and New Testaments.

- **Pursuing a reward is too mercenary.** Some say we should not be concerned with being rewarded for living a Christian life. (Someone actually said this to me.) I think Christ, the Servant, would argue this. He Himself valued it enough to pursue it to the sacrifice of His life, and it sustained Him through His ordeal. I would not scorn something that my Savior valued, nor would I dismiss what appears to be a significant element in God's Highway Project.

    The person who argues this assumes that a reward is something they can, of their own free will, choose to pursue or not. This person labors under the misconceptions that 1) the reward is necessarily a good thing, and 2) not all people get rewards. This is contrary to what Christ tells us this in Revelation 12:22:

    "And behold, I am coming quickly, and My reward is with Me, to give to every one according to his work." – Revelation 22:12 (Note: this

same statement is found in Isaiah 40:10 and Isaiah 62:11. It is one of the inclusios that bookend this study of Isaiah.)

As we read in the text, it is not our choice to pursue a reward or not. Everyone will get a reward. But that doesn't mean that the reward will necessarily be a good thing. The concept of reward comes from the idea of recompense or earning wages. The "reward" is in reaping what you sow, for better or worse. It has nothing to do with a mercenary pursuit of goodies or gold stars. It has everything to do with how well you lived your life for the glory of God. There is a judgment and recompense for every deed under the sun, and all will be reckoned in the coming kingdom.

- **The reward was for Christ but not for us.** Isaiah is going to refute that notion in Isaiah 53 and 55, 56, and 62 (we will talk about it more when we get to the end). The New Testament teachings also refute this notion. There are a number of passages that urge a pursuit of a reward, even a crown; however, there are different doctrinal stances on how a "crown" is defined.

We will come back to the discussion of the eternal reward in upcoming chapters, so I will leave it for the moment. As a personal observation, I admit that while I believe the LORD offers us an eternal reward, even to the point of extending the honor of royalty in the Messianic (Millennial) kingdom, that reward seems so far down the road that it is actually of little comfort to me when I am locked in some struggle in life. There are times when I need more immediate comfort.

Q: Is the promise of a future heavenly reward a comfort for you?

Maybe, yes. Maybe, no. But it is the only strategy that brings comfort for those facing death. There is a comfort in knowing that the one you love is a believer and when they die, they will go to be with Christ in heaven. That hope makes grief easier to bear. But for the rest of us facing lesser, non-lethal trials, it can be a marginal comfort simply for the fact that it seems so far off. It isn't a tangible, immediate comfort.

Q: Are there other, more immediate forms of comfort that the LORD offers to battle despair?

The Comfort of Knowing Your Experience Will Help Others

The Servant gives His trial over to the LORD to accomplish what the LORD wants with it, but what that experience does, in effect, is cast the Servant into an intercessory role where He now connects with suffering people through a shared experience. This is the second kind of legacy that the LORD offers the Servant here—the reward of knowing that the LORD will use that experience to make a difference in the lives of the people.

> **Q:** Is there reward in knowing that the trial you are enduring will make a difference in the lives of other people?

There can be, but it takes an unselfish, others-focused perspective to consider it in that light.

> **Q:** When you are struggling through a personal trial, do you ever stop to think how the LORD is equipping you through that trial to be a comfort to someone else?

This section describing the Servant is capped off with the command to sing. Sing, for the LORD has comforted His people! But what is Israel's response? Despair.

READ

Isaiah 49:14-26

DISCUSSION

Isaiah 49:14

For the first time, Israel enters openly into conversation with God. While all creation sings, she laments.

> *"But Zion said, 'The LORD has forsaken me, and my Lord has forgotten me.'"* – Isaiah 49:14

Before we move into a discussion of Israel's response, let me just ask:

> **Q:** Did Christ the Servant ever say words like this? (Matthew 27:46)

Christ, the Sin-bearing Servant, identifies very deeply with Israel's experience. In His mortal flesh, He, too, experienced the outpouring of God's wrath and the feeling of despair when the Father turned His face away from Him.

> **Q:** Even though He cried out like this, was this moment a crisis of faith for Him? Was He contemplating rejecting a relationship with God the Father?

No, He was not, and neither are we. It is okay to cry out to the LORD when you are under severe circumstances, but it should not be something that shakes your faith to the point where you seek comfort apart from God.

Here in Isaiah, Israel is not at the extremity that Christ was on that cross. Yes, she is oppressed and in distress, but God has spoken comfort to her. He has promised that her oppression will end shortly and commanded her to sing for joy.

> **Q:** God had proven His faithfulness to Israel in word and deed. Why would she still insist that she has been forsaken and forgotten? Why would she refuse to be comforted?

First of all, I think she has come to a place of weariness. Weariness can be a stumbling block in a good way because it stops a person from continuing forward under their own power and prompts them to turn back to God (or, at least, it should). So long as there is hope for the future, despair should not grip Israel, which is why, for the past eight chapters, God has been trying to instill hope in her. He has put the full force of His Godhead on display. He is omnipotent. He has power over creation, kings, and idols. He knows all things past, present, future, seen, and hidden. He orchestrates all events and is ever-present in Israel's affairs. He loves her. He has claimed her and redeemed her. His word endures forever, and with it, His covenant promises to His people. Though she is hard-pressed, she should not despair. But she does.

> **Q:** Why would a despairing person refuse comfort, in general?

I think there are a few reasons. One reason is because they don't want to acknowledge that their sin has caused their oppression and change their ways, which is the case with Israel. As God pointed out back in Isaiah 42, the Babylonians aren't the source of her problems. Her relationship with Him is. Her current exile was caused by her own sin because she would not walk in His ways, was disobedient to His Law, and pursued idolatry instead. It does not occur to her to reflect on her own behavior or even the true source of her torment, and as a result of her stubborn refusal to acknowledge her own sin, she will not be comforted by Him. She has hit a stumbling block, but instead of turning back, she mulishly refuses to budge from that place of unrepentance.

When hope and assurances are offered and still rejected, then the issue is no longer despair but self-pity. Suffering people may comfort themselves by saying, "My suffering is other people's fault, not mine." They play the blame game. We will talk about this more in a moment.

Another reason the person might refuse comfort is if the comforter hasn't "been there," that is, the comforter lacks an identification with their suffering. We can sympathize deeply with a person going through a particular trial, but our attempt to comfort can fall flat if the person doesn't feel that we identify with their particular circumstances. The sufferer might think that only a parent who has lost a child to cancer can truly identify with another parent who has lost a child to cancer. The identification aspect is often necessary to give effective comfort.

So, Israel's cry reveals that she has run up against a stumbling block that is keeping her from being comforted. How does the LORD address this? He begins by offering three verbal reassurances.

Isaiah 49:15-16

First, He addresses Israel in her immediate circumstances and draws a parallel between Himself and her. He appeals to her as a parent to a child, an experience with which she herself can identify. Have you forgotten your own children already? Why would I forget Mine?

God reminds Israel that while people may forget her, He will not. The truth is that people do forget. We get prayer requests all the time, and while we may remember to pray for the needs in the moment, how often do we continue to pray for an extended length of time, even for years until the issue is resolved? People may sympathize deeply but fleetingly. God doesn't. And this promise is not just for Israel but for all who are called by God's name. When we, as believers, see our world beginning to crumble around us and feel powerless to do anything, He reassures us that this is not the end. We are not forgotten. If He brings calamity on us, it is only for a time and a purpose.

Isaiah 49:17-21

The LORD's second reassurance is to cast a vision of a better future. Israel may be in captivity—may even die in captivity—but He guarantees her that while she may lose a legacy of children in this generation, a remnant will be preserved.

> **Q:** When we see dark days coming as Israel did, what worries do we have for our children and grandchildren? Do we despair over the direction our current generation is taking in life?

Greater persecutions were in store for Israel's children than what she herself was experiencing when Isaiah delivered this message. The same is true for us. Will our children remain faithful when the persecution begins in earnest? Will they resist the world's bombardment or walk away from the faith and be lost to us? These are genuine concerns, and they can bring us to despair when we realize how little power we really have to protect or even prepare our children for what lies ahead. But God promised Israel a return of future generations to a renewed land. Many would be lost, but a remnant would return and flourish in the coming kingdom. Keep in mind, this is a promise for Israel specifically, and will be accomplished in her near future when Cyrus releases her from exile to return to Israel. But there is another kingdom promised in a more distant future, and one in which everyone called by God's name, Jew and Gentile alike, will have a place according to faith. The Millennial Kingdom will be both a physical and spiritual kingdom, and the future generations that come into that kingdom are not defined by physical bloodlines, but spiritual faith-lines. While we cannot foresee how the thread of our faith will continue, many may be brought into that kingdom on account of us. In that sense, we, too, may exclaim, "Whose children are these? Where did they come from?"

Isaiah 49:22-26

God's third reassurance is a promise to remember Israel's oppressors. As He brings back her children, He causes her oppressors to bow to her, even as He did with the Servant in 49:7. The oppressors are mighty, but He is mightier, and He will take back what is His.

This reassurance is interrupted by a question—a doubt—on Israel's part.

> *"Shall the prey be taken from the mighty, or the captives of the righteous be delivered?" (Isaiah 49:24)*

> **Q:** Israel has witnessed God's mighty works in the past. Why would she express a doubt that He can do this in her present circumstances?

The LORD immediately quells this doubt with a very strong statement that she doesn't need to worry about her oppressor. It is true that no one can enter the strong man's house and plunder his goods unless the strong man is first bound, but God is stronger and that is exactly what He intends to do. He will contend with those who contend with her. He will feed them their own flesh and give them their own blood to drink, and everyone will know that He is her Savior. The promise of vindication and vengeance is a potent comfort God offers His people, and yet it seems to fall on deaf ears.

When a person stubbornly refuses comfort as Israel is doing, they must find comfort in a very crooked sort of way through self-pity.

GOD'S HIGHWAY PROJECT

The False Comfort of Self-Pity

Despair is a necessary thing to bring a person to the end of their own effort of empowering themselves and prompt a return to God. God lets Israel wear herself out until she has come to this stumbling block. But despair only exists so long as there is no hope. Once hope is given, there should be no reason for despair. Thus, God begins to exhort her with reason after reason to hope.

Even so, Israel stubbornly resists. She throw up illogical arguments. She perseveres in doubt and despair even after all God's reassurances and demonstrations of His power and sovereignty over her circumstances. She refuses to be comforted, choosing instead to entrench herself in self-pity at that stumbling block. Self-pity offers a twisted kind of comfort and empowerment and can become a stronghold that a person builds around themselves that the LORD must then tear down. Let's talk about self-pity.

> **Q:** Most of us have met someone in life who is sunk in self-pity. What is self-pity? What are self-pitying people like?

At heart, self-pity is self-focused, self-promoting, and self-indulgent. It demands that others continually lift up and support the victim to the point that the effort becomes oppressive to the comforter. There is a twisted form of power in self-pity because it has a perceived "just claim" backing it (I have been wronged! I have been hurt!) and it can sway people's sympathies toward supporting its cause—for a while. Self-pity is like a fire, though. It seeks out the audience who will feed it. It takes every opportunity to complain and point the finger because it is easier to turn the blame on others and make the problem someone else's responsibility to fix rather than acknowledge a personal failing. Thus, self-pity makes a person willfully blind and unwilling to deal with their own sin. They don't want to take responsibility for their actions or change their ways, and so they choose to remain in their oppressed state, even when justice is rendered over their "just claim" (in Israel's case, when God humiliated Babylon to avenge her, back in Isaiah 47). If left unaddressed, self-pity can develop into a permanent mentality.

> **Q:** Have you ever tried to comfort someone who is sunk in self-pity? If so, what did you say to them? Did it help?

> **Q:** How do you keep from empowering self-pity?

We are not immune from despair or the temptation to seek the false comfort of self-pity.

> **Q:** What strategies can we use to keep ourselves from falling over this stumbling block and succumbing to self-pity?

I have talked about the motif of reversals that runs through Isaiah's text—exalted things brought low, low things lifted up, mourning turned to joy, deserts to gardens, etc. Coming out of oppression requires a reversal of actions or attitudes that then brings about a reversal of condition. So . . .

> **Q:** If self-pity is self-focused and self-indulgent, then what reversal or change of focus might break this kind of oppression?

Maybe becoming others-focused? One of the comforts that God offered the Servant was that the trial that He was enduring would benefit the people in the future. A blessing would flow to others from that sacrifice. God helped the Servant combat His despair by turning self-focus into an others-focused goal.

Even as He confronts the need for repentance, God recognizes the need for a comforter to identify with a victim's struggle. Keep in mind, this is not a simple process. God's strategy for overcoming despair and self-pity will actually encompass the next several chapters.

LESSON 13

The Comfort of One Who Has Been There

READ

Isaiah 50:1-11

DISCUSSION

In Isaiah 49, we talked about some reasons why a despairing person might refuse comfort when hope was given. One reason was because sin was the cause of their oppression, and they refused to change their ways, preferring instead to sink into self-pity as a way of comforting themselves. The other reason was because they didn't feel that the comforter was qualified to give comfort because they hadn't "been there." They didn't know what it was like to struggle this way. They couldn't identify.

In Isaiah 50, God and the Servant together will address both of these reasons. They are systematically tearing down Israel's reasons for despair. God is also going to return to the doubt Israel expressed in the previous chapter over His ability to redeem her. There, she made this statement:

> *"Shall the prey be taken from the mighty, or the captives of the righteous be delivered?"* – Isaiah 49:24

God answered the first part of that statement in the last chapter. Babylonia might be strong, but He is stronger. Strength is not the issue. Now He is going to pick up on the second half of that question in the opening verses of Isaiah 50.

Isaiah 50:1-3

The chapter opens with God's frustrated reply. Where are the divorce papers? To whom have I sold you? Both questions have to do with legal transactions made according to the Law that make a person's return difficult, if not impossible. One is divorce, and the other is being sold to creditors as a slave. Both are very poignant experiences of being forsaken and in very binding ways, yet the LORD points out that these reasons for despair are groundless in Israel's case.

First, the LORD brings up the issue of their mother's divorce. According to Deuteronomy 24:1-4, if a man divorces a wife and she marries another, she can never return to the first husband. The LORD had previously brought a charge against Israel, that she had been unfaithful and married herself to other husbands (that is, her idols), and that is why He sent her away into exile. But He points out that no divorce papers were ever filed. There is no reason on His end for her not to return to Him.

The LORD then brings up the issue of being sold to creditors. This is in response to the doubt Israel had previously expressed in Isaiah 49:24, when she questioned if the captives of "the righteous" could be delivered. "The righteous" does not mean the godly. Babylonia is anything but godly. This kind of "righteousness" is in the legal sense of having a right or just claim to something or someone under the law. When a woman is sold away to creditors to pay a debt, her children are sold into slavery with her and must be purchased back at a price. This might describe Israel's condition, but the LORD declares that He did not sell her to Babylonia in such a way that Babylonia has any justifiable claim to her and her children. In fact, He did not sell her away at all. She did this to herself. She was the one who ran away from Him and pursued her pleasures by serving idols. And yes, He was angry, but the relationship is far from over. He still loves her. He sees that she is suffering horrifically as the result of her unfaithfulness, and He is moved to pity for her. He is willing to redeem the relationship, but when He tries to comfort her and bring her back to Him, she refuses to respond when He reaches out to her. He asks two more questions,

> "Why, when I came, was there no man? Why, when I called, was there none to answer?" – Isaiah 50:2

In other words, "When I came, no one was there. When I called, no one answered." This is God's frustration. He can dry up the sea and make the rivers a wilderness, He can move heaven and earth, but He cannot reach her heart. She won't open the door to Him. She won't answer the phone. She is completely unresponsive to Him.

Divorce is something that has touched almost all of our lives, and whether we have gone through it ourselves or witnessed the struggle of a relative or friend, we might understand the wife's withdrawal from the husband here, even though she was at fault (as in Israel's case).

> **Q:** Why would she not want to return or be comforted by her husband?

If the husband is perceived (rightly or wrongly) as abusive or oppressive, that would certainly explain a wife's refusal to return or be comforted by him. This is why it is important for God to point out that He is not the one to blame for the oppression Israel is in. She may blame Him for being cruel for having sent her into exile, but, in reality, she is suffering the consequences of her own actions.

On the other hand, she might not return or be comforted by her husband because, in his perceived abandonment of her, her perception of her own self-worth had become skewed. She cannot feel love because she believes she is unlovable or unworthy. Abandonment is an experience which spawns a number of other stumbling blocks including fear, shame, anger, or withdrawal into self-pity. Some of us might have experienced abandonment personally or have grappled with another person or a child suffering from it. This is often the experience of adopted and foster children. My own mother struggled with this all her life. The abandonment may not have been the person's fault, but it can create a skewed perception of self-worth that can cause them to refuse love or comfort.

> **Q:** Have you ever tried to comfort someone suffering from abandonment issues? If so, what does it take to release a person from that torment?

On one hand, the person may have been sent away—divorced or abandoned—unwillingly, but sometimes they initiate the removal by their own choice. Like the prodigal son in Jesus's parable, they might have chosen to cut themselves off from parents or spouses to pursue their own desires, and when their circumstances become desperate, they might still refuse to come home, even though grace is extended to them.

> **Q:** Why wouldn't they accept the grace extended to them?
>
> **Q:** How else can God (the Husband/Father) reach Israel (the unresponsive wife/child)? If she won't listen to Him, who will intercede for Him?

Perhaps she will listen to another person who has suffered the way she is suffering. This is where the role of an intercessor becomes vital. Now, the Servant inserts Himself into this frustrated dialogue between God and His people to intercede as much on God's behalf as Israel's.

Isaiah 50:4-9

The speaker speaks of Himself only as "Me." He explains how He Himself has suffered like Israel has suffered and, therefore, is qualified to comfort her because He has been there. He begins with a statement about His qualifications. He has been given the tongue of the learned, meaning He can speak from experience and is able to comfort someone "in due season." I like that phrase, "due season." It means an appropriate moment somewhere down the road. You may not know at the time of your personal trial exactly how the LORD is going to use that experience, so you just have to deposit that lesson in your "experience" bank. But that also means you have to be looking for the lesson in that experience as you go through it.

As the Servant points out, you have to use your ears first. Before you speak to someone else's experience, you have to listen to what God is teaching you in your own experience. Unlike Israel, the Servant does not turn a deaf ear to what God is teaching Him but listens wisely when God sends Him into a trial. And He goes willingly into that trial, without being rebellious and turning away from the hard thing God is requiring of Him.

Verse 6 details the abuse He received, which was not unlike the abuse Israel suffered—being beaten, hair pulled out, shamed, and spit upon. His words on the cross are even an echo of hers when He says, *"My God, My God, why have You forsaken Me?"* in Matthew 27:46. But He submitted to that ordeal because He knew God had a reason for sending Him into that trial. There was a purpose for it, and God would help Him. Therefore, He determined to go through it and learn what the LORD's purpose was. The shame and disgrace that the world heaped on Him didn't matter because He would not stand ashamed before God. There is great comfort for me, personally, in knowing that there is only one Person in the world to whom I have to look for my worth and validation, and the Servant has already paved the way for His approval.

Verses 7-9 are bookended by that conviction, *"Surely the LORD God will help me!"* The Servant's response to His abusers is defiant. Who will condemn Him if God doesn't? The world? What is the world but a moth-eaten garment? The world is worthless. Its opinion is worthless.

So, the Servant comes alongside Israel, He identifies with her, and then gives her some instruction on how to overcome the mental battle of despair and fear of abandonment. Just because she is going through a trial does not mean that God has forsaken her. It means He has a lesson for her that she needs to learn! When the world heaps abuse on her, God sees the abuse. He will deal with those who contend with her. If God stood by the Servant, will He not stand by His children as well? This is the faith challenge that the Servant is modeling for Israel. These are His words that Israel needs to internalize for herself: "It does not matter what the world thinks of me or does to me. They are the ones who are worthless. They are grass and moth-eaten garments. The LORD will help me. I will not be ashamed. If God does not condemn me, then who can?"

> **Q:** Imagine yourself as having been abandoned by someone in life. Do these words help overcome that feeling of abandonment, fear, and despair? If so, how?

The Servant's words are really an argument for personal worth—how the Servant sees His own worth and on what that worth is based. Self-worth is something with which an abandoned person grapples. That abandonment makes them feel like they are unworthy and undesirable, but that is the world's evaluation of them. Unfortunately, it is a lie that they come to believe. Getting them to divorce themselves from the world's fleshly opinion and convincing them of their eternal worth in God's eyes is the greatest part of the battle to comfort them.

God could not convince Israel that she was not forsaken, but an intercessor might because He has been there. Perhaps we have been there. If we have, the Servant's words might serve as a model for comforting our own struggling person.

> **Q:** How can we take the words of the Servant and make them our own when comforting someone who feels forsaken in life?

This passage puts to rest the second reason for Israel to refuse comfort. She cannot say that her Comforter doesn't know what it is like. He is her Wonderful Counselor, but will she listen to Him?

Isaiah 50:10-11

Notice the change in speaker. A third-party observer now issues a challenge. There is a choice to be made. Who fears God and obeys the words of the Servant or who wants to seek comfort their own way?

The Servant has been tasked with shedding light on Israel's darkness. He has been sent into this horrific trial specifically to identify with her and offer her comfort. He is qualified to give her that comfort. He has modeled how to deal with despair and respond to oppressors. The observer says, let the despairing person follow the Servant's example.

Having described those who walk by the Servant's light, the observer then addresses people who seek a light and comfort of their own making—they kindle their own fire and encircle themselves with sparks.

How much comfort does a kindled fire give? A little. Maybe a lot, depending on how much of a conflagration you whip up with your self-pitying cries. But that fire dies pretty quickly when people sour of giving you sympathy.

How much light does a spark offer to guide a person through the darkness? Even less.

This analogy takes us back to the opening theme in Isaiah 40:6-8. God's instruction began with the statement that all flesh is like the grass, but the Word of the LORD endures forever. He set up a comparison between the sufficiency of God and His provision to that which is fleeting, unsustainable, and dies quickly—like a spark. God says to Israel, I have reassured you and given you light and comfort through an intercessor who identifies with you personally. He has been through the trials

Himself, and He can speak words of wisdom to your situation and to My faithfulness. But if you refuse His help, this is what you get: fear, despair, and torment.

GOD'S HIGHWAY PROJECT

Tackling Despair, Part 1

God began addressing Israel's despair in Isaiah 49 with promises, but promises only go so far. Sometimes we need an actual, tangible comforter who can speak to our struggles from first-hand experience. Like Israel, we are faced with the same challenge over where to seek comfort and instruction: from the words of our Savior and the people He has uniquely equipped to help us, or from our own self-pitying effort to find our own way to cope.

The role of the intercessor is highlighted in this passage. While we understand "Me" is Christ in the big picture, when we read this in the first person, it is hard not to envision "Me" as ourselves in this role. God sends me into trials for the purpose of helping others in similar trials. So how do we model Christ in this passage? Change the "Me" to "I" in the following questions.

> **Q:** Have I endured suffering in life that has made me uniquely able to comfort others, offer timely words, or serve as a role model?
>
> **Q:** Did I enter into that suffering willingly?
>
> **Q:** How did I respond to being unjustly wronged?
>
> **Q:** To whom did I look for my justification and validation?

When we look back on the Servant's experience, we see that the LORD had a purpose for putting Him through that trial.

> **Q:** How does that change our perspective of going through trials? (Can there be a reason why bad things happen to good people?)
>
> **Q:** Is there any comfort in the knowledge that God might use our experience to help another person?

Part of avoiding the pitfall of self-pity is to turn your focus outward to others. I think the Servant's model challenges us to take a higher view of our circumstances in light of what God is trying to accomplish in us. Sending us into trials is needed not just for our refining but for our equipping as well. The words of the Servant were meant for our enlightenment, and we are called to model Him as an expression of God's love to others, to bring them out of their darkness in which they suffer from torment, fear, and despair. But we can't do that unless we have been there first.

Paul explains:

> *"For it is the God who commanded light to shine out of darkness, who has shone in our hearts to give the light of the knowledge of the glory of God in the face of Jesus Christ. But we have this treasure in earthen vessels, that the excellence of the power may be of God and not of us. We are hard-pressed on every side, yet not crushed; we are perplexed, but not in despair; persecuted, but not forsaken; struck down, but not destroyed—always carrying about in the body the dying of the Lord Jesus, that the life of Jesus also may be manifested in our body."*
> – 2 Corinthians 4:6-10

And again, in regard to following Christ's model, Paul writes:

> *"For even Christ did not please Himself; but as it is written, 'The reproaches of those who reproached You fell on Me.' For whatever things were written before were written for our learning, that we through the patience and comfort of the Scriptures might have hope. Now may the God of patience and comfort grant you to be like-minded toward one another, according to Christ Jesus."* – Romans 15:3-5

In the context of Paul's letter to the Romans, this principle is applied specifically to those of weak conscience, but I think the principle can be applied generally to bearing one another's burdens.

The Balance of Power and Love

Fear has been the chief stumbling block we have discussed so far, and in Part 1, God tackled that with a grand display of muscle—His sovereignty and power. But now despair and self-pity have entered the picture, and He changes His tone to an outpouring of love. Power or love by themselves cannot conquer the fear. It takes a balance of both, paired with a sound mind. This brings us back to our key verse in 2 Timothy 1:7:

> *"For God has not given us a spirit of fear, but of power and of love and of a sound mind."* – 2 Timothy 1:7

This was our key verse from Part 1, but it extends into Part 2. Chapters 40-48 focused heavily on the power aspect of God's comfort. Chapters 49-56 will develop the picture of His love. We should note that while Cyrus's work was the manifestation of God's power in Part 1, the Servant's work becomes the manifestation of God's love in Part 2. That is significant to our understanding of His purpose.

Love is meant to relieve the stumbling stone of despair but also the underlying fear that is part of it. God's love, embodied in the Servant's experience, was first and foremost meant to relieve the fear of being abandoned because of His judgment, but also from the torment that fear produces. As it was with Israel, so it is with us. As John wrote in his first letter,

> *"Love has been perfected among us in this: that we may have boldness in the day of judgment; because as He is, so are we in this world. There is no fear in love; but perfect love casts out fear, because fear involves torment. But he who fears has not been made perfect in love."*
> – 1 John 4:17-18

God does not abandon us permanently because of sin and faithlessness, though sin may separate us from Him for a time. There are no divorce papers. There are no creditors to satisfy. The debt has been paid in full. And yet, despite all His assurances, the fear that our separation can become permanent can keep us from experiencing His love and being comforted. We can be very much like Israel in this way.

God ends this chapter with a warning to those who willfully reject His comfort. In the next chapter He will address the faithful who are willing to accept the comfort but still struggle with fear.

LESSON 14

The Pursuit of Righteousness

READ
Isaiah 51:1-8

DISCUSSION

Here in Chapter 51, the Servant turns His focus to instructing and strengthening those who fearfully pursue the LORD and His righteousness but struggle with facing persecution from a furious, oppressive world. Again, the speaker in this chapter is "Me," the Servant. Christ is speaking—pleading, really—with Israel to listen to Him. The command is repeated three times: "Listen to Me, listen to Me, *listen to Me!*"

Isaiah 51:1-3

With the first "listen to Me," the Servant appeals to those who "follow" after righteousness. In other words, they run after it in order to attain it. They are looking for something to which they can cling, and He tells them where to look.

> *"Look to the rock from which you were hewn, and to the hole of the pit from which you were dug."* – Isaiah 51:1

This is a rather cryptic statement. To what event might this be referring? It might be referring to their genesis. In the Hebrew, the rock and the pit both refer to places that have been quarried—wells, pits, or cisterns. When these places have lost their usefulness, they are turned into prisons or sepulchers for the dead. Thus, the statement might refer to being taken from places of imprisonment likened to the grave. (The verb used here is in the perfect tense, which means that either it has been completed, or it is so assured that it is counted as complete.) We know from where we stand in history that the Servant Himself would go through a particular experience of being brought out of a hole in the rock—His resurrection after His crucifixion.

> **Q:** In what senses do we all start out imprisoned "in the pit"?
>
> **Q:** What sets us free?
>
> **Q:** Why is it important for those who pursue righteousness to remember the pit from which they were dug?
>
> **Q:** How does that help battle despair?

Those who seek after righteousness are then pointed toward a second example in verse 2.

> *"Look to Abraham your father, and to Sarah who bore you; for I called him alone, and blessed him and increased him."* – Isaiah 51:2

Notice that this example is not focused on Israel's genesis as a nation—her coming-out-of-Egypt experience—as it was in Isaiah 40-48. The Servant is speaking to individuals about their individual faith, and the genesis of that faith was in Abraham and Sarah.

> **Q:** The Servant is addressing those who follow after righteousness. On what was Abraham's righteousness based? (Hint: Genesis 15:6)

Abraham is the rock of their beginning. He was called out of an idolatrous country, and he went where the LORD sent him by faith, even though he didn't know where it would lead him in life. The LORD also promised him a blessing of children, and he believed that, too, although it seemed impossible because Sarah was barren. (Isaiah will address barrenness more fully in future chapters, so we will keep Sarah in mind.) The LORD counted that simple act of belief on Abraham's part as righteousness and blessed him for it. Here in Isaiah, the Servant points to Abraham and Sarah as the models of righteousness that is based on faith and faith alone. Faith is what Israel is lacking and why she is overcome by despair.

> **Q:** Is this promise of blessing only for Israel who is descended from Abraham by blood, or is there an application for us as well?

Paul tells us that all who are of the faith of Abraham share in his blessing:

> *"So also Abraham 'believed God, and it was credited to him as righteousness.' Understand, then, that those who have faith are children of Abraham. Scripture foresaw that God would justify the Gentiles by faith, and announced the gospel in advance to Abraham: 'All nations will be blessed through you.' So those who rely on faith are blessed along with Abraham, the man of faith."* – Galatians 3:6-9 NIV

Is there comfort in that? Yes, if you have faith in that covenant. Keep in mind that this exhortation in Isaiah is being given to a people who may die in exile, and yet they are still called to live by faith and with hope, the same as their ancestors did. The writer of the book of Hebrews exhorts us in the same way with the great "by faith" passages. He points out:

> *"All these people were still living by faith when they died. They did not receive the things promised; they only saw them and welcomed them from a distance, admitting that they were foreigners and strangers on earth. People who say such things show that they are looking for a country of their own. If they had been thinking of the country they had left, they would have had opportunity to return. Instead, they were longing for a better country—a heavenly one. Therefore God is not ashamed to be called their God, for he has prepared a city for them."*
> – Hebrews 11:13-16 NIV

Here in Isaiah, the Servant speaks specifically to Israel, but universally to all who pursue righteousness, in saying that their only hope is by faith and faith alone in the promises of God. We know that regardless of whether we are of the blood of Abraham or not, we are children of Abraham if we pursue righteousness with the faith of Abraham and trust in the promise of God that was realized in Isaac, Jacob, and finally, the Servant, Jesus Christ. (Romans 9:6-9)

After telling the righteous where to look for encouragement, the Servant then casts a vision of a future blessing that is promised for the pursuit of righteousness in verse 3. It is likened to a return to Eden. In this heavenly future, God promises a complete reversal of conditions: the wilderness into which sin sent them will again become a garden in which there will be joy and gladness and thanksgiving. But to receive this future blessing, they must persevere in righteousness according to the righteousness of Abraham. Faith is the condition around which Israel's restoration pivots.

Side note: We can fix our sights wrongly on getting back to life the way it had been—returning to the country we left. (Remember, Abraham came from a wicked and idolatrous country.) As the writer of Hebrews pointed out in Hebrews 11:15, we can go back to the old worldly life any time we want, but we should have a higher pursuit in mind. God calls us to cast our expectations toward a heavenly kingdom instead of an earthly one, toward Eden and not Ur.

Isaiah 51:4-5

The second "listen to Me" appears in verse 4 and is addressed to the nation. The Servant reminds them of His tasking. He is the righteous Servant-King who is coming to save His people and establish His law and justice as a light for all people. He speaks in the first person—"My justice," "My righteousness," "My salvation." The law will proceed from "Me." The coastlands will wait upon "Me," and "on My arm they will trust."

In the previous chapter, the Servant came alongside Israel and offered her one kind of comfort—the comfort of shared suffering. Now, He offers the comfort of anticipation—the assured hope of vindication and restoration. The Prince of Peace will come and will establish a new world order under His law that will bring universal peace.

> **Q:** Why would those who seek after righteousness need this kind of reassurance?

When we take a righteous stance, especially one for our faith, we need the assurance that there is a greater authority backing us that will stand with us when we face our contenders. In the previous chapter, the Servant looked to the LORD for His justification (Isaiah 50:7-8). Having been justified, the Servant now justifies those who pursue His righteousness. He gives them the same assurance of justification.

Isaiah 51:6-8

The final "listen to Me" in verse 6 addresses those who know righteousness and keep the Law in their hearts. Even though they have that understanding, they still fear the reproach and insults of the oppressor. The command not to fear in verse 7 is the main exhortation, but it is sandwiched between verses 6 and 8, which set up a comparison between fleeting things and enduring things (the same theme with which we began in Isaiah 40).

In both places, the eternal element is His righteousness and salvation. It is everlasting, from generation to generation, never to be abolished. Now look at the progression of the fleeting things. In verse 6, the Servant begins with the command "lift up your eyes" and look at the great things—the heavens and earth. How will they end? The heavens will go up in smoke. The earth will grow old like a garment. He then includes all those who dwell in the earth. They will die in like manner. In verse 8, the Servant switches to pictures of lesser things—garments and wool. These get eaten up by even littler things—moths and worms. The world and the people in it are like these garments. They get eaten up by little things and will end as useless, moth-eaten rags.

> **Q:** In the middle of these big and little comparisons, the LORD places the reproaches and insults of men. Are these big or little things?

The world's reproaches and insults seem like big things when, in fact, they are little things—at least, in God's eyes. They come from a world that is itself a little thing consumed by little things. Doesn't this just describe us today? We live in a world consumed by little things, although, in the world's eyes, they are big things, and when we fail to exalt them as the world exalts them, we get some severe backlash. Bullying, shaming, humiliation—these are all common experiences in our current culture, and they are used as ways of making us conform to and support the world's values. For us, as believers, it becomes an effort in maintaining perspective. Regardless of whether it is a big thing or little thing, it is a fleeting thing without eternal value and should be treated as such.

The Pursuit of Righteousness

In verses 1-8, the Servant addresses those who know what is right in God's eyes, who pursue that righteousness but fall victim to the insults and reproaches of the world in which they live because the world's idea of righteousness is very different from God's. So, the heart of the conflict really lies in the definition of righteousness.

> **Q:** What is righteousness?

In a broad sense, it means that something "is as it ought to be" in regard to being acceptable, but acceptable to whom? The first thing that must be defined is who is the approving authority—who decides what is acceptable. Who provides the wisdom, guidance, validation, and vindication: God, the world, or perhaps a certain faction within the world? (The world itself isn't a united entity.)

Understanding righteousness as a society is vital because it defines what is right, just, or ethical in regard to human behavior, justice, and government, and it drives social norms. Thus, there needs to be a guiding rule or foundation for that righteousness. Here in Isaiah, Israel is encouraged to look to the Law (Hebrew: *torah*) as that guiding source for God's standard of righteousness and the way things ought to be. Isaiah has repeatedly stated that the Messiah's law will form the backbone of His government.

> **Q:** On what does the world base its righteousness (its idea of the way life ought to be)?

We have a certain set of laws that govern us nationally, but those can be redefined or neglected altogether depending upon the rulings of the justice system. Moral relativism tells us that the rules are what we make them, which is fine if you are the last person on earth or living by yourself on a deserted island. It is not so fine when your idea of how life ought to be clashes with an opposing idea held by your neighbor next door. And how much worse when it clashes with God's ideals? God sees life very differently and has a very different opinion of how life ought to be.

Recent generations have seen the rise of a victim-based "righteousness." The world promotes a sense of righteousness for being part of what it considers "just" causes, and, interestingly, one of those causes is pursuing an Eden of its own making. A return to Eden is an outworking of God's righteousness, but the world is trying to accomplish the same thing according to its own righteousness while shutting God out of the garden. That isn't how life in Eden should be.

> **Q:** God's goal is world peace—an end to all conflict—and a future in a restored Eden. What goals and future does our culture pursue?

Pretty much the same goals, but the world goes about attaining them the wrong way. Moral relativism ensures there will never be an end to conflict. It is impossible to live at peace in a society where everyone is living by their own definition of what is right. The world may pay lip service to wanting world peace, so long as it doesn't have to let go of its own sense of righteousness and align itself with God's values and teachings to achieve it.

Even strong believers can still grapple with despair. Knowing this from His own experience, the Servant—the Wonderful Counselor—delivers His strategy to strengthen the righteous who are struggling to stand against an angry world and need help in maintaining perspective. Realigning His people to His perspective and His definition of righteousness is the third step in God's Highway Project: Straightening crooked ways.

The basic strategy is:

- **Remember the unshakable foundation of your faith**—the pit from which you were taken by faith and the faith of righteous Abraham. Righteousness is accounted to person according to faith and faith alone in God (through Christ, the Servant) and being willing to rest in His promises and go where He leads, not where the world leads. Blessing, comfort, and peace will only come if you cling to that faith, regardless of what the world says.
- **Remember that the righteous King is coming.** He will justify you when He comes to re-establish the law and judge the world in true righteousness and justice. He will put an end to the reproach and

insults that the unrighteous world heaps on those who have kept His law in their hearts, and He will vindicate them.

- **Keep the world in perspective.** The world seems indomitable, but it is a little thing eaten up by little things. It holds out a counterfeit version of God's blessings—support, comfort, empowerment, peace, and a return to Eden—in return for conforming to its idea of the way life ought to be, but it will never be able to deliver on any of those. Its reproaches are as fleeting as its promises. Do not let the fear of fleeting things consume you.

Maintaining perspective is the key. The righteous are called to discern what the big things and little things are in life and resist being eaten up or eroded by the little things. Consider what is of eternal value versus what is fleeting. We should know what makes for true peace and pursue what is eternal, regardless of the shame and reproaches we get for doing so. There is a blessing that awaits those who persevere through persecution.

The Wonderful Counselor who gives instruction to the righteous for maintaining perspective here in Isaiah also gave similar instruction to His disciples in His Sermon on the Mount.

For further study, read Matthew 5:3-12 and 6:25-34.

> **Q:** What comfort does Christ give to the oppressed in Matthew 5?
>
> **Q:** How does Matthew 6:25-34 use a comparison of big and little things to offer comfort?

LESSON 15

Facing Fury

READ

Isaiah 51:9-23

DISCUSSION

Earlier in this chapter, the Servant gave some instructions to the righteous—those who were still seeking God and kept His law in their hearts but struggled with facing their hostile and abusive world. In verse 7, Israel was given the command, "Do not fear the reproach of men, nor be afraid of their insults." The verbal assault is the first conflict God's people face when our understanding of godly righteousness runs up against the world's idea of righteousness. Now, things are going to heat up. Israel is suffering a lot more than verbal abuse over ideology. We see that she is actually facing abusive fury, even physical abuse. We pick up now in verse 9 with Israel's response to the command not to fear.

Isaiah 51:9-11

There is a change of speaker from verses 1-8. In verses 1-8, God (or perhaps the Servant) laid out His strategy for dealing with despair, which basically boiled down to having faith, and then commanded Israel not to fear.
This is Israel's response. It is a lamenting exhortation for the LORD to do something. Do something!

Have you ever been struggling, really, really struggling, with some issue in your life that is causing you no end of grief? But when you voice your struggle to a fellow believer, they just pat you on the shoulder and give you some infuriatingly simplistic answer like "Don't worry, it will be alright. You just have to have faith." It's so simplistic that it seems almost dismissive.

Q: How does that make you feel?

> **Q:** How do you respond?

Clearly they are not comprehending the depth of the problem that is making your life a struggle every single day with no relief in sight. So, maybe you vent a little. Maybe you lament. You do have faith, but nothing is happening. Someone needs to do something at this point because you are at your limit.

> **Q:** How do we expect our friend to respond in return?

> **Q:** What if our friend was God?

I think we can appreciate Israel's words here, and yet we cannot overlook all that we know about the conversation that she has had with God to date. This isn't the first time He has told her not to fear. That command resounded through Chapters 40-48 where He laid out His plan to deliver her from Babylonia. He is more than able to do it. His plan to send Cyrus to take her out of her abuser's hands is already in the works, and He has told her about the humiliation he intends for Lady Babylon. All this has already been discussed even as she voices this lament, and it is a lament.

When we read this in our English translations, we might take Israel's tone as more of an exhortation to God to act, but Jewish scholars remark that these verses have the character of a classic lament in how they speak of God's heroic victories in the past as a way of goading Him into action, if only for the sake of His own reputation.[1] Israel reminds Him of the things of which He is capable, and implores Him with an almost beseeching wail to awake—to rouse Himself. Get up! Do something! As if He hasn't done anything. There is a disconnect here. Is God not awake to her plight? Has He done nothing so far to comfort her?

> **Q:** What is driving this lament?

Again, we have this lingering issue of Israel's failure to internalize the hope God and His Servant are offering her.

> **Q:** Have you ever had a child cling to you with moaning despair, pleading for help after you have already told them what to do to fix

---

[1] The opinion of the Jewish scholars was taken from the side notes accompanying the text in my Tanakh Study Bible. Here is the citation for it: Adele Berlin and Marc Zvi Brettler, editors; Michael Fishbane, consulting editor. The Jewish Study Bible: Jewish Publication Society Tanakh Translation. Oxford; New York: Oxford University Press, 2004, pg 888.

the problem? (Usually, it's because they don't like your solution.) Where do you go from there in dealing with them?

Isaiah 51:12-16

Now we have the LORD's reply. His patience is phenomenal. He ignores the emotion-laden goading and answers her cry with a question that should provoke rational reflection. Building off the comparisons of eternal and fleeting things that He had previously presented in verses 6-8, He asks, "Why are you afraid of a man who will die like the grass? Have you forgotten who I am?" In other words, let's put this in perspective. You are like grass, but so is your oppressor. This abusive, overbearing person in your life might seem so strong and hold such power over you, but they are just as fragile as you in My hand, and they are going die the same as you. They are nothing. They are grass.

Before we come down too hard on Israel, we should acknowledge that she is still in the power of her abuser at this point and what God and the Servant are asking her to do is a very hard thing. She isn't just afraid of the reproaches and insults of men in verse 7. She is facing the fury of an oppressor who is seeking to destroy her in verse 13. The phrasing in the Hebrew conveys the idea that while the oppressor may be bent on her destruction, he may not actually have the wherewithal to accomplish it. There is only a perception of power. Nevertheless, the actual experience is a very intimidating kind of fury that she is facing. The Hebrew word for "fury" means rage, anger, indignation, even poison.

Q: Have you ever faced a poisonously furious person? What forms did that anger take?

Q: How does a person cope with that fury if they can't escape it?

Q: God describes the fear that the exile faces in verse 14. How does that fear of the oppressor's fury affect decision-making and actions?

Note: The Hebrew word translated as "captive exile" means one who is bent, stooped, or "tipped over." Jeremiah uses this term figuratively to describe a man as a vessel used by seasonal wine-workers. They use the vessel until they are done with it, then tip the vessel over, pour it out, and leave it empty and broken. These oppressors are transient—they come and go in a season—and yet this is the state in which they leave the vessel. That describes the exile here. Israel has been put into the hands of rough handlers who didn't care about her well-being or whether they broke her, but used her as it suited their purpose.

Depending on which English translation you are using, verse 14 will be rendered either:

> *"The captive exile hastens, that he may be loosed, that he should not die in the pit, and that his bread should not fail." – Isaiah 51:14 NKJV*

or

> *"The exile will soon [hastily] be set free, and will not die in the dungeon, nor will his bread be lacking." – Isaiah 51:14 NASB20*

In the King James and New King James Versions, it is the captive who acts hastily to appease the oppressor. In the New American Standard Bible and other versions, it is God who acts hastily to set the captive free. The different translations are not in conflict with one another. Both are true, and both have merit, considering the context. God promises Israel that He will act hastily on her behalf, but I think it is also accurate to say that the behavior of a fearful person is often marked by haste. Fear can rob a person of a sound mind, and when facing the abusive fury of an oppressor, the victim moves hastily and makes decisions hastily, often out of self-preservation. They may think that by pleasing or appeasing the oppressor they might escape that fury, so they quickly bow and bear the burden for fear that they will be denied necessary things like food and shelter. They fear being caught in "the pit." This is a different kind of pit than the one mentioned in verse 1. This pit is more like a snare by which something marked for destruction is trapped (like a pit used for catching wild beasts). You walk on eggshells around angry, abusive people, fearing a trap—fearing how the abuser will react to something you say or do because, once snared, you are at their mercy, and there is little to stop them. They may very well cast you in a pit and leave you to die.

In verses 15-16, the LORD describes how the oppressor bends the exile to a fleeting purpose, but then makes another comparison with a not-so-fleeting purpose that He Himself has given Israel. He has put His words in her mouth that He wants her to speak. That phrase, "put My words in your mouth," is a phrase that crops up a number of times in Scripture, particularly when describing prophets (Deuteronomy 18:18, Jeremiah 1:9-10, Isaiah 59:21). The prophets were commissioned to be messengers, watchmen, and witnesses, but it is really a commission in which all of Israel shares. It is also a commission with which we are tasked (Romans 10:8-9).

> **Q:** How does a fear of an oppressor's fury circumvent the LORD's purpose?
>
> **Q:** Does keeping silent make things better or worse? Does it end the oppression or enable it?

Fear can make a person keep their mouth shut when they ought to speak up, and their silence empowers the oppressor even more because nothing ever changes. God's people are not to be silent. We are called to speak the truth—the truth about God's definition of righteousness, His power, His love, and our redemption in Christ. This is part of the Great Commission.

When we face furious oppressors—and we will—it is a battle to let go of our concern over our fleeting, earthly life and cling to our faith and hope in that future heavenly kingdom. When we do, we bear witness of the value we place in the eternal kingdom, just as Abraham once did, and that faithful witness preserves for us a legacy that will be rewarded in that future kingdom, even though our abusers may leave us as broken vessels in this life. In the comparison of big and little things, God's commission is so much greater than that of our fleeting oppressors, however much they may roar at us. We are not to fear their fury or even what we might suffer as a result of our witness, but speak boldly the words of truth and hope.

It all boils down to maintaining a correct perspective.

Now, God kicks the comparison up a notch. Fear of an oppressor's fury seems to be the overwhelming problem, but what is Babylon's fury compared to His fury?

Isaiah 51:17-23

God's anger is the reason Israel is suffering at Babylonia's hands. He belabors the condition she is in. She has drunk the cup of His fury—she is reeling from it like a drunk person. Her sons are without strength to save her. Her own actions have brought ruin and destruction, famine, and sword upon her. God goads her just as she goaded Him. Who will be sorry for you? By whom will I comfort you? What do you expect Me to do about it?

But then He puts it in perspective for her. It isn't the human oppressor's fury from which she has to fear. It's His. And because it is His fury, it will end when He decides it will end. The power is in His hand to control what happens to her. And He now tells her that He is ending it (51:22-23).

In verse 17, God declares that Israel's ordeal is over. She has drunk the cup of trembling and now it will pass to her oppressors. He picks up the same thought again in verses 21-23, but in between, He brings up a picture of the sons who have suffered on account of her sin. Out of all the sons she has borne, none of them was able to save her. They have fallen under the oppressor's snares and made to endure the full fury of an angry God.

While He will, in the end, deliver Israel from a physical oppressor and avenge her, the sin factor has not been overlooked. There was a sacrifice that had to be made to appease an angry God.

> **Q:** By whom is an angry God appeased when sin is at the heart of the problem?

I can't help reading these verses through Jesus's eyes. He would have identified deeply with Israel's sons here in Isaiah 51. When God presented Him with that cup of fury, He knew how it would play out. He understood the sacrifice He was being asked to make and the reason for it, and while He prayed in agony that the cup might be taken from Him, He knew it would not. He was a son of Israel and the sacrifice to appease an angry God. But when He had drunk that cup to its dregs, He believed He would awake and arise, and then the cup would pass to His oppressors.

> **Q:** Why was He able to do this when the rest of the sons of Israel could not?

One son of Israel did what the rest could not do, but then He was not just a son of Israel but also the son of God. The Son's death atoned permanently for sin so that God's wrath would not have to fall on His people again as it had in the past.

GOD'S HIGHWAY PROJECT

The Stumbling Block of God's Fury

God, in His righteousness, models the destructive power of anger here in Isaiah 51. We see the effects of it as His wrath pours out on Israel. But God's anger is a righteous anger, and it is tempered with love and mercy. He offers the promise of a coming salvation that would take the cup of wrath from everyone, and it is meant as a comfort. But we know that Israel, as a nation, refused this comfort when it was realized.

> **Q:** Can we, as believers today, follow Israel's example in refusing to be comforted, even though we have been told that the cup of wrath has been taken from us?

I think we can, depending on the perspective of God's fury with which we have been raised. I have talked in previous chapters about reasons why a person might refuse to be comforted, and a fear of God Himself might be part of the reason a believer might shrink from His comfort. We all shrink from the hand of our comforter when our comforter is also an oppressive presence in our life.

This chapter has been speaking to the righteous, those who know God's law and diligently seek it, and yet they are plagued by a fear of reproach that stems from man and not from God. Sadly, this can be a scenario that believers face today. Faithful, conscientious believers who have been brought up in oppressive church environments that beat them over the head with fire-and-brimstone messages of God's judgment can be plagued by a fear of God's continuing fury and how to appease that fury. Even though these believers know that the penalty has been paid for their sin, guilt and fear of losing their salvation grips them, and they get no comfort from God's grace.

> **Q:** How do you help a believer struggling with a fear of God's fury?

The apostle John's words in 1 John 5:13 echo the Servant's instructions here in Isaiah 51. John's letter presents the dual picture of God's righteousness and His love, and is expressly written to believers that they may know for certain that their salvation is assured.

"I write these things to you who believe in the name of the Son of God so that you may <u>know</u> that you have eternal life." – 1 John 5:13 NIV (emphasis added)

You may know, without question. God balances the picture of Himself as being a God of power and of love, of righteousness and of mercy. The understanding of His righteous fury is needed to keep the issue in perspective and induce repentance, but He does not leave His people with that one-sided view of Himself, because it will create despair. We should not leave our struggling person with that one-sided view, either.

The Stumbling Blocks of Anger and Silence

God has made the comparison between the oppressor's fury and His own.

> **Q:** How is human anger different from God's anger?
>
> **Q:** This chapter began as an address to those who seek after righteousness. Is an angry response a way to achieve that righteousness?
>
> **Q:** This chapter has focused on maintaining perspective. How does God's fury bring human fury into perspective?

God's anger is a righteous anger, and it is tempered with love and mercy. Human anger—not so much. We are not as holy, righteous, or just as God is, and when we strike out in anger, even what we consider righteous anger (anger that life isn't the way we think it ought to be), it is often destructive because it is self-serving at heart and not tempered with love. We are warned in the book of James,

"So then, my beloved brethren, let every man be swift to hear, slow to speak, slow to wrath; for the wrath of man does not produce the righteousness of God." – James 1:19-20

> **Q:** Anger is destructive. Is silence equally destructive? If so, how?

Silence plays out in a desire to hunker down into defensive positions, hide behind barriers and walls, and withdraw into places where the enemy cannot get to us. But silence and withdrawal are equally destructive. They cut us off from the fellowship that would strengthen us. They also derail our calling to be witnesses and watchmen for the faith. We can let angry people silence us when we should speak the truth to a fallen world because we fear their persecution. We can also let angry victims silence us when we try to comfort them or help them address the sin in their life that is keeping them in oppression.

Anger and silence are empowering. They are tools that oppressors use to control their victims, but they are also tools that victims use to empower themselves and guard themselves against their oppressors.

Outbursts of anger can be fueled by a desire for justice, validation, vindication, and vengeance. Withdrawing into silence can also be a way that anger manifests itself. Giving someone the silent treatment is actually an act of aggression. Silence is a way of communicating our rejection of a person and bolstering our sense of self-righteousness. When the silent finally do speak out, it can be with explosive and destructive anger. Thus, silence is entwined with anger.

In the end, neither of these achieve God's goals of ending conflict and reconciling people, and they can become stumbling blocks that can keep us from moving forward mentally, emotionally, and spiritually even after the source of oppression is lifted.

This chapter has been about maintaining perspective, and the more our culture loses its perspective of God's righteousness, His fury, and His mercy, the more we see outbursts of anger, withdrawal into unhealthy isolation, and subsequent oppression. When we see outbreaks of violence like shootings in schools, for instance, we often discover after the fact that the shooter was a very isolated person, and that isolation warped their perspective of themselves, what they perceived was the problem with their world, and their sense of justice and values. The problem of isolation has been exacerbated by our absorption with technology. The more we withdraw into our online worlds, the more isolated we become, the more warped our perspective of the real world becomes; and when that isolation reaches a breaking point, it often erupts in frustration and anger.

If we are going to survive times of oppression and help others who are also struggling, we cannot stumble by responding to antagonists with angry words or actions which only fuel hate and strife. Neither can we withdraw into our own sense of self-righteousness or let angry people drive us into silence. Witnesses are not called to be silent but to speak the truth of what they see and know of God's fury and His grace. Here are some questions for self-assessment. Judge yourself . . .

In regard to silence:

- Witnesses are called to speak the truth of what they see and know. Why is speaking the truth necessary when removing stumbling blocks from a struggling person's path?

- Have you remained silent at a time when you should have spoken the truth? Why?

- Is there something about which you should speak up now?

In regard to anger:

- Is there anger in your life that you are holding onto? Why?

- Does your anger take the form of remaining silent?

- When you have spoken the truth, have you done it without using destructive or angry words?

- Has anger undermined your effort to communicate God's love and mercy to people?

- God has expressed His goals to end fighting and pardon sin. Does acting or speaking in anger achieve these goals?

LESSON 16

The Comfort of the Good News

READ

Isaiah 52:1-9

DISCUSSION

We have become so skeptical in life. We get bombarded daily by ad campaigns, advice columnists, and health gurus telling us that they have the "miracle" solution to our ills and problems, and for the most part we tune them out. They sound too good to be true, anyway. So, we turn the channel, ignore the flashing ads on websites, and throw the mailers in the trash. But what if, in the middle of all the messages that we are ignoring, there really was a solution that would bring world peace? God's message has to compete with the deafening roar of the world around us, and too often His good news falls on deaf ears. But He keeps saying it and saying it, hoping that it will eventually sink in.

Isaiah 52 is a continuation of the conversation begun in Isaiah 51:9 where Israel stubbornly implored the Arm of God to "awake, awake!" on her behalf, ransom her, and lead her out of exile. God immediately parroted those goading words back to her in Isaiah 51:17, telling her she is the one who needs to rouse herself and get moving. He has taken the cup from her and given it to another. This is good news! She has no reason for despair.

Isaiah 52:1-3

The chapter begins with the LORD's repeated imperative to "Awake, awake," this time as He calls to Jerusalem. This message picks up where the last left off on the theme of vengeance. It is not obvious at first because we are only given a picture of Jerusalem here in Isaiah 52, but this passage is the counterpart to the picture of Babylon in Isaiah 47. Jerusalem is the reigning city of Israel just as Babylon is the reigning city of Babylonia. Both are addressed as royal daughters and given a series of parallel commands. Compare the imperative commands in each passage.

> In Isaiah 47, God said to Babylon, *"Come down ... sit in the dust ... sit on the ground ... take the millstone ... grind meal ... remove your veil ... take off your skirt ... uncover your thigh ... pass through the river."*

> In Isaiah 52, God now says to Jerusalem, *"Arise ... shake off the dust ... sit down (on your throne) ... loosen your bonds ... put on strength ... put on your beautiful garments."*

Babylon has been dethroned, and Jerusalem reigns in her place. Jerusalem is presented as a beautiful bride, strong and purified. She has been redeemed, and now she rises from the dust, unfettered, to resume her throne like a queen.

> **Q:** Is this how Jerusalem looked when Israel returned to her after the Babylonian exile?

> **Q:** Is this her condition even now?

We read in Ezra and Nehemiah that Jerusalem was in shambles when the exiles returned, and it took the work of several generations to restore her to even a semblance of her former glory. Even today, she is overrun and embattled with oppressors. Isaiah's words imply that this picture of Jerusalem in her restored glory will be accomplished imminently, and yet, from where we stand today in the historical timeline, it remains, as yet, unfulfilled. But it is coming, according to Revelation 21. It is important to remember that some prophecies have a relatively near fulfillment, like Cyrus overthrowing Babylon. Others have a distant fulfillment, like the restoration of Jerusalem here in our passage. A few do dual duty. They may have a partial fulfillment, or a number of partial fulfillments over time before having a final, grand fulfillment. I will show you one of these when we get to Isaiah 60.

You would have thought that a queen's ransom would have been paid for Israel's release, and yet, the LORD says in verse 3 that since she sold herself for nothing, her redemption will be purchased without money. This is an echo of something the LORD said back in Isaiah 50:1, where we find the same phrase "you have sold yourselves."

> *". . . For your iniquities you have sold yourselves, and for your transgressions your mother has been put away."* – Isaiah 50:1b

Israel has sold herself into bondage in pursuit of her sin and lusts—and for nothing. God adds that comment now, and we should pay attention to that phrase. "For nothing" is the English translation of the Hebrew word *ḥinnam*, and while it is an accurate translation, it doesn't fully capture the meaning of that word. *Ḥinnam* means "freely, gratuitously, for nothing, without cause," but it comes from a word family that focuses on the characteristic of grace—something that is given freely or graciously. Here is the word family:

- (Adverb) *ḥinnam* meaning "freely, for nothing, without cause"
- (Verb) *ḥanan* meaning "to be gracious, merciful, to show favor"
- (Noun) *ḥen* meaning "grace or favor" in appearance or manner, like a graceful woman or wise man's words, or "graciousness and favor" that is granted as a sign of acceptance (by men or by God). For example, in Genesis 6:8, we read, *"But Noah found grace [ḥen] in the eyes of the LORD."*

The LORD uses the word *ḥinnam* to evoke a picture that is negative on one side, but positive on the other. On the negative side, Israel is like a beautiful, graceful woman who, gratuitously and of her own free will, gave her favors away to those who would abuse her, and it was for no reason and for nothing in return. He emphasizes the "nothingness" in her actions, but even more so, the freeness of her actions. Israel was given freedom of choice as to where she chose to grant her favors, and she exercised that freedom in pursuit of her sinful desires. We can see from her model just how destructive that choice became for both mother and children.

But then God turns the tables on her situation, and He, too, makes a choice of His own free will. He redeems her as freely as she once sold herself. He chooses to be gracious to her, to extend His favor to her, and grant her new life again—not because she merits it and not because she can pay for it. Simply because He freely chooses to do it, by His grace. This is the superiority of God. He takes Israel's own negative, self-destructive choices and rebalances the scales with His own positive, healing action. Thus, He cancels the debt through grace. The granting of grace is the first piece of good news for Israel—and for us.

Isaiah 52:4-6

In verses 4-6, we see another twist in the redemption plan. The picture begins with a build-up of God's reputation. Israel's past oppressions are remembered: the oppression of Egypt, then Assyria (remember, Assyria took the northern tribes captive but was then overtaken herself by the Babylonians). While exile is a necessary evil to turn God's people back to Him, it causes the Gentile nations to scoff at Israel for having been driven from her land, as if the God she served was too weak to prevent it or even redeem her. Therefore, when God brings her out of the nations, He does it not for her sake but His own, to reestablish His own reputation in the eyes of those nations and also in the eyes of His own people. (Ezekiel 36:17-32 explains this more fully.)

Then comes the twist in verse 6:

> *"Therefore, My people shall know My name; therefore on that day I am the one who is speaking, 'Here I am.'" – Isaiah 52:6 NASB*

Pay attention to that little phrase, "Here I am" which, in the Hebrew, is the phrase, *"hinneni."* This phrase is similar to "Behold, your God!" (*hinne Elohekem*) in Isaiah 40:9, but it is opposite in tone. *Hinneni* is almost always the response of one of lesser status to one of greater status. It is used, for instance, when:

- A man responds to God's calling, such as Isaiah saying, "Here I am!" (Isaiah 6:8)
- A son responds to a father or mentor, such as Samuel to Eli (1 Samuel 3)
- A servant responds to a master (1 Samuel 14:7, 22:12)

A man, a son, and a servant each respond to the authority above them with this form of the word. On a rare occasion, a father will answer a beloved son with *hinneni* (Genesis 22:7, 27:18), but only here in Isaiah (Isaiah 52:6, 65:1) does God use this phrase Himself. Even as He presents Himself in the greatness of His glory and declares that He is taking back His reputation, He humbles Himself to His people with this simple Hebrew phrase, "Here I am." He allows Himself to be summoned like a servant by His own servants. It is a complete reversal of roles and a shocking contradiction.

Q: Why would the LORD humble Himself to be a servant?

So, this is the good news as it is unfolding. Grace is being extended. God Himself, taking the form of a Servant (the Servant), will accomplish it for His own glory.

Isaiah 52:7

Tell them the good news! Proclaim peace! Proclaim salvation! Bring glad tidings! This is a reiteration of commands given back in Isaiah 40:9. We should note the word used for salvation in verse 7. The particular Hebrew word for salvation here is *yeshua*. *Yeshua* is the common word from which the proper name, *Yeshua*, springs. When that name gets translated into the Greek, it becomes *Iesous*. In English, it is *Jesus*. Proclaim Jesus to His people!

There is a difference, though. In Isaiah 40, Zion and Jerusalem were the ones being commanded to get up to the mountains and proclaim to the world. Here, it is opposite. Zion is the one who has to be told, instead of being the one doing the telling. She has failed as His witness. Even so, God calls the faithful watchmen not to stay silent.

> **Q:** If this command to share the good news is not directed to Israel, then to whom is it directed?

Paul quotes Isaiah 52:7 in his letter to the Romans.

> *"How then shall they call on Him in whom they have not believed? And how shall they believe in Him of whom they have not heard? And how shall they hear without a preacher? And how shall they preach unless they are sent? As it is written: 'How beautiful are the feet of those who preach the gospel of peace, who bring glad tidings of good things!' But they have not all obeyed the gospel [good news]. For Isaiah says, 'LORD, who has believed our report?' So then faith comes by hearing, and hearing by the word of God."* – Romans 10:14-17

Even if the gospel messengers are doing their job, God's message of good news does no good if it falls on deaf ears. Isaiah has been belaboring the fact that despite God's every effort, Israel has been unresponsive to Him. She refuses to believe Him and be comforted. Even the Servant bemoaned the fact that His labor had been in vain (Isaiah 49:4).

> **Q:** Was there a use for Israel's blindness and hardening of heart? How did that rejection work out for us? (Hint: Read Romans 11.)

Q: Is Israel's rejection permanent?

Even to this day, Israel still resists the good news, which is why God's Highway Project is still ongoing, and the Gentile believers have a role to play in that process, if only in provoking Israel to grapple with her understanding of grace.

Isaiah 52:8-9

Picking up again in verses 8-9, we find commands to sing. The watchmen will sing when the LORD brings back Zion. The waste places of Jerusalem are given the imperative command to sing because the LORD has comforted and redeemed His people. Those verbs are in the perfect tense, as if the work is already finished. We have talked about the "sing" passages in previous chapters. They are always in conjunction with proclamations of coming deliverers.

GOD'S HIGHWAY PROJECT

The Comfort of the Good News

The command to proclaim the good news in Isaiah 52:7-9 is the climax of the chiastic structure for Part 2 and fulfills the command to comfort God's people. In the chiastic structure, it is sandwiched between the picture of God's cup of wrath being poured out on His people and the picture of the Suffering Servant who took that cup in their place. God told Isaiah to comfort Israel by pointing them to this picture of salvation, but this salvation is not just for Israel's comfort. It is for our comfort as well, and it is the ultimate comfort to which we must point other struggling people. Jesus Christ is the one through whom all peace and comfort flows. Proclaiming the good news is part of our witnessing effort to the world. We are exhorted by Paul's example in Romans 1:16, where he says,

> "For I am not ashamed of the gospel of Christ, for it is the power of God to salvation for everyone who believes, for the Jew first and also for the Greek." – Romans 1:16

Consider your own witnessing effort. How have you worked out this command to proclaim the good news in your own life?

> **Q:** Have you ever used the good news of salvation to comfort a struggling person? If so, how did you present it?
>
> **Q:** Israel is still in need of comfort and salvation. As antisemitism grows around the world and sparks all manner of oppression, what kind of salvation might they look for and from whom?
>
> **Q:** Have you ever had a chance to witness to a Jewish person about Jesus (Yeshua)? If so, how did it turn out?
>
> **Q:** If you had a chance to witness to them and didn't take the opportunity, what stopped you?
>
> **Q:** If you did, did you use the Old Testament Scriptures or just the New Testament Scriptures?

We, as Church Age believers, often use the book of Romans to explain how to accept salvation. We call it the "Romans Road" to salvation. But the Romans Road rarely resonates with Jewish people. Do you know how to build a similar road (we might call it a "highway") out of the Old Testament Scriptures? The apostle Philip did. According to Acts 8, he began with Isaiah 53, which is where we are heading, but we could as easily begin laying the foundation for that coming picture with some of God's statements here in Chapter 52. So let's begin building a salvation message just from our verses today.

> **Q:** In Isaiah 52:3, God presents the gift of grace, saying, *"You have sold yourselves for nothing, and you shall be redeemed without money."* How can we build off of that statement to explain to someone about God's grace?
>
> **Q:** In Isaiah 52:6, God humbles Himself to the form of a servant, saying, *"Hinneni! Here I am!"* How do we explain to someone why God would humble Himself like that?

LESSON 17

The Glory of the Sacrifice

READ

Isaiah 52:10-15

DISCUSSION

At the beginning of this chapter, the LORD began to challenge Israel's understanding of glory by modeling how He Himself establishes His own reputation. Shockingly enough, He begins by emptying Himself—by humbling Himself to be called as a servant by His servants. "Hinneni. Here I am," He said in verse 6. Now, as we enter the downward swing of Part 2 with the closing arguments in our chiastic structure, He is going to return to this idea of sacrificing glory to gain glory, and it is going to confound Israel.

God's Highway Project began with the comparison of the world's fleetingness to God's eternality. Let's apply this to the ideas of glory and sacrifice. Let's begin with the worldly side:

> **Q:** What kinds of pursuits do people of the world think will bring them glory?
>
> **Q:** Pick one of those pursuits. What kinds of sacrifices come with that pursuit?
>
> **Q:** Is the sacrifice of a man's life in the course of that pursuit enough to gain him the glory of immortality?

Now let's ask the same thing of the godly side:

> **Q:** What pursuits do God's people believe will bring them glory?
>
> **Q:** What kinds of sacrifices come with godly pursuits?
>
> **Q:** Is the sacrifice of a man's life in the course of that pursuit enough to gain him the glory of immortality?

Jesus once said to His disciples:

> "... 'If anyone desires to come after Me, let him deny himself, and take up his cross, and follow Me. For whoever desires to save his life will lose it, but whoever loses his life for My sake will find it. For what profit is it to a man if he gains the whole world, and loses his own soul? Or what will a man give in exchange for his soul? For the Son of Man will come in the glory of His Father with His angels, and then He will reward each according to his works.'" – Matthew 16:24-27

> **Q:** Why does Jesus qualify the statement "whoever loses his life" with "for My sake"?

In this lesson, we will see what is glory-worthy in God's estimation, and how it then applies to us.

Isaiah 52:10

The command to proclaim the good news was the key point of the chiastic argument. Now we begin to revisit the opening arguments with some closing comments.

Opening Argument: (Isaiah 52:4-6) The LORD humbles Himself to become a servant
Closing Argument: (Isaiah 52:10) The LORD lays bare His holy arm

In chiastic structures, the closing argument resolves or further develops the opening argument. These two pictures might seem like an odd pairing, but the connecting thought lies in the understanding of the role of the arm of the LORD. The LORD has been developing a picture of His "arm" through the Old Testament Scriptures to prepare Israel's understanding for the coming event in Isaiah 53, so let's take a moment to gather that picture of the "arm," which is the Hebrew word *zeroah*.

The Zeroah (the Arm)

The word *zeroah*, or arm, is a symbol of strength in its Scriptural use. An arm can be a source of literal, physical strength in an animal or man, or it can be figurative of strength in a man or nation. A man's "strength" is embodied, figuratively, in his son(s) and the lineage that he begets.

A nation's strength is embodied in its governmental "arms"—its king, its political might, or its military forces. Back in Isaiah 40:10, the LORD Himself appoints His "arm," that is, His king, to rule for Him. Here in Isaiah 52:10, the LORD now lays bare His Arm—His Son, His King, and the symbol of His strength—to purify His people. (Purifying the people is the theme of this passage.)

But here is the twist. However strong a bull's or ram's *zeroah* may be, that strength is what it renders to the LORD at its death when it becomes a sacrifice for sin. Thus, that which is physically strong becomes weak, and yet, in that moment of mortal weakness, it takes on a different kind of strength—a spiritual strength that has the power to redeem and purify. The *zeroah* becomes figurative not just of kingly might but the priestly power of intercession. The *zeroah* of the sacrificial offering is the portion allotted to the priesthood (Deuteronomy 18:3).

Thus, two contrasting qualities are embodied in the imagery of the "arm." One is the greatest expression of physical strength. The other is the greatest expression of spiritual strength and redemptive power through the rendering up of that strength and the assumption of physical weakness. This is the picture of the *zeroah* in general. Now let's apply that understanding to the Arm of the LORD here in Isaiah 52.

The Zeroah of the LORD ("Son of God")

In the opening argument (Isaiah 52:4-6), the LORD brings Israel's experience in Egypt to mind. In Egypt, He promised her that He would deliver her from bondage and redeem her with His "outstretched arm" in a mighty display of strength (Exodus 6:6), which He did through the plagues on Egypt, the parting of the Red Sea, etc. And yet, before those powerful demonstrations of the LORD's *zeroah* were seen, Israel's redemption was purchased by the death of the firstborn sons and the blood of the Passover lamb spread on the doorposts. That redemption has been celebrated through the ages at Passover, and the Passover seder plate that holds the symbolic foods representing that story includes a bone from a slain lamb. That bone, in Hebrew, is referred to as the *zeroah*. Thus, it is symbolic both of the LORD's mighty work and the sacrifice which caused Israel to be passed over the night that the firstborn sons were killed. Keep the remembrance of that picture in mind as we build forward.

Based on that model of the experience in Egypt, it is understood that when the Zeroah of the LORD begins His redemptive work, the intercessory sacrifice is performed first, followed by physical deliverance—in that order. It is the same order of events now, here in Isaiah, and I think it is the reason why the Exodus was mentioned in the opening argument that is paired with this closing argument. Israel has called to the Arm of the LORD to awake and deliver her as it had in the past, expecting powerful demonstrations of physical strength, but she should not forget that her spiritual redemption had to be purchased first with the sacrifice, not money, as implied in Isaiah 52:3.

Thus, Isaiah is priming Israel for the coming work of the Arm of the LORD in His intercessory role. Even as the LORD humbles Himself as a Servant, crying "hinneni!" to His people, His holy Arm also renders up its divine strength for this sacrificial service, likened to the Passover lamb. This time, however, the LORD's outstretched arm will manifest itself in the outstretched arms of a firstborn son and Messianic king who will be crucified on a cross, and whose intercessory death will become the spiritual salvation not just for Israel but for the world. And the ends of the earth will see this salvation—the *yeshua*—of God, as it says in Isaiah 52:10. (Remember, *Yeshua* is translated as "Jesus" in English.) The spiritual deliverance would be accomplished in His first advent. The physical deliverance would follow in His second advent.

So, we have another piece of the salvation roadmap. The Arm of the LORD is the extension of the LORD Himself and symbolic of His strength and legacy in the way a human man's son would be or a nation's king would be. The *zeroah* takes on the human form as the "Son" of God who will also be God's ruling King over Israel. This kingly "Son" is of the same condition and character as the LORD (the Father), and He follows the Father's example. Just as the Father put aside His reputation and humbled Himself to be called a Servant, so this "Son" will humble Himself, relinquishing His strength and reputation to perform an intercessory act that will purify the Father's people. This is the resolution to the opening argument, that the redemptive work now devolves on the Arm or "Son" of God.

Isaiah 52:11-12

Opening Argument: (Isaiah 52:1-2) Awake, awake, purified Israel!
Closing Argument: (Isaiah 52:11-12) Depart, depart, purified Israel!

The purification of the people has been the goal in verses 1-12. The chapter began with "Awake, awake!" Now God says, "Depart, depart!" and gives another litany of commands to the newly purified people: *"Go out ... do not touch ... be clean."* The purification of Israel, once begun, is now accomplished. Those who bear the LORD's vessels are clean, and they proceed out of exile with stateliness and security, almost as if escorting a king. Isaiah's command in Isaiah 52:11 is directed at those who bear the vessels of the LORD (meaning the Temple furnishings) on the return journey out of Babylonian captivity. We know from Ezra 1:7-11 that Cyrus returned to Israel the Temple items that Nebuchadnezzar had taken from Jerusalem, and the released captives took them back to the land of Israel.

Isaiah 52:13-15

Opening Argument: (Isaiah 51:12-23) Israel endures the cup of God's fury
Closing Argument: (Isaiah 52:13-15) The Servant-Son endures the
    fullness of the cup of fury on Israel's behalf

In the opening argument, God declared that Israel had drunk the cup of His wrath and He would now take that cup and give it to her enemies, seemingly on the grounds of the suffering she had endured. But even as He makes that pronouncement, He remarks on her sons who have suffered on account of her sin. Out of all the sons she has borne, none of them were able to save her. They have all fallen under the oppressor's snares and been made to endure the full fury of an angry God. The Son of God now reveals that He is also a son of Israel in this regard. He is both Son of God and Son of Man.

"Son of Man"

In Isaiah 52:14, it says that the Servant's appearance will be exceedingly marred, more than any man, more than the sons of men. That phrase, *"more than any man ... more than the sons of men,"* lends weight to the statement but seems redundant. It is, in fact, a formulaic statement that we see often in the Old Testament (Numbers 23:19; Job 25:6, 35: 8; Psalms 8:4, 80:17, 144:3, 146:3, Isaiah 56:2). Where this phrase is used, man and son identify with each other not according to blood relationship but by their shared character, condition, or experience. For instance, Ezekiel was called "son of man" repeatedly because the LORD tasked him with identifying the people's condition, often by pantomiming it. This dovetails with what we talked about earlier, first in regard to the Zeroah of the LORD (the "Son") being of the same character and condition as the LORD (the "Father") the way a son is similar in character or condition to his human father. It was the same with the Servant becoming the representative "Son" of men (speaking of Israel) in their suffering condition. The use of this formulaic statement clues us to the fact that there is a kind of identification going on—in this case, the Servant is identifying with the condition of the people.

As we move from the opening argument to the closing argument, the promise God made earlier to Israel as a whole applies now to the Servant, the Son of Man. The Son takes the cup in Israel's place as her representative. And when the cup of fury had been drunk to the dregs, the cup will be taken from Him and given to His enemies as the LORD promised in Isaiah 51. Thus, Israel is not saved on the merit of her own suffering, as it seemed in the opening argument. Instead, she is saved on the merit of this one Son, the Servant, who is representative of her collective suffering. He resolves the conflict for her.

The Servant: Son of God, Son of Man

Twice in this chapter we have seen a role being passed to a representative. The first was when the Arm of the LORD became representative of the LORD Himself as the "Son" of God who offers Himself as the intercessory *zeroah* of the sacrifice. Now we see this same Servant as representative of Israel, suffering sacrificially for her sins. The two representative are of the same character and condition, and I would argue that they are, in fact, the same man who is labeled both the Son of God and the Son of Man. This Son provides a salvation that none of Israel's earthly sons could accomplish by their own strength because, even though He represents Israel in bodily form, He also embodies the Godhead. What the sons of men could not accomplish, the Son of God did, and He is glorified as a Messianic king and deliverer of His people.

The Servant's Glorification

In the aftermath of that suffering, the Servant will be glorified higher than any king. He is, in fact, the coming king heralded by the "sing" command a few verses ago.

Here in verse 13, there is a three-fold description of the Servant's glorification. In the New King James Version, it says He will be "exalted, extolled, and very high." Other versions might say "raised, lifted up, and highly exalted." The words seem redundant in English, which is why we pass over them so quickly, but we should look at the meanings of the three Hebrew words behind the translation because there is more to the picture. The three kinds of glorification mentioned here in the Hebrew are *rûm* (pronounced room), *nasa*, and *gabah*.

- *Rûm* means to be raised up and set on high, like a king ascending his throne.

- *Nasa* means lifted up, but in several different senses. It can mean simply to lift up something. The lifting-up action carries the sense of bearing up under a burden or heavy load that is being taken away (like carrying a cross). Figuratively, it means to endure or suffer something in order to relieve another of a burden. Depending on how it is used, it can describe a person lifting a burden from someone else and carrying it themselves, but in another sense, the person can become the burden that is being lifted up and taken away (like a man on a cross). Thus, this word has those somber undertones of suffering and even being taken away, presumably, in death.

- *Gabah* means to soar (like an eagle), to mount up, or be exalted in dignity and honor.

Order is important. Note the progression of these words:

1. It begins with *rûm*, being exalted, like a king at his triumphal entry.
2. Then, *nasa*—being lifted up, made to endure suffering by bearing another's burden, and finally taken away altogether, presumably,

in death. The full picture of the word *nasa* incorporates all of that understanding at once. It is a big picture word.

3. And then *gabah*, soaring up majestically to be exalted and glorified.

The triumphal entry isn't hard to grasp, nor is the soaring ascension in the end, but the middle experience described by *nasa* is complex, so complex that it gets unpacked in Isaiah 53.

Remember, God's Highway Project has required both processes of lifting up and tearing down to accomplish God's goals of peace and pardon for sin. Here we have the description of a lifting-up action—something being made high and exalted—and yet there is a tearing-down act in the midst of it.

This is the nature of some highways. Have you ever come out of a driveway wanting to turn left onto a highway, but you couldn't because there is a barrier blocking the turn? So, what do you do? You turn right and travel for a ways until you can make a U-turn. And then you go left and proceed in the direction that you really wanted to go. It feels like you have lost ground unnecessarily, but in the end, you get where you want to go and where you are meant to be. Highways in life are like this. Sometimes you have to turn right before you can go left, and sometimes you have to go south before you can go north. The Servant is going to be glorified in the end, but He is going to have to go south for a bit before He goes north. He has to be torn down before He can be lifted up, but this tearing-down is the most vital step in the highway-building process. No further progress can be made until it is accomplished.

The People's Reaction

In verse 15, the text says He will sprinkle (some translations say "startle") many nations. Sprinkling and startling are two very different actions in our English understanding, but not in the Hebrew. The Hebrew word simply means "to leap." Leaping can describe water or blood leaping from its source in a spurting, sprinkling, or spattering manner, or it can describe a startled or leaping-up action. When we consider Jesus's death on the cross, we see both the "sprinkling" effect as His blood becomes the covering for sin for all nations and also the "startling" reaction that He inspires. Thus, the fullness of that word is gathered together in one instance.

The salvation that this Servant brings and the means by which He attains it is astonishing. It's confounding. The kings of the earth will look at Him and consider in their hearts what this means. Kings are men who have achieved the pinnacle of glory as men reckon glory, but is this a picture of kingly glory?

Those who serve kings are often expected to sacrifice themselves so that these kings might attain glory over other kings.

> **Q:** How does the Servant's death bring glory to God the King?

Isaiah 52:13-15 blends seamlessly into the next chapter, where the *"nasa"* part of the Servant's glorification gets unpacked in great detail. But before we move on, I want to look at John 12. Here, Jesus Christ, the Messianic King, has just made His triumphal entry into Jerusalem (John 12:12-16), and the people expect Him to be the conquering Messiah-King who will overthrow Rome and make Israel glorious again. They want to see the *rûm* and *gabah* versions of His glorification and share in that glory with Him. But instead, He stands up before them and begins to talk about being lifted up in death to the glory of God the Father—the picture of *nasa* described in Isaiah 52:13-15. His words reference this Isaiah passage, so let's look at John 12:23-41 and consider what Jesus understood about His life's purpose from it.

John 12:23-41

Keep in mind that in Jesus's day, the Hebrew words in Isaiah are a little difficult to understand because the common language of Israel is no longer Hebrew but Greek, and the Greek translation of the word, *nasa*, doesn't capture the full depth of its meaning any better than our English translation. In the Greek, *nasa* comes across as being exalted and honored like a king but loses the sense of being made to endure a burden and be taken away. So, there is a translation difficulty. To recapture that sense of the Hebrew word, Jesus clarifies it in John 12:32 by adding that He will be lifted up "from the earth." In other words, He isn't just lifted up like a king being paid homage. He will be literally lifted up and taken away from earth, out of this world. He is going to heaven, which means He is going to die. But how can that be? (Sometimes you have to go south, before you can go north.)

Jesus has been referring to Himself alternately as the Son of God and Son of Man throughout His ministry. He employs the formulaic as a way of expressing His identification with God, but also with the people. The people question Him about this here, in verse 34.

> "... We have heard from the law that the Christ remains forever; and how can You say, 'The Son of Man must be lifted up'? Who is this Son of Man?" – John 12:34

In their eyes, the Son of Man is obviously the Son of Israel, her representative King, who has just made His triumphant entry into His kingdom, but He is not identifying with that glorified condition or experience. Quite the opposite. This is a problem because the people of Israel expect to share in His glorification as a king, not in this appalling picture of suffering and death. They have already suffered and died enough over the ages. And so they question Him sharply. Who is this Son of Man? What is this identification? Explain the analogy to us.

They should know it already, so Jesus doesn't explain it. Instead, He answers with His own twist on that formulaic phrasing (John 12:35-36). Instead of using the "man" and "sons of men" analogy, He uses "light" and "sons of light." Again, this should be a clue to the people. He is playing off Isaiah's description of the Servant-King who would bring light to the world (Isaiah 42, 49, 50, and 52).

The Servant passages should have connected the dots for His questioners, but they don't. The apostle John sums up this exchange between Jesus and the people with quotes from Isaiah 53:1:

> "But although He had done so many signs before them, they did not believe in Him, that the word of Isaiah the prophet might be fulfilled, which he spoke: '_Lord, who has believed our report? And to whom has the arm of the LORD been revealed?_' – John 12:37-38 (emphasis added)

John then quotes Isaiah 6:10 to explain the reason for the people's lack of understanding:

> "Therefore they could not believe, because Isaiah said again: '_He has blinded their eyes and hardened their hearts, lest they should see with their eyes, lest they should understand with their hearts and turn, so_

that I should heal them.' These things Isaiah said when he saw His glory and spoke of Him." – John 12:39-41 (emphasis added)

Through the words of Isaiah, the LORD revealed the full program for the Servant's glorification through which the people could then be restored and glorified. But it confounded Israel because being "lifted up" in suffering and death didn't fit their idea of glorification. And yet God had made it clear from the beginning that the reversal of their condition and circumstances could not begin until the sacrifice had been paid for their redemption and purification. Only then could the journey toward their glorification begin.

GOD'S HIGHWAY PROJECT

The Glory of the Sacrifice

In his letter to the Philippian church, Paul fleshes out the transformation of Christ, the Servant and Son of God, into the Son of Man who would become the sacrifice for the people's sin. Read Philippians 2:9-18.

> **Q:** What is Christ the Servant's reward?

> **Q:** This Servant is the Light, and His followers are "sons of light." To be a "son of" someone means to be of their character and/or condition. What then does it mean for us to be "sons (or daughters) of light"?

Building a Salvation Message From the Old Testament

Now, let's return to the list we began in the previous lesson and continue building out the salvation message from the Old Testament. So far, we have seen these salvation elements in Isaiah 52:

- **Isaiah 52:3** – *"For thus says the LORD: 'You have sold yourselves for nothing, and you shall be redeemed without money.'"*

    We first talked about the grace aspect being expressed in the "for nothing" phrase. God purchases Israel back as freely as she once gave away her favors. She is saved by grace and grace alone on

God's part, and that redemption is purchased by a sacrifice and not money. But what is the nature of the sacrifice that redeems her?

- **Isaiah 52:4** – *"For thus says the Lord GOD: 'My people went down at first into Egypt to dwell there...'"*

A subtle reminder of Egypt is inserted into the text. In that deliverance, Israel was redeemed first by the sacrifice of the Passover lamb, now immortalized as the *zeroah* portion on the Passover seder plate. Only after this, was she saved by the might work of God's outstretched arm (*zeroah*). The *zeroah* is associated with both the intercessory sacrifice that caused God to pass over His people at the death of the firstborn sons, as well as the miraculous works that freed her from her oppressors. But, in the salvation program, the sacrifice comes first, and then the physical deliverance—in that particular order.

- **Isaiah 52:6, 10** – *"Therefore My people shall know My name; therefore they shall know in that day that I am He who speaks: 'Behold, it is I,'... The LORD has made bare His holy arm in the eyes of all the nations; and all the ends of the earth shall see the salvation of our God."*

The freewill sacrifice for sin is made by God Himself. First He humbles Himself to the status of a servant, crying, *"Here I am!"* in verse 6. Then, He lays bare His own arm in verse 10. His arm is an extension of Himself and figurative of His strength the way a man's strength is reckoned through his son or a nation's strength is reckoned in its king. The "arm," therefore, takes the human form of both a son and king who delivers Israel. When God's kingly, firstborn "Son" renders up His strength to become a sacrifice for sin, He fulfills God's promise to redeem Israel without money. He displays a priestly strength by interceding for the sin of the people as their representative. He is the salvation—the Yeshua (in English, Jesus)—of our God.

- **Isaiah 52:13** – *"Behold, My Servant shall deal prudently; He shall be exalted and extolled and be very high."*

For His sacrificial service, God's Servant is glorified as a king with a three-fold expression of glory: *rûm, nasa,* and *gabah. Rûm* and *gabah* both portray a king's exaltation, but *nasa* paints the picture of a different kind of "lifting-up," one that involves enduring suffering to lift a burden from a person and carry it away, even at the sacrifice of life. This is the same sacrifice that the zeroah of God performs.

- **Isaiah 52:14** – *"Just as many were astonished at you, so His visage was marred more than any man, and His form more than the sons of men;"*

  Even as the *zeroah* is representative of God (the Son of God) to the people, He is representative of the people (the Son of Man) before God as He takes up the cup of wrath and drains it to its dregs. He endures God's divine wrath on His people's behalf. While the kingly sons of Israel could not save her, the kingly Son of God could.

Do you see how God is establishing the salvation plan here? We as believers in Christ, familiar with the "good news" gospel accounts, can easily fill in the picture. The command to proclaim the good news is at the heart of this chapter, where all these salvation elements are on display. There remains only to flesh out the details of the complex picture of the *nasa* form of glory.

Just as the first messianic deliverer, Cyrus, was given a grand introduction in Isaiah 44, followed by the details of his tasking and reward in Isaiah 45, the Servant has now been given a grand introduction in Isaiah 52. From here we move to the details of His tasking and reward in Isaiah 53.

LESSON 18

The Way Out of a Crooked Place

READ

Isaiah 53:1-12

DISCUSSION

After the Servant's glorious introduction in Isaiah 52, we now see the details of His tasking and reward in Isaiah 53. Isaiah 52 presented the glory of His sacrifice; Isaiah 53 now explains how that sacrifice was meant for comfort.

Before we get into the text, let me just ask you: Is there comfort in sacrifice?

No, of course not, and yet, maybe. It depends on what sacrifice is being demanded, how the person making the sacrifice views it, and what benefit they hope to achieve by it. Parents make sacrifices for their children all the time. Sometimes children make sacrifices for their parents. Husbands and wives make sacrifices for one another. A person might sacrifice time and resources for a good friend or a good cause. The sacrifice might even be something as serious as giving up one's life. First responders risk death to save people who are often complete strangers to them. Soldiers give their lives for their king and country. Making that sacrifice declares the value a person places on that relationship or greater cause.

Paul remarks,

> "For scarcely for a righteous man will one die; yet perhaps for a good man someone would even dare to die. But God demonstrates His own love toward us, in that while we were still sinners, Christ died for us."
> – Romans 5:7-8

Q: What does this tell us of the value God places on us?

Q: What is the comfort in that?

Isaiah 53: The Way Out of a Crooked Place | 193

There is great comfort for the one receiving the benefits of another's sacrifice, but what about for the one making the sacrifice? God engages us as His co-laborers in this Highway Project and tasks us with lifting up hurting and struggling people. That task often demands a sacrifice on our part. Think of a sacrifice you personally have made and what it cost you.

> **Q:** Why did you do it?
>
> **Q:** What kind of sacrifice(s) did you make to lift up or comfort that person? How far did you go in giving of yourself?
>
> **Q:** Did you get to a point where you wondered if the ordeal was worth the effort?
>
> **Q:** What kept you going in your endeavor? What was your end reward?
>
> **Q:** If the person into whom you have poured your energy and support walks away seemingly no better off, would you feel your effort has been without reward?

Now let's change the perspective a little. So far, the Servant has been the one entering into another person's suffering (Isaiah 49 and 50). What if He was the one who has suffered for the sake of God's glory, and He now asks you to identify with that goal and share in His suffering?

> **Q:** What kind of sacrifice is required on your part to identify with Him?
>
> **Q:** How much are you willing to sacrifice so that God might be glorified?
>
> **Q:** Is there comfort in knowing that your effort glorifies God, even if there is no earthly reward for it?

Today, the intercessory role of the Arm of the LORD will be on full display. Will anyone believe it?

Isaiah 53:1-10

Opening Argument: (Isaiah 51:9-11) Israel exhorts the Arm of the LORD to save her
Closing Argument: (Isaiah 53:1-10) The Arm of the LORD is revealed, but Israel doesn't accept Him

Israel once wailed *"Awake, awake, O arm of the LORD!"* The prophet now replies, good news! The Arm of the LORD is here to save you! But there is a problem. Israel doesn't believe the report. The Arm of the LORD is revealed in all His glory, but He doesn't fit her mental picture of the hoped-for Messiah. He should be more like Cyrus. He should conquer the oppressor, put her enemies under His feet, and reign on the throne. (Cyrus set the bar pretty high for a messianic figure in that regard.) She wanted Him to be stately and kingly. She wants a hero. Instead, He is inglorious in His appearance. He looks a lot like—her.

The Servant's identification with Israel's condition is what equips Him to offer comfort, and the wincing description here in Isaiah 53 is as much a description of her as it is of Him. In her bondage, Israel has no beauty. She is not desired. She is despised and rejected, acquainted with sorrow and grief. The Hebrew word for grief actually means sickness or affliction. The Servant is the very reflection of her, and she hides her face from that reflection. He identifies with her, but she does not want to identify with Him. She considers herself to be a victim, but this man has clearly been stricken by God for some sin. That, too, is a denial. God told Israel that her own sin was the reason she had been stricken by Him. This is part of her blindness, that she doesn't see herself in the light.

When we don't like what we see in the mirror, we hide from our reflection, don't we? We have previously talked about why a person would refuse comfort, and one reason was because they don't want to acknowledge their own condition and it becomes a stumbling block. This is why, when a victim is faced with the reflection of their true condition in their comforter, they will want to deny the association. They will stab a finger at the comforter and say something like, "I am nothing like you! You deserved what you got. I did not! I am a victim!" They will reject the association and scorn the comfort. That is what Israel did to her Comforter. Thus, He became a stumbling block for her. Instead of admitting her sin and accepting the redemption He offered her freely by grace, she went on trying to redeem herself by her own effort. She could not accept the gift of grace, not from His hands.

In verse 5, the prophet forces Israel to identify with the Servant as the trespass offering for her sin. He endured this for her. He bore the affliction silently. (Note: the Servant, who has been speaking for Himself in previous passages, goes notably silent in this chapter. The only speakers are the prophet in verses 1-10, and the LORD in verses 11-12. The Servant's silence is deafening.)

There is a particular word that we should savor in verse 5. It is the word "wounded" in the NKJV; other translations say "pierced." In the Hebrew, it is the word *ḥalal* (pronounces ha-layl with a phlegmy "h"). The word is rich in meaning. Let's delve into it a little.

In a literal, physical sense, *ḥalal* means to be pierced, as with a sword or spear, so as to inflict a mortal wound. The wound causes contamination in the body that leads to death. In a similar context, *ḥalal* can describe a woman being raped—when a man enters into a place where he had no right to go and contaminates or defiles her. That defilement begins to consume her mentally, emotionally, and even spiritually, the way that contamination from a wound consumes the body.

In a spiritual sense, *ḥalal* means to be defiled or profaned. Just as corruption enters an open wound so that the man becomes sick and dies, so spiritual defilement enters a man and pollutes him and he dies.

To *ḥalal* is, in essence, the act of making a way. The corruption or defilement would not have happened without that initial beginning. Thus, *ḥalal* is also translated as "to begin" to do something (Genesis 4:26, 6:1, 9:20, 10:8, 11:6, 41:54). There is a *ḥalal*-ing moment where a way is opened, a beginning is made, and a train of events then unfolds as a consequence. The beginning act might be something innocuous or seemingly harmless, such as, Noah began to be a farmer. But when we follow the train of events from that beginning, it ultimately leads to death, separation, or defilement. But it doesn't end there. Out of that experience comes a new beginning. For example, the Flood was the end result of a train of events that began with a *ḥalal*-ing moment:

> "Now it came to pass, when men began to [ḥalal] multiply on the face of the earth, and daughters were born to them, that the sons of God saw the daughters of men, that they were beautiful; and they took wives for themselves of all whom they chose." – Genesis 6:1-2

The sons of God joined physically with the daughters of Adam. The sons of God entered into a place where they had no right to be, and the physical defilement led to physical and spiritual profaning. The human lineage that was meant to lead to salvation was corrupted. As a result, the earth was corrupted with idolatry and filled with violence. The people corrupted their ways to the point where everything had to be destroyed, and then God brought the Flood. And yet, out of that destruction, God made a way for restoration by saving Noah and his family. New life began again under a new covenant. That is *ḥalal*-ing in its fullest sense.

Here in Isaiah 53, the prophet says that the Servant was *ḥalal*-ed for our transgressions. He was pierced physically. He was profaned spiritually. He bore (*nasa*-ed) our "griefs"—our disease and anxiety (sickness of body and mind). The corruption caused by our sin was placed upon Him. The piercing and defilement led to His death.

Verses 8-10 detail the Servant's death. There is no doubt that this is a death, and the LORD's hand was in it. The LORD was the one who gave the Servant the cup of fury to drink, and He drank it to the dregs. But then, in verse 10, there is a reversal, mid-verse. The Servant, who was dead, has somehow prolonged His days. He will see prosperity and a return for His labor. Thus, that death was not an end but a new beginning. His resurrection initiated new life under a new covenant. His inglorious death was a *ḥalal*-ing moment, and yet it was the means by which God created a way out of a crooked place not just for Israel but all of humanity.

The chapter ends with a reward for the Servant, just as it did for Cyrus.

Isaiah 53:11-12

This closing argument is paired with the opening argument in Isaiah 51:

Opening Argument: (Isaiah 51:1-8) The eternality of God's righteousness and His reward for those who pursue His righteousness
Closing Argument: (Isaiah 53:1-10) The eternality of the Servant's reward for His righteousness, which He shares with "the strong."

Notice how the speaker shifts in Isaiah 53:11-12. A third-party has been speaking of the LORD and the Servant, but now the LORD Himself speaks.

"I will divide Him a portion with the great..." This is the LORD Himself rewarding the Servant for the sacrifice He made, and this is the reward on which the Servant set His sights when it seemed His effort was in vain (Isaiah 49:4). Having come through the ordeal, the Servant now sees the result of His labor and is satisfied, meaning He feels fulfilled and overflowing, like a cup that runs over with fine wine.

The LORD grants the Servant a portion with the great, and the Servant, in turn, shares His spoil with "the strong," much like His ancestor David who was accustomed to sharing his spoil with his mighty men. Who, then, are "the strong"? What defines a "mighty man" (or woman)? It depends on whose definition and values you use.

Q: Who are the strong by the world's definition?

Q: Who are the strong by the Servant's definition?

By the world's definition, the strong are the biggest bullies on the block. They are the most popular candidate who receives the most number of voters at a polling booth or the influencer with largest number of supporters for their social cause. But as imposing as it might appear, that kind of strength has no eternal power. The strongest nation can be broken in one day. The LORD proved that with Babylonia. The strongest athlete can be broken with one injury. The strongest support can evaporate overnight with one controversial statement. The strongest anything that is of this world can be reduced to nothing if God merely blows on it.

Those who are strong by the world's standard are not the ones with whom the Servant shares His spoil. The strong, by the Servant's definition, are those who look beyond the fleetingness of the earthly riches and sacrifice all in pursuit of God's glory and an eternal reward, just as He did. They identify with Him as disciples and follow in His footsteps, as He said:

> *"And whoever does not bear his cross and come after Me cannot be My disciple... So likewise, whoever of you does not forsake all that he has cannot be My disciple." – Luke 14:27, 33*

The Servant has been the one coming to us and identifying with us in our suffering, but now He invites us to come to Him and identify with Him in His suffering as a way of testing our strength. To those who bear the burden and endure as He did, He divides the spoil. But what is the spoil?

> **Q:** The reward that the Servant receives is a crown and a kingdom. Is the crown, or the extension of royal status, something that He shares with the strong?

It is. When we look at the pairing in the chiastic structure, we see that the reward for pursuing righteousness is a crown and kingdom granted by righteous God to His righteous Servant-King. The Servant-King then extends that same reward of royal honor to those who pursue righteousness. This is the resolution of God's address to the righteous in Isaiah 51. If they faithfully endure, they will have this reward in a future kingdom. We will come back to a discussion of the reward when we get to the kingdom picture in Isaiah 55.

The Servant's glorification pronounced in Isaiah 52:13-15 has come full circle. The *rûm* glorification played out at His triumphal entry. The lifting-up act described in the word *nasa* then played out. The Servant was lifted up as an offering and made to bear the burden of the people's sin. As He was taken away, He took that death, guilt, and judgment with Him. And finally, He was *gabah*-ed. He is lifted up once again, this time to heaven to be seated at the right hand of the Father with all the dignity and honor of an eternal king.

GOD'S HIGHWAY PROJECT

The Way Out of a Crooked Place

The Servant's sacrifice is the turning point in God's Highway Project. Isaiah 53 marks the exact center in the span of chapters between Isaiah 40-66 and presents the pinnacle act of salvation that ends the conflict on the spiritual plane and straightens the path that will lead to the final end of all conflict. From this point forward, God's Highway Project will begin to focus on straightening the path—realigning Israel's understanding of God's righteousness and how to be a holy people. Israel needs healing from the inside out because it was the internal, spiritual problem that got her into her destructive, conflicted lifestyles and eventual oppression.

Once her internal values are set right, then the external oppression will be more easily and thoroughly conquered.

This is an important fact to remember when comforting a struggling person and why it is vital to turn them to Christ for that way out of their crooked place. The internal condition must be addressed first because simply changing external circumstances doesn't have any eternal benefit so long as the inner person remains the same. The inner person is what needs healing, and only Christ can heal from the inside out.

God sends us into furnaces of affliction for our equipping as much as our refining, so that we can identify with people who are struggling as we have struggled and offer words of comfort in due season. While comfort can be achieved through shared experience, sometimes it can have the opposite effect. The struggling person may resist our comfort, particularly if our experience required us to confront sin in our life, because a victim won't want to be convicted of their own sin. We can be too much of a reflection of something they wish to avoid. But there is only one way out of the crooked place they are in, and that is through an identification with the Servant and His atoning death. It is the only way to be released from the bondage of sin and guilt.

Have you ever had a ḥalal-ing moment in life? Perhaps it began as an innocent pursuit, but having begun down that path, you found yourself deep in a crooked place. Maybe into debt. Maybe into an addiction. Maybe into a toxic relationship. Maybe the ḥalal-ing moment began with a crime committed against you that defiled you as a person and consumed you physically, mentally, or emotionally as a result.

> **Q:** How does Christ make a way out of that place for you?
>
> **Q:** Have you ever shared that ḥalal-ing moment with someone else who was struggling with the same thing?
>
> **Q:** When they found out you had a similar experience, did it bring them any comfort?
>
> **Q:** Did sharing how Christ brought you out of that crooked place help them find the way out, as well?
>
> **Q:** If they are still in that crooked place, what is keeping them there?

When I delved into the "griefs" aspect which Christ bore, I was surprised to find that the "sicknesses" that word describes includes not just sickness in the body which leads to death, but sickness in the mind—our anxieties—which also lead to death if we let them master us. Anxiety is a sign of fear, which is a stumbling block we have addressed in the past, but we didn't touch on the anxiety issue.

> **Q:** Are you, personally, given to anxiety? If you are, you are not alone, but, we should ask the question, why?
>
> **Q:** Where has that anxiety led you? What have been some of its effects on your life?
>
> **Q:** How has anxiety overrun our culture? What is its cause(s)?
>
> **Q:** How does Christ's death on the cross comfort our anxieties? In what way does He bear this burden for us?

LESSON 19

The Stumbling Block of Shame

READ

Isaiah 54:1-10

DISCUSSION

In the last lesson, we studied the death of the Sin-bearing Servant, which was the prophetic vision of Jesus's death on the cross. That sacrificial death achieved the pardon for sin that ended the spiritual conflict between God and His people and paved the way for Israel's return to Him. Ending the spiritual conflict was only one of the two main objectives in the Highway Project, and just because the way has been made for spiritual reconciliation, that does not mean that the work is finished.

Isaiah now embarks on the new theme of abundant life in the coming kingdom. This theme begins after the death of the Sin-bearing Servant in Isaiah 53 and will span Isaiah 54-57. The theme opens with a discussion of Israel's fruitless past. Before she can enter into the abundant life God has in store for her, she must overcome another stumbling block—the stumbling block of shame.

Before we get started, let's briefly discuss the topic of shame. We have all experienced shame in life. It's a universal human experience.

Q: What is shame?

Q: What are some scenarios where a person might feel ashamed?

In Isaiah 54, shame is a byproduct of Israel's sin and oppression, and it is felt two-fold. First, in regard to oppression, there is the shame and humiliation she has suffered at the hands of her furious antagonists. That shame, once internalized, gives her a crooked view of herself that must be straightened and realigned with God's view of her if she is to recover her well-being.

Secondly, in regard to her own personal sin, Israel grapples with shame over her past failings. It is hard enough to face conviction for sin under neutral circumstances, but when a victim has suffered injustice and humiliation at the hands of an abuser or oppressor, facing conviction for his or her own sin can be an overwhelming obstacle. Even if the sin is acknowledged, the shame from that can be crushing, especially when added to the shame and humiliation suffered at the hands of an oppressor. This dual aspect of shame is what God now addresses with Israel.

We are continuing the comparison of opening and closing arguments in the chiastic structure. Here is the pairing for this chapter:

Opening Argument: (Isaiah 50:1-11) The Servant endures the shame to comfort Israel

Closing Argument: (Isaiah 54:1-17) Israel's shame is removed after the Servant's death

Isaiah 54:1-6

The chapter begins with joyous imperative commands to the barren woman: "Sing! ... Break forth!" Why? *"For more are the children of the desolate than the children of the married woman"* (54:1). The LORD is speaking to Israel, but notice how He describes her. He calls her barren.

> **Q:** Why would the LORD describe Israel as barren?

> **Q:** According to Old Testament Law, of what is barrenness a sign?

Barrenness equates to fruitlessness in the human experience and is an outworking of disobedience as prescribed in the Mosaic Law. The LORD promised Israel abundant life so long as she obeyed His commandments, and the fruit of the womb was part of that covenant blessing according to Deuteronomy 7:14. But if she disobeyed, He promised He would curse her with unfruitfulness of field and womb. A woman suffering from barrenness was looked upon as cursed, and, therefore, was shamed and shunned by her peers. A good example of this is Samuel's mother, Hannah, who was barren and wept because of the continual taunting and harassment she received from her sister-wife, Peninnah in 1 Samuel 1.

According to the Law, barrenness and exile were the curses for disobedience. When Israel broke that covenant relationship between them, God took from her the abundance that would have come from that relationship and sent her into exile and oppression, just as He had warned her that He would in that Law.

In the Hebrew, the word for "desolate" invokes the essence of silence—silence in a land or a life that has been laid to waste. The desolate are the ones who have been shamed into silence. We previously talked about being reduced to silence in the face of fury. Silence is also a reaction to shame. And yet, it is the silent who are now called to sing. The fruitfulness of the one who was barren will now eclipse the fruitfulness of the one who has many children by a husband.

Now the LORD commands her: *"Enlarge the place of your tent! . . . Do not spare! . . . Lengthen your cords! . . . Strengthen your stakes!"* There is a glorious sense of anticipation. The barren woman will soon have children—so many that she will need a bigger tent.

> **Q:** What brought about the reversal of condition? What lifted the curse?

The death of the Sin-bearing Servant in the previous chapter. Repentance and return on Israel's part are necessary, but the payment for her sins still had to be made. The Servant's death lifted the curse caused by her disobedience and satisfied the Law so that she could enter into that blessing of abundance and new life again. The lesson of grace is embodied in the figure of the barren woman. All barren women in Scripture had to endure that condition for a time to show that the problem could not be lifted by human effort or will. They had to come to the end of their own resources before they could experience abundant life gifted by God's grace and grace alone. And so the picture of the barren woman becomes an illustration of salvation by grace, according to the promise.

The LORD has extended grace to Israel. She has been redeemed without money as He promised back in Isaiah 52:3, and not just redeemed but promised an explosion of abundant life.

> **Q:** This is the beginning of the kingdom pictures in Isaiah, and it is a kingdom full of children. But what kind of kingdom is coming into view—an earthly kingdom full of earthly children, a spiritual kingdom full of spiritual "children," or both?

The immediate focus for Israel will be on the return of a future generation of physical children—a remnant that the LORD saves in the sense of preserving them throughout the exile—and theirs will be the task of rebuilding the earthly Jerusalem after the Babylonian exile. There is a near fulfillment of this in a very physical sense. But what stake does a barren woman have in this kingdom if she does not bear physical children to rebuild her legacy? Perhaps it is in how we define "children."

Q: How do we define "children"? Who is your child, and in what sense?

In Old Testament thought, Israel's children are not defined strictly by physical bloodlines. A person is considered your "child" if you have a part in their care and upbringing, even if they are not your child by blood (such as Naomi and Obed in Ruth 4:16-17, or Mordecai and Hadassah in Esther 2:7). If you are their teacher or a mentor responsible for their spiritual upbringing, then they become your children in a spiritual sense, as well. Thus, the barren woman can have many "children" figuratively of a spiritual nature, born of her relationship with God, and in greater abundance than the physical children born to the married woman by a physical husband.

This is important because, while the immediate focus is on rebuilding a physical Jerusalem, there is another Jerusalem on the horizon—a heavenly Jerusalem—and it is filled with spiritual children who are born of a spiritual Husband and by grace. God is beginning to expand Israel's vision toward a more eternal goal.

This is a comfort to me personally, because I identify with this model of the barren wife. After 28+ years of marriage, I have never been able to have children, though not for lack of trying. I am a barren woman, now past my child-bearing years. Is a woman like myself barred from this promise of abundant life for lack of physical children? No, of course not. I am grateful that the LORD's promise of abundant life is not defined by the number of earthly children I have. I would never experience abundant life if it was defined purely by earthly possessions like children, who are a fleeting comfort at best. I, too, can be fruitful, and in a more enduring way, because my "children" are of a different nature. They are children I have brought forth in the faith, and if I persist in faith and pursue a legacy of children along that line, I will see the fruit of that when I enter the kingdom. And I am content with that, although, sadly, I have met many women in life who are not. There are many women in life whose sense of personal worth is often wrapped up in their role as mothers, and I have met many of them in Christian circles. I was once harangued by a woman for fifteen minutes after a Sunday Bible class for not adopting children. Another wept in despair when yet another attempt at in-vitro fertilization failed. She and her husband had sunk thousands of dollars into fertility clinics to no avail. The pursuit of physical children was almost an obsession with these women, and they could not understand why I wouldn't go to the ends of the earth to have them.

What none of them understood is that the LORD does not withhold abundant life from the barren woman, and the fleeting pursuit of physical children can become a form of bondage. I have had a greater freedom to pursue the tasks that the LORD has given me—tasks that I might not have done if I had been constrained by children—and I have experienced abundant life in my own way. It all boils down to how you define abundant life. Realigning our understanding of how abundant life is defined and achieved is the next stage of God's Highway Project.

Verse 4 begins with the imperative command: *"Do not fear, for you will not be ashamed, neither be disgraced"* (54:4). A barren woman enlarging her tent with this kind of anticipation is like Noah building the Ark. The world, and even her own people, will view the effort with amusement, derision, taunting, and scoffing. They shame her for her hope as well as her cursed condition. Thus, the shame of yet another seemingly fruitless pursuit becomes something she fears, and a stumbling block she must overcome if she is to enter into abundant life.

God uses a number of Hebrew words in verse 4 to describe the experience of shame. (These are the words as they appear in the New King James Version. Your Bible version may render them differently, which is why we are looking at the original Hebrew text behind them.) Let's look at their definitions:

- **Ashamed**, Hebrew: *boosh* meaning simply to be ashamed.
- **Disgraced**, Hebrew: *kalam* meaning to wound or hurt, to insult, shame, humiliate, make blush. A person can deal out that disgrace

Isaiah 54: The Stumbling Block of Shame | 207

or be the recipient of it—to be ashamed, be put to shame, be reproached or humiliated.

- **Shame**, Hebrew: *khapher* meaning to blush or be ashamed in the sense of being detected by someone digging away at you or prying into your life. Thus, there is a fear of one's hidden side being discovered and brought to light.

- **Shame**, Hebrew: *bosheth*. This is a noun variation of the adjective, *boosh*, meaning a shameful thing (like an idol). Thus, "the shame of your youth" translates into a past lived in pursuit of shameful, fruitless things (like idols).

- **Reproach**, Hebrew: *kherpa* meaning to taunt, carp at, reproach, defy, jeopardize. It comes from the root word, *kharaph*, which literally means to be "pulled off" in the sense of being exposed as if by stripping, like a fruitful tree stripped of fruit and leaves. It can mean to scorn in the sense of counting one's life as of little worth.

The LORD describes all the kinds of shame that can be felt and then applies them to women in various life experiences: the youth, the widow, the forsaken woman, and a youthful wife who has been refused. All of these women share the experience of "barrenness" or unfruitfulness that results in shame. The text pairs the youth and widow together first in verse 4.

- **The youth.** "Youth," in the Hebrew, describes a kind of juvenile vigor. The youth has a fruitful life ahead of her, and yet there is an experience of shame in it. What kind of shame is associated with one's youth? Perhaps it is in the things she pursued. Perhaps she put her energy into running after trivial things that had no lasting value or, worse, a life of dissipation that got her off the path and into sin. Looking back, the sinfulness and fruitlessness of her early life can be a source of regret and shame.

- **The widow.** The widow is at the opposite end of the spectrum from the youth. Her fruitful days are past. In Old Testament times, widows suffered a lack of support after the death of their husband and lived on the margins of society as charity cases. They were often victims of neglect and denied justice in court. The widow is the one who suffers the *kherpa*—the taunting, the stripping of her value, the exposure and neglect. Her life is of little value in the world's eyes.

The LORD then addresses women who have experienced shame and a loss of fruitfulness because of a broken relationship with their husband: the forsaken woman and the youthful wife who has been forgotten. Remember Israel's cry in Isaiah 49:14, *"The LORD has forsaken me, and my Lord has forgotten me."* She has cast herself in this role, and the LORD answers her as such.

- The forsaken woman is like the widow in verse 4. "Forsaken" describes a woman who has been "loosed" from a husband or left behind when a husband deserts her. There is a shame associated with that abandonment and loss of fruitfulness.
- The youthful wife is like the youth. She has all the promise of fruitfulness in her, but that fruitfulness is denied to her by a husband who has developed an aversion to her and refuses to have relations with her.

Isaiah 54:7-10

In verses 2-3, God commanded the barren woman to enlarge her tents in hope. In verse 4, He command her not to be afraid of being humiliated for speaking out and stepping out in faith. Why? Because He is her Husband, and He is calling to her.

Q: What reassurances does He gives her in verse 7-10?

Do you feel the tenderness in the LORD's words? Don't we ache for tenderness from our spouses when we have been at odds with one another? He is a merciful Husband. He put her away for a little while, but He promises that He will gather her again with "great mercies." His words describe a deep, deep compassion for her, like the compassion a mother has for the child she carries in her womb (that is the sense of the Hebrew word for mercy or compassion in verse 7). He says He will have mercy on her and show her an everlasting kindness.

Israel is the youth who pursued her lusts. She is the widow who has reaped a bitter end. She is the woman who grieves over being abandoned for her unfaithfulness and suffers a fruitless life as a result, but now God holds out His arms to her.

In verses 9-10, God gives Israel a comparison to help illustrate His mercy. He says that Israel's exile is like the "waters of Noah" (the Great Flood). That was another instance of His outpouring of fury on sinful and idolatrous people, and yet He preserved a remnant who would enter into abundant life in a new world.

> **Q:** What covenant promise did He swear in the aftermath of the Flood?
>
> **Q:** What similar covenant promise does He swear to Israel now in Isaiah?

God promised not to be angry and punishing to His people forever. He didn't let His anger and judgment rule His relationship with them permanently. His mercy and kindness toward them will always be there, and He desires peace with them.

GOD'S HIGHWAY PROJECT

The Stumbling Block of Shame

Shame is a universal experience for all people, and it has its uses, for better or worse.

> **Q:** How can shame be healthy?
>
> **Q:** How can it become a stumbling block that prevents health and healing?

There is a healthy shame that convicts us of sin and that shame is necessary to motivate us to repent and return to God. This is the kind of shame being addressed in this passage. God is able to remove Israel's shame by providing a substitutionary sacrifice for her sin through the Servant's death. The Servant identified with that shame. He took it from her and bore it Himself, then took it to the grave with Him. That pivotal act was meant, above all, to remove guilt and shame, and not just for

Israel, but for us. Because of our identification with Christ and acceptance of His sacrifice for our sins, we now have that same covenant of peace with God the Father and there should be no reason to stand before God our Husband, naked and ashamed. It remains for us to experience an abundant life with the King in His coming kingdom.

Q: So, why do we still grapple with shame?

Shame enters only when we let go of that identity with Him—when we don't cling to that cross and God's grace. That is when we stumble back into shame, and with it, fear and despair over not being loved. God's grace and forgiveness were meant to empower us and protect us from the world's condemnation, and when we let go of those and seek validation for our works instead, we open ourselves to the world's condemnation because the world has its own skewed values and social norms. The world does not understand grace, and it will never, ever, grant us grace.

Shaming and humiliation has become a severe problem in our modern culture. It is a bullying tactic used by people who seek to dominate and force compliance with their skewed ideals. It is also used for amusement. God forgives and forgets, but the world never forgives, and social media never forgets. Every mistake and ill-spoken word can be captured and broadcasted to the world in the blink of an eye. And that is just the stupid stuff we do. What happens when they catch us taking a stand for our faith? It's brutal. And the world loves it. They support it and encourage it. But it destroys a person's worth, and those feelings of inferiority and guilt linger long after the oppressor is gone or a different video has gone viral.

Shaming and humiliation have also become methods of punishment that God never, ever intended to be used. When He laid out the rules for punishing someone, it was to be done in a way that was just and brought about repentance, but did not rob a person of personal worth or value in the eyes of society. According to Deuteronomy 25:3, there was a set punishment for a set crime, the person knew what that punishment would be before they sinned, and when the punishment was delivered, that was the end of it. There was a distinction made between a controlled punishment and a beating. A controlled punishment was meant to bring repentance so a person could be restored to fellowship. A beating was forbidden because it was humiliating and destructive and prevented a person from returning to fellowship with others afterward.

But our culture has skewed God's values on this. Here is an example that I have seen play out over my own lifetime. I grew up in the generation that believed in corporal punishment and spanked children, and, granted, there were abuses of that form of punishment. But when society saw a child being physically beaten, instead of realigning with God's values and punishing the individual abuser as God would, it banned all forms of physical punishment and substituted verbal punishment instead. You talk to the child. You reason with the unrepentant little tyrant. My generation soon discovered that was not effective very often, and so parents began to resort to verbal shaming that was just as humiliating as a physical beating. Again, God forgives and forgets, but people don't. This has been the work of several generations, but we now have a generation of children who have perfected the art of verbal abuse and humiliation, and we have given them social media as a platform on which to practice it. And for the record, the world's solution hasn't stopped the physical abuse at all. In fact, it is more rampant than ever. Substituting physical punishment with verbal punishment only amplified the problem.

> **Q:** We have created a culture that has become saturated with shaming and humiliation and is overly sensitive to it. How is our current generation trying to curb it?

With more shaming. Any criticism that might be considered to undermine a person's worth, even when it is good, healthy counsel given in the person's best interests, is labeled as shaming, and the alleged shamer then gets shamed in return.

> **Q:** Has our culture's effort to deal with shame and humiliation relieved the oppression or just become another form of oppression?

It is bad now, but it is going to get worse. This generation is straying so far from God's highway that eventually they will refuse the instruction of the Word of God altogether, as Paul warns in 2 Timothy 4:2-4.

The world shames us when we run counter to its values but even more so when we step out in our faith as a witness for Christ. The world loves nothing more than to dig up our past failings and throw them in our faces, and when we offer faith-based comfort, it blows back at us with a vengeance. The fear of being shamed or humiliated can impact our witness for Christ, but we are warned against being sway by this. We are called to take up the cross with Christ. Jesus said in Mark 8:38,

> *"For whoever is ashamed of Me and My words in this adulterous and sinful generation, of him the Son of Man also will be ashamed when He comes in the glory of His Father with the holy angels."* – Mark 8:38

Straightening crooked places requires maintaining a proper perspective of the world in relation to God. In Isaiah 40, God challenged Israel over where she sought comfort and empowerment: in fleeting, earthly things or an eternal God. In Isaiah 51, God asked, what is the oppressor's fury compared to Mine? I was the one who sent you into exile because of your sin, just as I warned you I would do if you were faithless to Me. I am the one with whom you need to reconcile. You have lost the correct perspective. We should be more fearful of being shamed by Christ than by this world.

Q: What are we telling the world about Christ when we let guilt and shame rule us?

Q: When the world shames us for our relationship with Christ, what is our comfort?

There is beneficial shame that stems from God's conviction of us, and there is destructive shame that stems from the world's conviction of us. Once our shame before God is removed by the Sin-bearing Servant, human oppressors lose their power (or at least, they should). God promised Israel in the beginning that He would empower her.

Q: How is forgiveness an empowering experience?

Helping Broken People Overcome Shame

God models mercy for us in the way He handles Israel. While the promises He makes to release her literally from Babylonian exile and restore her to her land are made specifically to her in the immediate context, His character is universal, and He extends this same grace and mercy to all people to help deal with the issue of shame.

Israel is suffering from shame on two accounts. First, there is the shame she feels for her past sins, and second, there is the shame she feels because of the world's abuse. We see a reflection of Israel in broken people, perhaps even in ourselves. How do we comfort them, or ourselves, for that matter?

First, we need to separate the shame being felt for violating God's rules from the shame being felt for not abiding by the world's rules. Sometimes, the line between God and the world blurs.

> **Q:** Where do we point someone when they are feeling ashamed of the sin in their past? What essential truths do they need to know? (Hint: What essential truths did God present Israel in this passage?)

> **Q:** The Sin-bearing Servant's death removes the shame caused by sin. Does it remove the shame caused by our antagonists in life?

> **Q:** How do we restore a person who has suffered humiliation at the world's hands in a way that it has skewed their view of themselves?

Struggling men and women among us may actually have experienced the pain of being abandoned by a human spouse or suffer from one who is physically or emotionally distant. It is devastating when it happens with a physical spouse. Imagine what it would be like if it happened with our spiritual "Husband" as well. Fortunately, we have a merciful God who promises He will not abandon us, even when our earthly spouses do.

> **Q:** For those of you who are widows or widowers or have suffered abandonment by an earthly spouses, how has God been a "husband" to you?

Questions for Reflection:

In regard to the greater problem of shame that has beset our culture, perhaps the solution to shaming begins with us.

> **Q:** Have you ever shamed a person in how you speak to them or about them? Are you given to criticism, belittling people, or patronizing them? If so, why? What do you get out of it?

Q: God promised not to be angry with His people forever. Are you a person who stays angry forever over an offense? Do you hold that offense over the person's head and trot it out every time you want to punish them?

Q: Do you use humiliation (verbal or physical) as a punishment? It may be effective in achieving an immediate goal, but what are you communicating to the offender about their worth?

Q: What kind of punishment aligns with God's model?

Q: If you have suffered at someone else's word or hand, what would it take for that shame to be lifted? Perhaps that is what you need to do to restore a person you yourself have shamed or humiliated.

Shame is a stumbling block because it prevents healing and restoration to fellowship. Do not put this stumbling block in your brother's or sister's path.

We have dealt with the past. Now, on to the abundant future.

LESSON 20

Redefining Abundant Life

READ

Isaiah 54:11–55:13

DISCUSSION

Back in Isaiah 49, God made some opening promises to Israel, who felt forsaken and abandoned. He promised not to forget her or her children or her enemies. Now, we see the picture of the fulfillment of that vision.

Continuing the comparison of opening and closing arguments in the chiastic structure, we have this pairing:

Opening Argument: (Isaiah 49:15-26) The LORD promises that He will bring Israel and her children back into their kingdom

Closing Argument: (Isaiah 54:11–55:5) The promise fulfilled: Israel and her children are glorified as royalty in a future kingdom

The main goal of God's Highway Project is to return His people to Him and glorify them in their kingdom. Accomplishing that requires a change of heart, but also a change in thinking and acting. In this phase of God's Highway Project, God begins to straighten out the crooked places by challenging His people to consider His vision of ideal life and how to achieve it. What kind of salvation did they really need to release them from bondage? What kind of kingdom are they looking for in the future? Are their values based on the physical things that the world values or the eternal things that God values? What does God value? How does He view these things? Much of what is keeping them in oppression is a skewed view of what they should be pursuing, and He needs to bring those expectations back into alignment with His vision. Before we get into our verses for today, let me just ask you . . .

    Q: How do you define abundant life?

Isaiah 54:11-17

Notice how God describes Israel in verse 11. She is still afflicted and storm-tossed. After all of His promises, even the death of the Servant that released her from her spiritual bondage, she is still not comforted. We can appreciate her struggle, though. Even though we have the comfort of knowing Christ died for our sins and reconciled us with God, that does not mean our lives are free of antagonists and trials. We can still feel afflicted, tossed with tempest, and lacking in comfort during times of trial. It is part of the sanctification process. One of the problems early on in the journey has to do with adjusting to a new vision of the future and learning how to take comfort from it.

God presents Israel with this picture of a glorious future kingdom that is coming. It is like something out of a storybook, a gorgeous city laid with colorful gems and precious stones. It is a kingdom that the world, and even Satan himself, would envy because it is rich the way the world reckons riches.

> **Q:** But what else is of value, perhaps even greater value, in this kingdom, according to verses 13-14?

First, there are children, lots of children, just as the LORD promised the barren woman earlier in the chapter, and these children will be taught by the LORD. The Hebrew word for children is used twice in verse 13, and it can refer to children as being literal progeny but also, figuratively, builders of a house or kingdom. It can also mean disciples, those who are taught and understand. These are all "children," and all applications of this word fit the context here. The kingdom will be rebuilt and re-peopled by those with an understanding of the LORD. Think about that.

> **Q:** Why would children who are taught by the LORD top the list of valuable things?

> **Q:** What is the value of godly teaching? What are some of its out-workings?

One is peace, and not just peace but *great* peace.

> **Q:** Is peace something that this world values?

The world pays lip service to it, but how many wars and protests are waged in the name of peace? Peace for whom and according to whose values?

Righteousness is another key quality of this kingdom. "Righteousness" is a justice term. Justice is foundational to the peaceful running of a kingdom. Think of our own culture.

> **Q:** How has a lack of godly teaching affected our justice system?
>
> **Q:** What happens to a justice system when the citizens use the system to pursue wealth and build their own little kingdoms?

We get oppression. The Hebrew word for oppression in verse 14 specifically includes a sense of fraud and deceitful dealings—things that are the opposite of truth. What would it be like to live in a kingdom where truth reigns and there aren't scammers or hackers or fraudsters or identity thieves or any of the abuses that we fear in our current culture? What if all that was gone? Wouldn't that be heaven?

> **Q:** So, which is of greater worth—precious gems and worldly wealth, or peace and righteousness and a release from fear and oppression?
>
> **Q:** Is the kingdom's true wealth in its costly buildings or in its people?

Oppression and fear are pushed back as God brings Israel into a wide, safe space, but there are still antagonists in this place, according to verse 15. This may be referring to the experience that Israel had when she returned to Jerusalem after her release from Babylonian exile. The books of Ezra and Nehemiah describe how the returnees were beset by antagonists as they struggled to rebuild Jerusalem and the Temple.

But there is a difference about these post-exile antagonists. Unlike Babylonia, these antagonists will not overcome Israel. God was the one who sent Babylonia after Israel in the beginning, and there was nothing she could do to prevent it or save herself. Her time in the furnace of affliction had been decreed by the LORD. But these new antagonists are not divinely commissioned. She will still face combatants and revilers, but their power over her is broken. She can overcome them. This new position of power and authority is the heritage of the servants of God, but it is a power and authority that is granted by Him and sourced in Him.

One of the first promises God made back in Isaiah 40 was that He would empower the weak if they would wait on Him, and He makes good on that promise in this future kingdom.

There is a reason why these particular promises and conditions are presented after the picture of the Sin-bearing Servant's death in Isaiah 53. All of this comfort springs from that source. Now that the penalty for sin is removed, whatever power these antagonist had over God's children to condemn them is now broken, and this is a promise that extends to all God's people, even us. As Paul says in Romans 8:1, *"There is therefore now no condemnation to those who are in Christ Jesus..."* The penalty has been paid. The wrath is appeased. Now every tongue that rises against us in judgment will be condemned because our righteousness is in Christ. That is as much our right and heritage as servants of God as it is for Israel, and a very great comfort.

We have talked about the building and fabric of the kingdom. It is rich, but its real riches are in its people who understand God and embrace His values and in its character of peace, truth, and righteousness. Now let's look at life in the kingdom. Again, this is going to challenge Israel's understanding of what is valuable.

Isaiah 55:1-3a

This kingdom offers a rich abundance of good living—water, wine, and milk. There is an everlasting fountain of these. Water is needful for sustaining life, particularly in desert places. Wine and milk are luxuries, perhaps, but they are all things that the world values and on which it places a high price (similar to the costly gems of the previous verses). And yet, these things can be had for nothing in God's kingdom. They are not considered valuable as the world values them. The LORD's words challenge Israel to redefine her values. Why waste good money for what is not bread?

> **Q:** What is the value of bread?

Bread represents food that sustains the body in our earthly life. It is needful, but it is also a transient thing. A person buys it and eats it. It passes through their body with only fleeting benefit and comfort, and even though they eat it, they are hungry again afterwards. And so they go to work to earn money to buy more bread. Thus, their life becomes consumed with the pursuit of consumable things. Isn't that an irony?

Let's compare the bread to the costly stones in Isaiah 54. The world sees only the precious gems that are of worldly value, but God sees those gems as people—living stones that are of eternal value. The wealth of His kingdom is embodied in His people, not material things.

This kingdom picture that God is painting for Israel is not of a fleeting, earthly kingdom but an eternal, spiritual one. The nature of this heavenly kingdom is different from the earthly one; therefore, what nourishes and sustains life in it is also of a different nature. What sustains life in an eternal, spiritual kingdom? The Word of God. That is the bread. Israel needs to transform her thinking over what will give her an eternal kind of nourishment and what she needs to feed—body or soul.

"Listen to Me . . . Incline your ear . . . Hear and your soul shall live." (55:2-3a) The abundance of the kingdom is not achieved in the pursuit of what satisfies the body but what satisfies the soul, and nourishment is received not by the mouth but by the ear. Hear, and you shall have all that is needful for living. But it is not enough to simply listen. We have to consider the source that is speaking to us. The world promotes the pursuit of the kind of wealth and abundance that God's kingdom offers, but it does so by its own wisdom and its own definition. It craves the riches and abundance of God's kingdom but will try to achieve them by deceit, fraud, fear, and oppression. Even in our Christian circles today, we find prosperity cults who twist the definition of abundant living into a worldly pursuit of wealth. Believers can stumble back into bondage when they do not have a clear picture of the kingdom, its abundance, and how that abundance is achieved.

Isaiah 55:3b-5

In almost the same breath, verse 3 segues from talking about being fed by the LORD (that is, being taught by the LORD) to the practical application of running a kingdom. In verse 4, there is the mention of the covenant that was made with David—the promise of an eternal kingship. The covenant with David will come to fruition in this kingdom when the Messianic Davidic King takes the eternal throne—the same Messiah-king who was the Sin-bearing Servant in Isaiah 53. Like His forefather,

David, that Servant will divide His spoil with the strong, and surely, David himself is among those. I believe the LORD promises David not just an eternal kingship through his progeny, but also a personal place in the administration of that future kingdom under that Son. Christ will be King of all, and David will be a leader (prince) and commander of the people. But notice that this covenant isn't just made with David. The covenant is extended to "you." *"I will make an everlasting covenant with you . . . you shall call a nation . . . nations who do not know you shall run to you . . . for He has glorified you."* (55:3, 5)

    Q: Who is "you"?

God has been speaking to the nation of Israel throughout this chapter. When her remnant comes into the kingdom, He will extend the same everlasting covenant of royal rulership—the sure mercies of David—to them as part of their glorification. Thus, the kingship is being democratized, meaning, the ruling power is being extended to the people. Christ will be King over all. David will be given a high level of rulership in the kingdom under Christ. Beneath him are the people who are not just subjects but co-rulers. "You" will command and direct kingdoms, and "you" will know the abundance that is usually reserved for those of royal status.

I want to pause here and do a quick summary of this picture being laid out for us, because this promise of abundant life and even rulership is not just for Israel. It is for us as well. It is for everyone who has identified with the death of the Sin-bearing Servant in Isaiah 53 and has endured suffering even as He endured suffering in pursuit of God's righteousness and kingdom. It is an important comfort. The apostle Peter references this particular Old Testament picture in his first letter. Let's look at that.

1 Peter 1:22-2:10

In his first letter, Peter explains how we fit into this picture of a kingdom built of living stones. He begins by talking about the salvation and heavenly inheritance of which the prophets prophesied (1 Peter 1:3-12). He then talks about the transformation that comes out of that salvation. We now have new life and are nourished by the enduring word of God. He quotes Isaiah 40 to make his comparison between the fleetingness of corruptible life versus the incorruptible life we have through the

Word. Then, in Chapter 2, he speaks about us being the living stones in a spiritual house.

> *"Coming to Him as to a living stone, rejected indeed by men, but chosen by God and precious, you also, as living stones, are being built up a spiritual house, a holy priesthood, to offer up spiritual sacrifices acceptable to God through Jesus Christ.*
>
> *Therefore it is also contained in the Scripture, 'Behold, I lay in Zion a chief cornerstone, elect, precious, and he who believes on Him will by no means be put to shame.' Therefore, to you who believe, He is precious; but to those who are disobedient, 'The stone which the builders rejected has become the chief cornerstone,' and 'A stone of stumbling and a rock of offense.' They stumble, being disobedient to the word, to which they also were appointed.*
>
> *But you are a chosen generation, a royal priesthood, a holy nation, His own special people, that you may proclaim the praises of Him who called you out of darkness into His marvelous light; who once were not a people but are now the people of God, who had not obtained mercy but now have obtained mercy."* – 1 Peter 2:4-10

Just as the LORD exhorted the barren woman to embrace the promise and not to be ashamed of the reproach and rejection she might suffer for her hope—the hope that the death of the Sin-bearing Servant obtained for her—Peter exhorts us not to regard the world's rejection but embrace our new identity and calling.

The children of the barren woman are the builders of the kingdom who have been taught by the LORD. Hearing and obeying the Word is the basis for our inclusion in the kingdom. People who see only a kingdom built of costly gems but without an understanding of God's word and the saving knowledge of Christ's death stumble over the foundational cornerstone that is Christ Himself. He will become a stumbling block to them because of their resistance to godly teaching.

The sure mercies of David are now extended to a people who had not obtained mercy before, and a new class distinction described as a royal priesthood emerges in this coming kingdom. (Just as the kingship is democratized here in Isaiah 55, the priesthood will be democratized as well, as we will see later in Isaiah 61:6.) Peter gets this understanding from the kingdom pictures in Isaiah, and he applies these pictures to us as believers in this age.

Now, back to Isaiah 55 . . .

The LORD seeks to comfort Israel with this picture of the kingdom and all its benefits—its material riches, its peace, its righteousness that brings safety and security, its abundance, and all the benefits of royalty. The question remains: How do you enter this kingdom?

Isaiah 55:6-13

Faithless, idolatrous Israel once cried out in despair that the LORD had forsaken her and abandoned her to exile. Having provided a way to deal with the sin issue through the Sin-bearing Servant's death, He is now able to offer her reconciliation and relief from her despair. But the relationship isn't fully healed. He has done His part. Now she must do hers.

In the chiastic structure, we have this pairing:

Opening Argument: (Isaiah 49:14) Problem: Israel despairs that the LORD has forsaken her
Closing Argument: (Isaiah 55:6-13) Solution: Despair will be relieved when Israel returns to the LORD and aligns with His values

Notice, we are moving away from a simple, passive belief in God that was demanded in Isaiah 40-53 and into an actual practice of faith that will be the theme going forward. The way out of the crooked place has been made by the Sin-bearing Servant. God has laid the kingdom before Israel and is pushing her forward. If she wishes to enter into this abundant life, she must now take some proactive actions. *"Seek the LORD . . . Call upon Him . . . Let the wicked forsake His ways . . . the unrighteous man his thoughts."* Let's consider those commands.

> **Seeking the LORD** is a new kind of pursuit and very different from the old earthly pursuit of consumable things like wealth and bread. What are you seeking? An understanding of Him, how He sees things, and how He works. Where do you seek Him? In His Word.

> **Calling upon Him** is a step of faith. It means you believe He has the power to deliver and comfort you, and that He will answer your call.
>
> **Forsaking old ways** of acting and thinking means returning to God's ways and thoughts. God says bluntly in verse 8, *"My thoughts are not your thoughts, nor are your ways My ways."* If Israel is going to realign with God's vision and values, it will require her to let go of her earthly perspective and interests and pursue life with the LORD on an eternal, heavenly plane. The LORD offers abundant mercy and forgiveness to those who return to Him. This is the ultimate goal in God's Highway Project.

In verses 10-11, the LORD draws a parallel between an earthly experience of rain coming down from heaven to replenish the earth and the heavenly act of sending forth His Word to accomplish its task. Neither effort returns void or without fruit. Those who hear and receive this life-giving word will enter into abundant life. The chapter ends with the promise of a restored Eden, where the brier and thorns associated with the curse of sin are replaced with beautiful, aromatic trees and the sweet smell of eternal peace.

GOD'S HIGHWAY PROJECT

Straightening the Crooked Places

This vision of the kingdom seems like a rather glowing, almost storybook future that God is presenting Israel, but it is a distant future. This heavenly kingdom hasn't been established, even in our day. It is a comfort to those who are suffering, particularly under severe affliction to the point of death, and yet, we must be careful when presenting this kind of comfort to a beleaguered sufferer or even an unbeliever in this age because this is not a picture for this age. Setting false expectations of the Christian life can send a person back into bondage again, and we need to be realistic when we talk about having abundant life in this age.

> **Q:** Can we experience abundant life in Christ in day-to-day life, or is this an experience reserved for a future kingdom when it comes?

(Depending on your doctrinal stance, you might believe that the kingdom is only a spiritual one inaugurated at Christ's resurrection; thus, you might argue that we are living in the kingdom now. I would argue in return that the LORD's promise to Israel here is a literal kingdom, and that literal kingdom has clearly not come to fruition yet. I see the promise being fulfilled in the Millennial kingdom described in Revelation 20. Isaiah will talk more about this literal kingdom in the chapters to come.)

> **Q:** If we can experience abundant life in this age, what kind of experience is that? What does it look like? (Broken people will need to understand this if they are to take comfort from it.)
>
> **Q:** Even if the full kingdom experience is delayed, why is it important to set that expectation?

The Reward

As we move into this new stage of stepping out in faith, the issue of work and reward now comes into play. Reward is the recompense or wage for works (as opposed to salvation by grace and grace alone) and that recompense can be for better or worse. Here in Isaiah 55, God rebukes Israel for seeking an unsatisfactory return for her wages, and then holds out a better reward in the form of eternal life and an everlasting covenant of royalty in a glorious eternal kingdom:

> *"Why do you spend money for what is not bread, and your wages for what does not satisfy? Listen carefully to Me, and eat what is good, and let your soul delight itself in abundance."* – Isaiah 55:2

The pinnacle honor that can be achieved through works, as Isaiah defines it, is the crown of royalty. The crown is awarded to both of God's anointed deliverers, Cyrus and the Servant, for completing the tasking He gave them. In Isaiah 53, the Servant-King then shares His royalty with "the strong" (those who have diligently pursued righteousness and sacrificed themselves to gain that eternal reward in the same way that Servant did). The Servant valued the crown of royalty more than life itself, and the promise of it comforted Him as He faced death (Isaiah 49:4). Here, in Isaiah 55, the honor of royalty and rulership is extended to the people. Thus, this eternal reward flows from God the Great King to the Servant-

King to the people, and it plays a major part in comforting God's broken people, which is why this theme is one of the bookends of this study. Remember the inclusio I mentioned in the introduction? The repeated phrase about the reward is found in Isaiah 40,

> "Behold, the Lord GOD shall come with a strong hand, and His arm shall rule for Him; <u>Behold, His reward is with Him, and His work before Him</u>."
> – Isaiah 40:10

and again in Isaiah 62,

> "... 'Say to the daughter of Zion, "Surely your salvation is coming; <u>Behold, His reward is with Him, and His work before Him</u>."'" – Isaiah 62:11

Jesus Himself also repeats this statement in Revelation 22:

> "And behold, I am coming quickly, and <u>My reward is with Me, to give to every one according to his work</u>." – Revelation 22:12

There is still more to this picture of rewards, but I will hold the discussion of how it applies to us in the Church Age until the end of the study.

LESSON 20

The Promise of Equality

READ

Isaiah 56:1-12

DISCUSSION

In the last few chapters, we've been talking about the coming kingdom—its appearance, character, values, and the new ruling class that emerges in it. As God presents Israel with these pictures of the kingdom, He challenges her ways of thinking. Her thoughts and ways are not His thoughts and ways. Her idolatry has skewed her perspective of abundant life—what it looks like and how it is achieved—and has sent her in pursuit of a counterfeit version. If she wants this kingdom and the abundant life that the LORD is promising her, she needs to wrap her head around God's vision of things. In this chapter, He is going to challenge more erroneous thinking, this time over who is kingdom-worthy—who will enter into His peace and on what grounds. God has His own policy for diversity, equity, and inclusion among His citizens.

We are going to talk about what defines a kingdom-community and what it means to be a citizen of that community. Our current culture has skewed the concept of citizenship, so let's define this using our own country's definition as an example. (Go ahead and google it to answer the questions.)

Q: What does it mean to be a citizen in the U.S.?

Q: What benefits do citizens enjoy?

Q: What is demanded of them in return?

Q: What does it take for someone who is not a citizen by birth to become naturalized?

I looked up the answers to the questions on various government websites and found these answers. A citizen is one who is legally recognized as a subject of a kingdom, state, or community, who enjoys the rights, privileges, and protections of that community. In turn, citizens must align themselves with the laws and values that govern that community and agree to live by them and uphold them, e.g., participating in civic and military duty. There are some additional requirements for a person who wants to naturalize as a U.S. citizen. They have to be of good moral character, meaning they are not engaged in criminal activity or have a criminal record. They must pass a test to see if they understand the language, know how the government and justice systems work, and what their civic responsibilities are. That is the traditional textbook definition.

As it is in our own country, so it will be in God's kingdom. Those who enter must understand how it works and be aligned with its values to enjoy the peace and blessings of abundant life in that kingdom.

In this chapter, God begins by setting the standard for all citizens with some opening remarks and then goes on to address those within the community who will be facing marginalization in the new kingdom as well as those who, at the moment, are not citizens at all. And then, He is going to rid the citizenry of some very corrupt leadership.

Isaiah 56:1-8

You will recall back in Isaiah 49:13-15 that salvation was promised to the Gentiles when the Servant sets up His kingdom. That promise made in the opening argument, is now resolved here in the closing argument. Salvation is granted to the Gentiles after the Servant's sacrificial death, when He establishes His kingdom. In the chiastic structure, we have this pairing:

Opening Argument: (Isaiah 49:15-13) Salvation is promised to the Gentiles through the Servant's rule.
Closing Argument: (Isaiah 56:1-8) Salvation is granted to the Gentiles after the Servant's sacrificial death when He establishes His kingdom.

God prompts Israel to prepare herself for His salvation—His *yeshua*. This salvation would be facilitated by a messianic deliverer who is Himself named Yeshua. We saw His picture back in Isaiah 52–53. We also know He will fulfill all righteousness according to the Law and establish justice over the coming kingdom according to Isaiah 49. He is the Prince of Peace, and under His reign, the kingdom will become one of peace, well-being, and abundance. That peace will depend on a justice system that rules righteously, without bias, and according to the truth which stems from God's Word.

As incoming citizens, Israel is commanded to ready herself for the new administration and its values—keep justice, keep her hand from evil (do what is right), and keep from defiling the Sabbath.

The word "keep" is the Hebrew word *shamar*, and it is repeated three times. *Shamar* can mean one of two things:

1. It can mean to physically practice something—to observe or celebrate it, such as "keeping" a festival, or
2. It can also mean to have charge of it— to keep watch, protect, and preserve it, like being a watchman or a shepherd. This blends into the idea of preserving the understanding of something through teaching or study.

The wicked shepherds and lazy watchmen will be addressed at the end of the chapter, so let's talk about this aspect of "keeping" in regard to God's opening command concerning justice.

Q: What does it mean to preserve or guard justice as a watchman or shepherd?

Q: Is the act of "keeping" just leadership's responsibility, or is it the citizen's responsibility as well? Why?

Q: What happens to a community when its leadership wants to uphold justice, but its citizenry does not?

Q: What happens to a community if the leadership doesn't uphold justice for its citizenry?

Keeping justice is the first command. The second is like it. Do what is right. This command is mentioned twice, once in the positive ("do what is right") and once in the negative ("keep your hand from evil"). These commands emphasize a citizen's personal responsibility in keeping justice and righteousness.

The LORD is addressing Israel here, and Israel's understanding of His righteousness and justice comes from His Word—literally, the Torah—and the definitions of these don't change when she goes into exile. But now she is living under foreign rule where God's ideas of justice and righteousness are not the law of the land. Keeping God's definition of these can be challenging, if not impossible, in that foreign environment where there is a lot of injustice, oppression, and abuse.

> **Q:** How can the faithful uphold justice and practice righteousness while living in exile among the Gentile nations where injustice, abuse, and wrongdoing are rampant? (We might ask, how do we do this as believers in our current culture?)

In addition to preserving justice and doing what is right, Israel is specifically instructed not to defile the Sabbath. That command is very specific to keeping the Mosaic Laws, and it will raise a question for us when we see this command applied to Gentiles in a few verses. Let's finish the verses for this lesson first, and then talk about Sabbath-keeping and why God includes this as a command here in Isaiah.

As the LORD announces the imminent arrival of the kingdom, a cry immediately goes up from two classes of people who feel marginalized and cut off from the kingdom and its abundance. They are the sons of the foreigners who have joined themselves to the LORD and the eunuchs. The LORD addresses the eunuchs first, so we will start there.

Addressing the Eunuchs

> **Q:** First of all, who were the eunuchs and why would they feel like they didn't have a place in the Servant's kingdom?

Back in Isaiah 39:7, Israel was warned that some of her own sons would become eunuchs or *sarise* in the palace of the king of Babylon. The Hebrew word *sarise* primarily refers to a man who is castrated in the sense of being cut off physically, and thus left without seed or progeny by which he may build a dynasty. He is, poetically, a dry tree. But *sarise* in Scripture are most often described as officers of a high or honored rank in a king's service.

They are captains of his bodyguard or military men as seen in Genesis 37:36, 2 Kings 25:16). They are the chief cupbearers and bakers in Genesis 40:2. They are also the stewards of the royal family in Esther 2:3, 14. Not all of these influential officials were necessarily castrated, but many were, mainly to prevent them from using their powerful positions in government to establish a dynasty of their own which would threaten the king.

The eunuchs here are the ones who have been cut off and made servants in a foreign king's court. They are the male counterpart to the barren women in Isaiah 54 who are bereft of children and seemingly have no part in rebuilding the future kingdom. The barren women once despaired of having children, but the LORD promised them that they would have many children in the kingdom once their relationship with Him was restored. Similarly, the eunuchs contend that they themselves are "dry trees" because they no longer have the physical ability to beget physical children. As we discussed with the barren women, children don't necessarily have to be physical children, but there is this to consider with the eunuchs. While Israel's bloodlines are reckoned through the women of Israel, the transfer of inheritance is passed down through the men of Israel. The eunuchs see their inheritance—their place in the kingdom—as being lost in a very physical sense.

There is an additional problem for these eunuchs, however, that has to do with the place of royal privilege and honor they enjoyed in the foreign king's administration—a place that would be lost when they returned to their own land and people. Instead of enjoying privilege, their condition would stigmatize them in their community and deny them an experience of abundance that others enjoyed. It would also keep them from serving the LORD particularly in a priestly role.

The LORD offers them this reassurance and a gifting of grace. To those who remain loyal to the Him even in the service of the foreign kings, who cling to Him and His covenant, who choose what pleases Him and keep His Sabbaths, to these the Great King promises a place and name in His house. The position of honor and royal rank that they once enjoyed in the earthly king's court would be carried into the eternal King's court and even amplified. It is an everlasting name, greater than even those of physical sons or daughters, and an unshakable eternal place in the kingdom.

Addressing the Gentiles

Having answered the eunuchs, the LORD then answers the Gentiles who have joined themselves to Him but still feel ostracized. If they serve the LORD from the heart out of love for Him and His name, if they keep from defiling the Sabbath, and if they cling to His covenant, then they, too, will have a place in His kingdom.

This seems like a long list of to-do's that smacks of obeying the Mosaic Covenant for inclusion in the kingdom, particularly the part about keeping the Sabbath and clinging to "the covenant." Which covenant? We question that because we know from where we stand in history on the opposite side of the cross from Isaiah, that a change in covenant has happened as a result of Christ's death. We are no longer bound to the Old Covenant and its righteousness by works but are under the New Covenant of grace.

Covenant is important, because it defines a community's identity and purpose, and governs who is allowed into its citizenry and on what grounds. God is making a systemic change to the community here. He is redefining all these things. This isn't about bringing everyone into Israel's community. It is about bringing everyone *with* Israel into *His* community which is a universal community, as He says in verse 7.

> "... For My house shall be called a house of prayer for <u>all nations</u>."
> – Isaiah 56:7b

> **Q:** How did God create the universal community? (Ephesians 2:14-18)

> **Q:** How did He redefine its purpose? What is our new Great Commission? (Matthew 28:19-20)

Isaiah gives the commands to the faithful to keep justice and do righteousness, and I would argue that God's definitions of those have never changed, regardless of being under the Old Covenant or New Covenant. What *has* changed is how our righteousness before God is reckoned so that we can become citizens in His kingdom-community.

> **Q:** Now, anyone is allowed into God's kingdom-community, but on what grounds?

So, what about Sabbath-keeping?

Sabbath-keeping in a Time of Exile

Sabbath-keeping is a very specific requirement mentioned here, and it struck me as odd to require of a people who are in exile. Exile disrupts everything. It is a state of being separated from God. Israel is no longer in her land where God once made provision for her in Sabbath years, and her inheritance has been taken away so that she cannot return on the Jubilees and start over. Even the weekly Sabbath observance relies heavily on a community that restrains consumerism because all work must shut down in order to observe the Sabbath day. Everyone in the community, from the king and his administration down to the lowest servant, must keep the Sabbath or else no one keeps the Sabbath. This is why Nehemiah shut Jerusalem's gates on the eve of Sabbath, to keep the merchants out, because an unrestrained merchant class can break the system. Let me give you a personal illustration from my husband's experience on how an unrestrained merchant class sabotages Sabbath-keeping.

> My husband (now retired) was a postal carrier for the United States Postal Service (a government agency). Part of the reason he took the job was because it originally allowed him Sundays off so that we could go to church and participate in corporate worship. Midway through his career, the post office leadership signed a contract with a merchant, Amazon, to deliver Amazon purchases, including next-day deliveries. Consequently, any citizen who bought something on Amazon and clicked "next day delivery" obligated the post office (and, subsequently, my husband) to carry that item to them, even on Sundays. The merchant set the conditions for the government contract. The post office agreed to it and, in doing so, altered the terms of my husband's contract as a carrier so that he was no longer guaranteed Sundays off. My husband had no say in that decision, but he was obligated to perform the service. As a result, his ability to join corporate worship services on any given Sunday was determined by a merchant who needed to satisfy a random citizen-consumer. The unrestrained consumer didn't care if my husband got a day of worship and rest. They themselves rested comfortably at home while my husband delivered the product to them. The unrestrained merchant (Amazon) didn't care, either, because the sale meant profit for them. The governmental authorities saw no problem with it. Not

even the Christian community had a problem with it. There are a lot of Christians who, even now, take advantage of Amazon's next-day Sunday delivery and have forced their brethren in the postal service to go to court just to appeal their right to worship and rest on Sundays.

The system broke the moment an unrestrained merchant was allowed to drive the contractual agreements for the community, and the brokenness is perpetuated by every citizen-consumer who demands next-day delivery on Sundays.

I give you this example to help you understand why Sabbath-keeping is not possible for Israel during times of exile. When she is a slave to a master who does not keep the Sabbath, then she does not keep the Sabbath, either. She is thoroughly immersed in a works-based relationship with that worldly master. Whatever provision she has on the Sabbath day is purchased by her own effort in serving that master, not by God's grace.

The Babylonian exile is not the only time of exile that Israel has experienced. Because she didn't accept the salvation of the Servant-King when He came to redeem her, the Church Age became (and continues to be) another exile period for her. Even now, she is dispersed among Gentile nations and subjected to the laws of their lands, which pay little heed to the Sabbath. Over the ages, small islands of Jewish community have existed within the greater world community, and within those closed communities where the merchant class is forced to close on Sabbaths, Jewish people have been able to observe the Sabbath in a limited way—minus the death penalty for not keeping the Sabbath, of course, because that would be murder under Gentile law. Gentile Law trumps the Mosaic Law in times of exile. Even the Jews in Jesus's day had to appeal to Caesar to crucify Him because it was not lawful for them to do it themselves (John 18:31).

I think it is interesting that as God makes this transition from the old works-based form of righteousness under the Mosaic Covenant to the grace-based righteousness of the New Covenant, He does it in conjunction with Israel being in a state of exile when only a semblance of the laws can be kept and certainly not in a way that would afford her any righteousness in God's eyes.

This is the challenge to Israel's thinking. She has to let go of the physical keeping of the Old Covenant Laws for her righteousness and consider what grace-based righteousness looks like in the universal kingdom into which God is integrating her. To this end, God tells her to keep the Sabbath. To understand this, I think we have to ask a couple questions.

1. How does the Sabbath itself illustrate a transition from works-based living to grace-based living?
2. If Sabbath-keeping is part of kingdom living, to what kingdom is this referring?

Question #1: How does the Sabbath illustrate grace-based living?

According to the Law, everyone was to observe one day of rest at the end of each week. Just as the LORD rested on the seventh day after His work of creation was completed, so His people are called to emulate His model. We read that in Exodus 20:8-11, Exodus 31:13-16, and Leviticus 23:3.

The practice was instituted when Israel came out of Egypt, so it is associated with that release from bondage—the bondage of work. During the wilderness trek, the Sabbath was a day of grace, when the LORD provided bread (called manna) freely and abundantly for His people by His own hand, apart from their works. There can be no work on the Sabbath. The benefit of that day must come from God's provision alone. If man's works play any part in that experience of grace, it defiles the gift of grace. Thus, by commanding Israel to keep the Sabbath day, God began to condition her to the expectation of a day when works-based living would end and grace-based living would be the rule. Week in and week out, she made that transition from works to grace. The day of grace is coming. Prepare for the day. This was the first step in preparing her for the coming transition from the bondage of works, and righteousness based on works under the Old Covenant of Mosaic Laws, to the freedom of grace-based righteousness under the New Covenant. Even as God gives her these Sabbath laws to keep, it is with the understanding that He would, one day, tear down the mountain—the Old Covenant which bound her under the burden of works-based righteousness.

So, that is the picture of the Sabbath Day. It fits with the pictures of grace and abundant life that God has been incorporating into the understanding of the kingdom here in Isaiah 54-56. We have seen children gifted to the barren woman in Isaiah 54, the "priceless" provisions of abundant life gifted to the kingdom citizens in Isaiah 55, and now, a perpetual place is gifted to eunuchs and God's favor extends to the Gentiles in Isaiah 56. This is grace upon grace, and it is capped with the command to keep the Sabbath, which is the final picture that announces a covenantal transition from works to grace.

Once Israel enters the kingdom, the manna stops and the model changes. The Sabbath experience increases to include more extensive periods of rest. In addition to keeping the weekly observance, Israel is now commanded to keep Sabbath years and Jubilees. We read that in Leviticus 25. The time of rest wasn't just for man but extended to the land itself. Every seven years, the people would refrain from planting and, instead, live off of the abundance that the LORD had supplied in the sixth year, supplemented by what the LORD caused to grow of its own accord without being cultivated—and it did not matter on whose land the produce grew. Ownership of the land and its produce was relinquished as belonging to the LORD and was given over for community-wide use. Also, payments of debts were suspended during the seventh year since there was no income from crops. Thus, both the land and man had rest according to the LORD's provision. In the Jubilee (every fiftieth year), every man who had lost his inheritance and fallen into poverty on account of debts would have his debts canceled and his inheritance restored to him so that he could begin again. Slaves were set free. This grand gifting of grace was meant to be experienced at least once in a person's life.

Thus, the yearly cycle of Sabbaths and Jubilees became an economic model for God's kingdom. Every man began with an inheritance in the land from which he supported his family. All citizens were, in essence, small business owners. The Sabbath cycle allowed for periods of work and profit gained from work, but it also restricted consumerism by demanding a periodic ceasing of work and the canceling of debts. The practice of releasing slaves and bondservants and returning them to their inheritance in the Jubilee effectively prevented generational poverty from becoming rooted in the community (or it would have if Israel had practiced the Jubilees).

Gentile nations never employed a Sabbath economy because they never had that relationship with God. As a result, the world has come up with various economic models, all of which have their flaws. Think of the arguments that are raging in our own culture over which economic policy should rule our nation: capitalism or socialism?

> **Q:** What is the flaw in the capitalist model? What kind of oppression does it create?
>
> **Q:** What is the flaw in the socialist model? What kind of oppression does it create?

The communal living on the Sabbath is very socialist in reckoning every man's land as community property and allowing every person to take what they need from it, but it is not a perpetual state because it is not self-sustaining and does not work if God is not at the heart and source of it.

By the same token, the Sabbath model incorporates aspects of the capitalist system in regard to consumerism and profiteering in a merit-based system, but these, too, are given limits. If consumerism and the pursuit of wealth runs unrestrained, as they do in the world's model, they can bring a community into a form of bondage to that pursuit. If a person falls into poverty, there is little chance for recovery, and this gives rise to a perpetual poverty class. The rich get richer and the poor get poorer, and the inequality within the social classes creates conflict. The Jubilee year of the Sabbath model breaks the escalation of inequality.

The Sabbath, as an economy for a kingdom, combines the best of both worlds when it comes to ending conflict caused by inequality among social classes, while at the same time, being sustainable. It is a means of establishing peace in God's kingdom. But it only works because it is founded on grace that is sourced from and sustained by God. Without God's provision in the equation, the kingdom-community must fall back on a works-based model.

Question #2: If the Sabbath represents God's ideal economy for a kingdom, to what kingdom is this referring?

To answer that question, let's consider what Isaiah sees and doesn't see in the vision God is giving him.

> **Q:** Did Isaiah see the Church Age?

No, he did not. Paul makes it very clear that the Church Age was a mystery to the Old Testament prophets (Ephesians 3). Isaiah did not see the Church Age; therefore, the kingdom picture in Isaiah 56 is not a picture of the Church Age, or the Gentiles coming into the kingdom as a part of the Church Age.

A difficulty in this chapter arises because Isaiah incorporates the bringing the Gentiles into the kingdom, an event which we associate with the Church Age under the New Covenant of grace, with the keeping the Sabbath, which was a tenet of the Old Covenant of works. So, how do we reconcile this command to keep the Sabbath in a New Covenant context?

Obviously, the Sabbath is not kept as a way of being reckoned righteous before God. Righteousness is accounted to us only through Christ's death on the cross. It is granted by grace and grace alone, not according to works. In regard to keeping the Sabbath, the practice isn't possible in times of exile, and Israel is still technically in exile even today. The Sabbath can be practiced only in a very minimal weekly way (if at all) in a time of exile when God's people are under Gentile laws.

But what about in a future Messianic kingdom that hasn't been realized yet? I speculate about that. Zechariah talks about the Feast of Tabernacles being a requirement for the Gentiles to practice in the Messianic kingdom (Zechariah 14:16-19) and there is a Sabbath day associated with that feast. That feast is also a tenet of the Old Covenant laws, and like the Sabbath, it illustrates a picture of kingdom living. Isaiah speaks of the keeping the Sabbath in the coming Messianic Kingdom, in this chapter and in chapters to come. Even the apostle Paul declares in Colossians 2:16-17 that the feasts and Sabbaths are shadows of things to come:

> *"So let no one judge you in food or in drink, or regarding a festival or a new moon or sabbaths, <u>which are a shadow of things to come, but the substance is of Christ</u>."* – Colossians 2:16-17

Interestingly, even ancient Jewish scholars concluded from passages like this in Isaiah that the Sabbath is a metaphor for the kingdom in the Messianic age, which they called Olam Ha-Ba or the World to Come. I found this explanation on the Judaism 101 webpage.

> *"The spiritual afterlife is referred to in Hebrew as Olam Ha-Ba (oh-LAHM hah-BAH), the World to Come, although this term is also used to*

> *refer to the messianic age. Olam Ha-Ba is another, higher state of being.*
>
> *In the Mishnah, one rabbi says, 'This world is like a lobby before Olam Ha-Ba. Prepare yourself in the lobby so that you may enter the banquet hall.' (Pirkei Avot 4:16) Similarly, the Talmud uses Shabbat as an analogy for this World and the World to Come, 'He who prepares on the eve of Shabbat will have food to eat on Shabbat.' (Avodah Zara 3a) We prepare ourselves for Olam Ha-Ba through Torah study and good deeds."* [1]

The Sabbath is a metaphor for the Messianic kingdom. Even Jewish people who don't believe in Jesus understand this. We, as believers in Jesus, know that He is not just King of the Kingdom but Lord of the Sabbath as well. They are one and the same. That connection is made for us in Mark 2:23-28 (cf. Luke 6:1-5, Matthew 12:1-8). The grace and abundant life of that day is embodied in the King and in His kingdom.

We also know that the Sabbath has not yet been fulfilled. The writer of the book of Hebrews talks extensively about this transition from the Mosaic Covenant to the New Covenant and the reason for it, but in Hebrews 4, he explains,

> *"For if Joshua [or Jesus] had given them rest [Greek: katapauō], then He would not afterward have spoken of another day. There remains therefore a rest [Greek: sabbatismos, that is, sabbath] for the people of God. For he who has entered His rest has himself also ceased from his works as God did from His." – Hebrews 4:8-10*

The Sabbath reaches its ultimate fulfillment in the kingdom to come. I think this is why, as Isaiah is describing that kingdom to come, God injects this requirement for keeping the Sabbath, in anticipation of the day when the final kingdom will be realized. It is my personal belief that when Christ sets up His Millennial Kingdom, He will pattern its economy after the Sabbath economic model. The Sabbath will not be kept for the purpose of attaining righteousness before God as it was in the works-based Mosaic Covenant, but it might be used as a model for its economy. The Messianic Kingdom will be a physical kingdom, after all. It will have administrative needs.

---

1   Tracy R. Rich, "Olam Ha-Ba: The Afterlife," Olam Ha-Ba: The Afterlife - Judaism 101 (JewFAQ), 1999-2024, https://www.jewfaq.org/afterlife#:~:text=%E2%98%B0%20Olam%20 Ha%2DBa:%20The,expressions%20of%20approval%20or%20disapproval.

There is so much more that can be discussed about this, but I want to get back to Isaiah 56 and the topic of God's Highway Project. Let's finish the chapter, and I will give some final thoughts.

The LORD's address to the Gentiles ends in verse 7, voicing His desire to bring them not just into the kingdom but to His holy mountain and into His house—the Temple. We should recognize the phrase, *"My house shall be called a house of prayer for all nations,"* because Jesus quotes this as He drives the moneychangers and merchants out of the Temple (Matthew 21:12-13, Luke 19:45-46). This is the perfect segue to the last few verses in Isaiah 56. Israel's greedy, irresponsible leaders are being a lot like those moneychangers in the Temple, and now the LORD decommissions them.

Isaiah 56:9-12

These last few verses complete the chiastic structure of Part 2.

Opening Argument: (Isaiah 49:1-4) The Servant is commissioned and seeks His reward from the LORD
Closing Argument: (Isaiah 56:9-12) Wicked servants are "decommissioned" for rewarding themselves

This chapter opened with the picture of law-abiding people who felt cut off from the kingdom and its abundant life but, in fact, were not because they kept the LORD's justice and righteousness. Now we are given a contrasting picture. The LORD addresses those who have long been considered keepers of His justice and laws—the watchmen and shepherds—who are, in fact, lawless and enjoying abundant life off the backs of their own people in kingdoms of their own making. There is a scathing rebuke in how He describes them. They are dumb dogs. A watchdog should watch for danger, but these watchdogs are blind. They don't see danger. They are even ignorant of the danger. They don't bark. They don't say anything to warn or protect the people. They are lazy and love to sleep. They are also greedy and complacent. They seek an abundant life that doesn't come from keeping the LORD's ways but by doing things their own ways. Similarly, the shepherds have pastured themselves on their sheep. They have carved out their own little kingdoms and have achieved a version of abundant life, but in the most disgusting fashion and in a way that brings them into bondage. And they think they are safe from consequences.

The wicked keepers are the ones against whom the LORD sends the beasts of the field and the forest—the Gentile nations. He says, "Come and devour them. They oppress the people; therefore, they have no place in my kingdom of peace."

> **Q:** How do Jesus's actions in driving the moneylenders out of the Temple fit with this picture in Isaiah 56?

> **Q:** What is the end for the irresponsible and unrepentant watchmen and shepherds?

GOD'S HIGHWAY PROJECT

Tearing Down the Mountain

God tore down a mountain when He gave us the New Covenant of grace, of which the Sabbath is a picture. When God commands the faithful to keep from defiling the Sabbath, He is telling them not to defile that picture of God-gifted provision. It wasn't supposed to be a burdensome task, but a comfort that we have, knowing that we now live under grace and not works.

> **Q:** How can we defiled the experience of grace by falling back into works-based righteousness?

Personally, I don't believe we can truly "keep" the Sabbath in the Church Age. I see the Church Age as a time of exile for Israel and an age of the Gentiles that precedes the Kingdom Age. In a time of exile, the Sabbath day may be kept individually in as much as our dependence on the greater, non-Sabbath-keeping community allows. (Feel free to disagree with me, but I would challenge you to come up with a solution to my husband's dilemma with the post office that doesn't involve him leaving one of the few jobs in our area that pays a family-sustaining wage.) I do, however, think that believers should keep the Sabbath in the secondary sense of preserving an understanding of that future hope of grace, peace, and rest in the coming kingdom. It is a kingdom picture.

The Promise of Equality

There are a lot of ramifications to what the LORD is doing here in this chapter. It begins with lifting up a people who have been marginalized and outcast and ends with bringing down Israel's own oppressive leadership. It is bad enough to be under the thumb of the Gentile nations, but to suffer a similar abuse by her own people is even worse. God has leveled the highway, so to speak, by lifting up the valleys and taking down the mountains to make way for a universal community under the Servant's rule. This chapter presents God's diversity, equity, and inclusion policy in regard to people who Israel herself marginalizes and oppresses, and it challenges Israel's thinking in regard to citizenship in the kingdom.

> **Q:** What comforts are offered to the marginalized people in this chapter?

There has been a similar DEI push in recent years in our own nation. Let's compare God's policy with our culture's:

> **Q:** The marginalized people in this passage include those who have no means of begetting children or the foreigners. Who has our current culture identified as marginalized?

> **Q:** God elevates these marginalized people by granting them equal citizenship in His kingdom, but there are conditions they must meet. How has our culture elevated its marginalized group? Are there conditions for them to meet as well, or are they simply handed a place of honor? Is there merit involved, or simply an award?

> **Q:** Peace in the universal community has been God's overarching goal. Has the enforcement of the world's DEI policy brought peace and wholeness to the community or generated more conflict? Why?

The Struggle with Celibacy

I want to return to the topic of eunuchs because it is one which Jesus addressed as well. He said,

> *"... All cannot accept this saying, but only those to whom it has been given: For there are eunuchs who were born thus from their mother's*

womb, and there are eunuchs who were made eunuchs by men, and there are eunuchs who have made themselves eunuchs for the kingdom of heaven's sake. He who is able to accept it, let him accept it."
– Matthew 19:11-12

> **Q:** Who are the ones who have made themselves eunuchs for the kingdom's sake?

In a world where values are skewed toward the goals of building fleeting legacies in the form of fleshly children instead of spiritual ones, purpose can be lost for those without children or even spouses. As I noted in the Isaiah 54 discussion on the barren women, the focus on having earthly families and child-raising is a big push, even in Christian circles. Over the years, my husband and I have sat through so many adult Sunday School classes where the topic was child-raising. We were marginalized within those classes, and I, for one, felt it keenly. It would have been comforting to be part of a discussion that didn't focus on earthly children or family. I imagine a lot of single people feel the same way. Any believer who faces a life of celibacy and singleness, whether by circumstance or choice, can feel oppressed and despairing because they seemingly lack an abundance and purpose in life that they think other people have.

> **Q:** How do you comfort a single person who is despairing over their single state?
>
> **Q:** How do you redirect their understanding of purpose away from human expectations and onto a relationship with God? (Do you need help with developing this perspective in your own life?)
>
> **Q:** How do you keep from marginalizing them in community settings like small groups or adult Sunday School classes?

Homosexuality is a particular inclination with which even Christians can struggle, and celibacy may be the only lifestyle option for a believer who wishes to remain pure before God. These believers struggle deeply with this issue in their lives and can fall victim to the onslaught of messaging from a world that validates a pursuit of that lust where the Christian world condemns it.

> **Q:** How do we comfort them in that struggle?

God's Highway Project: Part 2 Wrap-up

Part 2 began in Isaiah 49 with the introduction of the next messianic deliverer, known only as the Servant. Where Cyrus's deliverance was the central theme of Part 1, the Servant's salvation became the central theme of Part 2. God's arguments in Part 2 shifted away from the topics of His sovereignty and power which He used to overcome Israel's fear and onto the topics of His love and grace, which He used to address her despair and shame.

The chiastic structure reached its pinnacle with the command to share the good news (the gospel), marking the high point of God's effort to comfort His people. The Sin-bearing Servant took the cup of God's wrath upon Himself in Israel's place and drank it to its dregs in a supreme act of mercy and grace. His death and resurrection accomplished one of God's Highway Project goals by ending conflict on the spiritual plane between God and His people. In its wake, we see the kingdom pictures begin.

The thematic thrust of Part 2 has been making peace—peace between God and His people, but also peace within the greater community. A new, universal kingdom-community is taking shape. The Servant has divided the spoil with the strong, democratizing the kingship for the righteous and faithful remnant who align themselves with God's vision and values. Outcasts, including Gentiles, are being added to Israel's assembly as God begins to gather the faithful into the coming kingdom.

Part 2 began with Israel in a very passive stance. All she needed to do was simply believe and bear witness of the work the LORD and Servant performed on her behalf. But as the narrative moved forward from the Servant's death in Isaiah 53, the LORD began to issue commands to Israel to do her part. He is moving her into the next phase of faith, which requires her to respond and step out in obedience, even if it is only in a limited capacity which her servitude in exile allows. She is to preserve the understanding of His ways of justice and righteousness, and the knowledge of His provisions of grace as she casts her eyes toward the future kingdom.

Part 2 ended with God dismissing the wicked watchmen and shepherds as the Servant-King prepares to enter His kingdom. The kingdom is about to be realized, but now, as we move into Part 3, we find that something is very, very wrong. There is a delay.

PART 3

NARRATIVE STRUCTURE

Chiastic Structure of Part 3 (Isaiah 57-66)

Opening Arguments:
- **1a:** The wicked kingdom where the righteous perish and the wicked flourish (57:1-21)
- **2a:** Israel seeks God, but God does not answer her (58:1-14)
  - God's charges against wicked Israel (59:1-8)
- **3a:** Israel's prayer of penitence/confession of sin (59:9-15)
- **4a:** The Battle: The Redeemer comes in vengeance (59:16–21)

   5: The Kingdom realized: God's people, the Servant, and God Himself glorified (60:1–62:12)

Closing Arguments:
- **4b:** The Battle: The LORD comes in vengeance (63:1-14)
- **3b:** Israel's prayer of penitence/plea for mercy (63:15-64:12)
- **2b:** God is found by those who did not seek Him and answers them (65:1)
  - Judgment between the righteous and wicked of Israel (65:2-16)
- **1b:** The new heaven and new earth and the new Jerusalem where the righteous flourish and the wicked perish (65:17-66:24)

The opening and closing arguments for Part 3 are mirrored around Isaiah 61–62 where salvation is proclaimed and then assured, the righteous kingdom is realized, and God, the Servant, and His people are glorified. The realized kingdom is the apex of the argument, and also closes out the theme for our study. Isaiah 62:10-11 marks the closing bookend of the dual inclusio begun in Isaiah 40 (Isaiah 40:3, 10), repeating the themes of preparing the way and the reckoning of reward word for word.

Isaiah 62 closes the book, thematically, even though it is not the end of the book. Thematically, the author's intent is to present the way of return that begins with oppression and brokenness and ends with healing and restoration. Thus, the exile and the kingdom represent the conceptual starting and end points, respectively. But the exile and kingdom are not just concepts. The exile was a literal starting point for Israel on her historical timeline, and the timeline will end in a literal, physical kingdom realized in the future. God is making promises to Israel here in Isaiah that He must fulfill not just in theory but literally. Thus, we cannot reduce the kingdom to a mere analogy of restoration.

While Part 3 is arranged primarily in a chiastic structure that resolves the conceptual theme, there is a second structure running in the background that fleshes out a linear timeline. Once we get done with our discussion of the theme, I will outline the prophetic timeline for you, starting with the pivotal point of the Servant's death in Isaiah 53 and ending with the new heaven and new earth in Isaiah 66. I will lay out the series of pictures in the order that Isaiah presents them and compare them to the events in the book of Revelation. And then we will draw some conclusions as to what Isaiah saw and didn't see, and how that impacts some of the information in previous chapters.

LESSON 22

The Reward of Peace

READ
Isaiah 57:1-21

DISCUSSION

We pick up now in Isaiah 57 with a startling reversal in the kingdom picture that has been building in Isaiah 54–56. The previous view of the coming kingdom was a kingdom of justice, peace, righteousness, and abundance. The exiles were called to align themselves with God's thoughts and ways, and prepare themselves for the Sabbath. (Remember, the Sabbath is an analogy to the messianic kingdom on the horizon.) Isaiah 56 ended with a rebuke to the wicked watchmen and shepherds, who didn't protect the flock, but instead pastured themselves on their own sheep. As a result, they and their flock are given over to be devoured by the predatory, beastly Gentile nations. That rebuke now carries forward into Isaiah 57 with a comparison between law-abiding, righteous citizens and the lawless idolaters. Funny that we should be back to the topic of idolatry again. We haven't seen that since Isaiah 46. Let's work through these verses in chunks.

Isaiah 57:1-2

The opening verse presents us with the jarring picture of righteous people perishing and merciful people being taken away. Law-abiding citizens are suffering from violent crimes, even murder, and their own leadership has done nothing to stem the lawlessness in the community. Yet no one considers why. Sadly, I see this very scenario as I look at the national news headlines today in the United States.

Q: Why doesn't the leadership, whether at the national, state, or community level, endeavor to stop the lawlessness and abuse?

Q: Why don't the citizens themselves take action?

Q: The community should benefit from having righteous and merciful citizens. Why are they killed or taken away?

Let's expand a little on the phrase, "taken away." The New King James and New American Standard Bible translations says "taken away from evil." The English Standard and Revised Standard versions translate it as "taken away from calamity." The New International version translates it as "taken away to be spared from evil." The difference in the translations stems from the Hebrew phrasing, which conveys the idea of the righteous being withdrawn from the community (presumably, in death) to be spared the evil or calamity to come. The Hebrew word for evil used here can also be translated as distress, misery, injury, adversity, or calamity.

The LORD rebukes the community as a whole for not considering how they got into their predicament and what would be the repercussions for removing righteousness and mercy from community life. But His rebuke also suggests that His own hand has been at work in this seeming miscarriage of justice. The community's intentions in killing off the righteous were meant for evil, but from the LORD's perspective, it is actually good, even merciful, for the victims.

Q: What comfort does the LORD offer these murder victims?

Those who have walked uprightly and held to God's highway have paid the ultimate cost for their righteousness, and the LORD promises them that they will enter into rest and peace as a result. The particular Hebrew word for "rest" used here is *nuach*, and it describes a sitting-down kind of rest that servants are given, particularly on the Sabbath. They don't just stop working. They are allowed to sit down as well, just as God sat down after He finished His creative work. It is also a positional kind of rest that implies having a permanence of place, particularly in the kingdom. This kind of rest is heavily associated with Joshua bringing the children of Israel into the Land and causing them to rest in the inheritance they possess. It is also the permanence of place that salvation through Jesus provides. (Joshua is a picture of Jesus.) Those who have been saved in the spiritual sense may lose their place in the physical world, but they are given a permanent place in the eternal kingdom, and an inheritance that can never be permanently lost.

Now we have a contrast. While the righteous experience rest in a bed of the LORD's making, the wicked idolaters go about making their own bed.

Isaiah 57:3-13

There hasn't been much mention of Israel's idolatry since the LORD's rebukes in Part 1. Part 2 focused heavily on the coming righteous kingdom, so heavily that it seemed like that kingdom should be realized now, but, instead, a wicked kingdom is still very much a reality.

The LORD strongly addresses the sons of the sorceress, the adulterer, and the harlot, and describes their idolatrous actions in wincing detail.

> **Q:** How does the LORD describe their actions?

In short, they pursue their own lusts with the things they idolize. They do it openly and are arrogant about it. They are rebellious and deceitful. They are murderous hedonists, and they are no longer afraid of the repercussions of their actions. Fear was one of the original stumbling blocks that had driven them to idolatry, but now it seems that all fear is gone, and their idolatry is pursued purely for pleasure. (Sounds like our own cultural experience, doesn't it?)

The LORD has been lifting His people up and up over the last eight chapters, and now they are exceedingly lifted up in their hearts but not to pursue the LORD's ways. The LORD remarks in verse 10 that even though they are wearied by their pursuits, they don't stop to consider that these endeavors have no future. This is the second time in this chapter that He has charged them with failing to stop and consider. God has held His peace as He worked them through the healing process so far, but now His forbearance is coming to an end.

> **Q:** Does it seem like there is any hope of redemption for these?

Isaiah 57:14-21

The command to "prepare the way" that opened this study is repeated in this chapter. This picture of a kingdom given completely over to wickedness now comes to an end, and we hear the herald announce that the Messiah-King is coming. Prepare the way for the king! Finish the King's highway! Remove the stumbling stones! It is almost like a rallying cry being given when the comforting effort seems to be waning.

> **Q:** Who does the high and lofty God of eternity lift up to dwell with Him?
>
> **Q:** What comfort is there for the backslider?
>
> **Q:** When the LORD says, "I have seen his [backsliding] ways and will heal him" (57:17b-18a), does that mean that the person can continue his/her backsliding ways with impunity? Will the LORD simply overlook the sin?

It is God Himself who creates the fruit of the lips—the heartening words that speak peace and healing to those who are near and those who are far off. Paul quotes Isaiah 57:19 in Ephesians 2:13 and 18. Read Ephesians 2:8-18 to see the larger context, then answer these questions:

> **Q:** Who does Paul identify as the ones who are "far off"?
>
> **Q:** By contrast, who is "near"?
>
> **Q:** According to Paul's identification of those God calls the "far and near," who are the backsliders in the Isaiah 57?

The last verse in Isaiah 57 is given as a final warning. There is no peace for the wicked. Wickedness is the Hebrew word *rasha*. It is a justice term meaning one condemned or guilty of wrongdoing, whether in civil, ethical, or religious relations. It can also refer to sin against God or man, or showing hostility toward God. There was a justice aspect that had to be dealt with before the conflict between God and His people could end and peace be made. Thus, those who are not reconciled with God can never enjoy the peace of that relationship. There is no quietness in wickedness, only the continuous, never-ending roar of conflict, rage, and commotion—like the tossing sea that boils up on the land, stirring up the mud.

The Reward of Peace

Peace and what makes for peace has been the topic running through these last nine chapters. It began in Isaiah 48 with this statement:

> "'There is no peace,' says the LORD, 'for the wicked.'" (48:22)

It now wraps up in Isaiah 57 with the same statement:

> "'There is no peace,' says my God, 'for the wicked.'" (57:21)

These two verses are the bookends (the inclusio) that frame the topic of peace. Peace is what Israel is lacking in her exiled state, and in an effort to comfort His people, God has delved deeply into this topic. He has defined peace as He sees it and what a kingdom-community of peace looks like. He has explained how it is achieved individually and on a community level. He has even extended His own arm to achieve peace between Himself and His people, sacrificing Himself so that the justice aspect might be resolved. He has done everything He can to remove the stumbling stones of despair and shame that were robbing His people of peace and instill hope in them. He now holds out peace as a reward for the righteous—those who cling to His covenant of salvation, His vision, and His ways. For those that depart from the highway, there is no reward of peace. There is only more judgment and calamity to come.

If there is anything that struggling people crave, in addition to comfort, it is peace. Peace can be experienced in different ways in life. External forms of peace might include simply having difficult circumstances resolved so that there is no more conflict. Another is by having relationships with others repaired. External circumstances aside, the overriding need is for inner peace—peace of mind and a release from anxiety, if only through escapism. We live in a culture beset by constant external, internal, and relational conflicts, and inner peace and "self-care" have become major, almost idolatrous, pursuits in our generation.

Q: How is inner peace achieved the world's way?

Q: How is inner peace achieved God's way?

> **Q:** Before you counsel someone else, consider what peace you have found in your own life. Is there something in your life that is robbing you of peace? If so, why?
>
> **Q:** If you have found peace, how would you describe the process you went through to find it? (This is an important testimony you can use to comfort a struggling person.)

The tone of this opening chapter in Part 3 is a sharp departure from the previous chapters in Part 2. Part 2 was all about love, grace, validation, and promises of a bright, abundant future. Diversity, equality, and inclusiveness became goals for the new universal kingdom—provisionally. There were some requirements in God's DEI policy. But now, in Part 3, judgment falls on the people in a strong rebuke. It seems that they have suddenly lost ground and are back to their old idolatrous pursuits (if they ever left them).

This kind of fall-back can happen when you are engaged in a lengthy discipleship with a struggling person.

> **Q:** What causes them to fall back into an old, destructive lifestyle?
>
> **Q:** What attitudes do they take when confronted with their failing?
>
> **Q:** At this point, does their departure stem from not knowing God's way or willfully rejecting God's way?
>
> **Q:** Does it make a difference in how you respond? If so, how?

God makes a distinction in His law between intentional and unintentional sin—sin that stems from not knowing versus willful rebellion—and He adjusts His response and judgment to fit the case. Under the Old Mosaic Covenant, a sacrifice could restore the ignorant, but there was no sacrifice for willful rebellion. There was only judgment.

At this point, Israel knows the way she should take. She is being willful about pursuing her own pleasures. God's rebuke is very sharp and ends with that stiff warning. He has done His part to make a way for her return. Now she needs to set herself straight. Judgment is coming.

LESSON 23

The Practice of Letting Go

READ

Isaiah 58:1-14

DISCUSSION

In Isaiah 56–57, God began a discourse on covenant and community. The peace of the kingdom community is grounded in justice and righteousness, and the community as a whole needs to align itself with God's version of these. This requires an understanding of Him, His values, His ways, and His way of thinking, which are not the ways and thinking of men. So, a transformation process has to take place in the hearts, thoughts, and subsequent actions of those who would enter the kingdom.

God promised at the end of Isaiah 57 that there would be redemption for the backsliders, and that He would make His dwelling place with the humble and contrite of heart.

> *"For the iniquity of his covetousness I was angry and struck him; I hid and was angry, and <u>he went on backsliding in the way of his heart. I have seen his ways, and will heal him</u>; I will also lead him, and restore comforts to him and to his mourners."* – Isaiah 57:17-18

On the surface, that statement seems to indicate that Israel's redemption happens automatically, that her sins would be reckoned to her past and the LORD would treat her with grace after her punishment in Babylonia was over. There doesn't seem to be anything that Israel actually has to do to be healed. God just heals her, as if she deserves grace solely on the merit of having endured that time of punishment. This notion is going to be challenged today.

God has promised to make His dwelling with those of contrite heart. Today, in Isaiah 58, we will see a people contrite of heart—they are fasting and crying out to the LORD—and yet the LORD is still angry with them. He brings a charge against those who have seemingly humbled themselves outwardly and yet there has been no transformation of heart. We are returning to a discussion of justice, righteousness, and keeping the Sabbath today as the LORD takes Israel to task over the act of fasting.

Fasting may or may not be part of our modern faith practice, but it was in the Old Testament, in Jesus's day, and in the days of the early church (Matthew 6:16-18, 9:14-15; Luke 18:12; Acts 10:30, 14:23; 1 Corinthians 7:5). Before we start, let's gather what we know about the practice of fasting as it relates to a relationship with God. What is fasting, as it is defined in Scripture, and what is its purpose?

In general, fasting is an act of abstaining from something, typically food, as a way of showing repentance and grief. The act can be associated with mourning over physical death or spiritual separation from God due to sin. It is meant to be an outward expression of repentance and a desire to reconcile with God, particularly when facing His judgment. It reflects an anguish of heart.

There were a number of corporate fasts that Israel observed in the Old Testament. Only one is Scripturally-mandated, and that is on the Day of Atonement in the seventh month. Fasting was a way of carrying out the command to "afflict yourselves" prescribed in Leviticus 23:27. Apart from the Day of Atonement, there were a number of corporate fasts instituted to commemorate the horrific events of the siege of Jerusalem and the destruction of Solomon's temple at the hands of Babylonia. Second Kings 25 describes the events, and Zechariah 8:19 lists the fasts that resulted:

- The fast of the fourth month commemorated when Jerusalem's walls were breached.
- The fast of the fifth month commemorated when the Babylonians sacked Jerusalem and the Temple. This same fast, known as Tisha B'Av (pronounced Tisha Bay-Av), later memorialized the sacking of the Second Temple by the Romans in 70 CE. Both events happened in the same month, though years apart.

- The fast of the seventh month commemorated the death of Gedaliah, the remaining governor in Israel who tried to keep the remnant of Jews still living in Israel from decamping to Egypt against God's command.
- Finally, the fast of the tenth month commemorated when the Babylonians' siege of Jerusalem first began.

In Jesus's day, religious people observed personal fasts in addition to the corporate fasts. The Pharisees, in particular, fasted voluntarily on Mondays and Thursdays to demonstrate their piety and righteousness through spiritual discipline. Their fasting was accompanied by outward expressions of mourning and penitence, and Jesus rebuked them for it in Matthew 6:16.

> **Q:** Can you go through the motions of fasting, and yet do it in a way that defeats the purpose?

Fasting is still practiced to greater or lesser degrees in the Church Age. When I taught this lesson in class, it just happened to coincide with the season of Lent. The observance of Lent requires a "fast" of sorts—giving something up for a period of time.

> **Q:** What kinds of things are given up for Lent and for what reason?

Here in Isaiah, the LORD rebukes Israel for the practice for much the same reason that Jesus rebuked the Pharisees. Let's look at the text.

Isaiah 58:1-4

God tells the prophet to lift his voice and trumpet Israel's transgressions without sparing their feelings. You can feel the sarcasm in the LORD's words as He lays His charge against them. By appearance, Israel is doing all the right things—seeking the LORD and His justice. They want to know His ways and be near to Him—as if they were a righteous nation that had not abandoned His commandments. As if. In other words, they aren't that nation. They have convinced themselves that they are such, and yet, in God's estimation, they are not. Either they are only putting on the appearance of such, or perhaps, they are doing it in a way that defeats the purpose because they haven't yet grasped the LORD's way of seeing things. A transformation is needed.

Notice that the LORD mentions being righteous, keeping the ordinances, and keeping justice. These were all the things that He told them to do to prepare for the coming kingdom back in Isaiah 56. Blessed is the man who does these things, He said. It is good to seek that blessing, but there are right and wrong ways of pursuing it and right and wrong reasons for pursuing it. By all appearances, Israel seems to be doing the right thing, but the heart that is motivating her actions is not aligned with God's goals and values. And so, she misses the mark, and her actions are reckoned as sin. God brings these charges against her:

- In verse 3, He says, *"... in the day of your fast you find pleasure, and exploit all your laborers."*

  Israel makes a show of wailing and fasting and afflicting her soul, begging to be delivered from her affliction, and yet, at the same time, she is exploiting and afflicting her own laborers. She makes a show of giving up something, but all the while she is still profiting. She really hasn't given up anything. And she, who has been forced to serve under Babylonia's abusive hand, should have more of a conscience toward not oppressing her own servants. It's the Golden Rule, isn't it? Do unto others as you would have them do unto you? (Matthew 7:7-12) Do you ask, seek, and knock at the LORD's door, looking for relief, and yet don't listen to those who are begging for relief from you? That's a problem.

- *"... you fast for strife and debate, and to strike with the fist of wickedness."* (58:4)

  Israel seeks divine intervention in her quarrels with her brethren. She points the finger, shakes the fist, and stirs up strife, then fasts in a grand show of being victimized. She puts on the pitiful face and begs the LORD to take her side and grant her justice in her case.

  God's goal is peace and an end of conflict, and yet there is strife in a congregation where there should be peace. To help flesh out the issue here, let me point to a couple New Testament examples. One is the issue in the Corinthian church that Paul addresses in 1 Corinthians 6:7-8. He says,

  > *"Now therefore, it is already an utter failure for you that you go to law against one another. Why do you not rather accept*

wrong? Why do you not rather let yourselves be cheated? No, you yourselves do wrong and cheat, and you do these things to your brethren!" – 1 Corinthians 6:7-8

The book of James also elaborates on this theme.

"Where do wars and fights come from among you? Do they not come from your desires for pleasure that war in your members? You lust and do not have. You murder and covet and cannot obtain. You fight and war. Yet you do not have because you do not ask. You ask and do not receive, because you ask amiss, that you may spend it on your pleasures." – James 4:1-3

"Asking amiss" in the Greek carries the sense of having a sickness inside you that is driving the request. God's people go to court with one another because of their grasping after earthly things, declaring themselves to have been cheated, and perhaps they fast, imploring the LORD to rule on their behalf. These are citizens of the kingdom who have not yet grasped an understanding of God's goal of peace and what makes for that peace, nor do they even desire it. What happens when peace for one person is gained through the loss of another's peace? It becomes an oppressive cycle. That's a problem.

Back to Isaiah 58 . . .

- Also in verse 4, the LORD charges Israel, saying, *"You will not fast as you do this day, to make your voice heard on high."* (58:4)

This is the irony. Israel is abasing and afflicting herself as a way of lifting herself up and making her voice heard on high. She is trumpeting her victimization. We talked about the stumbling block of self-pity a number of chapters ago. A victim can ask the LORD to lift them up and act on their behalf. That is one way of finding relief. Or they can turn, instead, to other people and demand that the people around them lift them up. They do this by putting on a pitiful face.

When we put on the pitiful face, it is a cue to the people around us that we need lifting up. But that pitiful face is for the people's

Isaiah 58: The Practice of Letting Go | 259

sake, not God's. God doesn't need the pitiful face as a cue. He sees. He hears. He knows our situation already, and He doesn't need goading to act. This is why Jesus said,

> "Moreover, when you fast, do not be like the hypocrites, with a sad countenance. For they disfigure their faces that they may appear to men to be fasting. Assuredly, I say to you, they have their reward. But you, when you fast, anoint your head and wash your face, so that you do not appear to men to be fasting, but to your Father who is in the secret place; and your Father who sees in secret will reward you openly." - Matthew 6:16-18

When we pull the long-face act, what we don't stop to consider is that God also sees and considers what else we are doing. He sees how we treat others and how we demand to be served. Even though we are a victim, are we also an abuser? That is a problem. Are we using our righteous victimhood—the long face and afflicted posture—as a way of empowering ourselves instead of relying on His power? That is hypocrisy and false humility, when we put on a show of seeking God that gets support and approval from men. It angers God because it hinders Him from acting. If He does anything to help us, it will only encourage us to continue in our false humility because we perceive that it gets results. It will only further empower our pride and selfish pursuit. God is not a man that He is taken in by pitiful faces that only reflect a selfish, hardened heart. And so God does not act. He takes no notice.

Israel raises this grievance in verse 3. She has wept and fasted and afflicted herself, and God has not noticed. Isn't that irksome, when someone doesn't take notice?

Isaiah 58:5-9a

God responds to Israel's complaint by challenging her over the way she is going about fasting and the reason for it. There are right and wrong ways and reasons to do this. She wants relief from her oppression, but also to know His ways and His laws—His ordinance of justice—and be near Him. She is preparing herself for the kingdom, as instructed, by humbling herself in a contrite manner. She is fasting because, in her mind, the act itself pleases the LORD. A day of fasting is deemed an acceptable day of the LORD, a day in which He delights and approves and shows favor.

The LORD challenges her. Does she really think He delights in seeing His people afflicted and bowed down, especially in the day of their salvation?

Israel missed the mark in her understanding. He doesn't want this kind of posturing in His citizens. He has lifted her up and granted her favor as a royal citizen of the kingdom, and yet she is still in the posture and mentality of a Babylonian slave. And she is under the erroneous thinking that a show of contrition equates with making peace with God. But the outward show is not what makes peace with God. What makes peace with God is the change in the heart and thinking, and that has yet to be demonstrated.

> **Q:** In verses 6 and 7, what is the LORD's idea of fasting?

Think of fasting as not just letting go of something temporarily, but letting go in a way that achieves God's goals of peace and rest.

- First, He says, *"Loosen the bonds of wickedness."*

  Wickedness is what is keeping God's people from entering into peace and rest. Sin is a bondage. It causes wars and strife within a community that should be free of that bondage. The wars and strife come from grasping after fleeting, earthly cravings which are actually just lusts of that old nature. How do we respond when we feel we have been wronged? Do we point the finger at each other? Do we go to the LORD seeking divine intervention and ask for a verdict that will grant our desires? What if we just let go of those desires? Wouldn't that also achieve peace?

  God says, let it go. Let go of the grasping and pride and sense of victimhood. You may be a victim, but that does not give you the right to become an abuser. Let go of your contentions and quarrels with each other—let go of the wrong and strife and be at rest. That is fasting. It will be a sacrifice for you to let these things go, much more than just giving up food for a day. Denying yourself food is nothing but a token gesture compared to this. What you need to deny yourself is those other cravings—the lusts of the flesh, the lusts of the eyes, the pride of life. That is the kind of abstinence that reflects holiness, righteousness, and justice. That is the kind of fasting that the LORD answers.

- Next, He says, *"Undo the heavy burden, let the oppressed go free, and break every yoke."*

  If you are going to deny yourself, then truly do it. Let go of your grievances and victimhood with which you burden others. Give up your demands to be carried and served. Let go of your pleasures and your profit. Give everyone a rest, and most of all, from you! That is God's idea of approved fasting.

- In verse 7, He says, *"Share your bread with the hungry, open your house to the poor, clothe the naked."* (my paraphrase)

  Don't just give up the food. Put it in someone else's mouth. Put your roof over someone else's head. Put your clothes on a person who has none. Don't hoard these things to yourself. Let them go. These last commands should be familiar to us because Jesus used them to describe how He will judge the righteous when He comes in His glory to establish His kingdom.

  Q: How will Jesus reward this kind of fasting?

This is fasting that is acceptable to the LORD. It is not about abasing or afflicting oneself. It isn't even about food. It's about letting go of self and doing what pleases the LORD and pursues His goals of peace and rest—and not just for you but for the community as a whole.

Isaiah 58:8-9a presents a "then" statement to the LORD's somewhat rhetorical question, "Is this not the fast I have chosen . . .?" There are glorious consequences to humbling oneself with godly "fasting."

In verse 8, the LORD tells Israel that it will be a transforming experience. She will no longer be a prisoner sitting in darkness but a person of light. Being children of light should not be a foreign theme for us. The New Testament speaks to a great extent of our own commissioning in this, but we will go into this more in the coming chapters.

In verse 9, her fasting becomes an act that the LORD answers, as opposed to the fasting that He did not answer because it wasn't from the heart. The LORD promised in Isaiah 57 that He would dwell with those who are humble and contrite of heart, which is aligned with His own servant heart. He answers them, Servant to servant. "*Here I am* (Hebrew: *hinneni*)." We talked about the Hebrew phrase *hinneni* in Isaiah 52. *Hinneni* means "here I am," but it is typically the response of the inferior to the superior—the servant to the master, child to father, etc. The LORD says *hinneni* to those who let go of their flesh-bound cravings and hoarding of earthly things and willingly humble themselves to serve rather than be served for the sake of making peace.

Isaiah 58:9b-12

Isaiah 58:9b-12 is the first of two "if…then" statements. If Israel fasts from her selfish pursuits and turns her heart to comforting and helping others rebuild their lives, then her own well-being increases exponentially. She is blessed with wisdom and understanding as the LORD equips and strengthens her. Nothing is lost with this kind of fasting endeavor except the fleeting things of life. Instead, there is an eternal blessing and honor for those who enter into the highway-building task. She will lay a foundation for generations to come.

The world reckons greatness by how a person is served in life, but the LORD reckons greatness by humility and self-sacrifice. In verse 12, the LORD gives the highway-builder a new name. He calls her Repairer of the Breach and Restorer of Streets to Dwell In.

Isaiah 58:13-14

Isaiah 13-14 presents the second "if…then" statement, and this one returns to the topic of the Sabbath and wraps up a discourse that started in Isaiah 56. There has been a progression building over the last few chapters.

- **Isaiah 56** addressed the righteous who kept justice, did not defile the Sabbath, and turned their hands from evil.
- **Isaiah 57** rebuked the unrighteous but offered a promise to the backsliders that the LORD would heal them if they did not persist in their wicked ways.

- **Isaiah 58** now addresses a people who appear righteous outwardly, but are still wicked at heart.

The LORD has been sifting Israel out as He goes. Isaiah 58 now concludes with a comment on the Sabbath, which is where we started in Isaiah 56.

> **Q:** How is the practice of fasting, by God's definition, like keeping the Sabbath?

Like fasting, the Sabbath can be viewed as merely a religious activity that requires giving up something for a day and going about it with a sober face. Meanwhile, there is a pining in the heart for a release from the restraint so that the person can go on with their own pursuits. There is no delight in the act. It's an obligation (or at least, it was for Israel). But to treat those activities that way receives no praise from the LORD. He wants a heart that delights itself in Him and has communion with Him.

Sometimes you have to go south before you go north. You have to sacrifice the fleeting pursuits of life to gain the higher eternal reward.

GOD'S HIGHWAY PROJECT

The Practice of Letting Go of Self

At first glance, the topic of this chapter seemed to be about fasting—something that was certainly part of Israel's faith practice but maybe not so much our own modern ones. But it really wasn't about fasting. It was about how their fasting compared to all the other things they were doing, and what that revealed about the true nature of their heart.

Israel bewailed the fact that she was going through all the motions she thought would please God so that He will do something in return for her, that is, release her from her oppression, and yet her oppression wasn't lifted because that was all she was doing—going through the motions. When we reach out to comfort struggling people, we might hear a similar cry from them that even though they are being repentant and sacrificing in their lives, they aren't getting any response from God. Now, we know that there can be a number of reasons why God doesn't seem to answer prayers at times.

Q: What some reasons God doesn't answer?

Israel is our case study. She is going through the motions of having a relationship with God, but her worldly lifestyle and ways of treating people in her life really haven't changed and are glaringly out of sync with the LORD's values and goals. It is as if she hasn't grasped the big picture and what God expects of her.

Our own struggling person might not fit Israel's model, but let's suppose he or she does. When we reach out to help a struggling person, addressing the cry of why God isn't answering them or helping them might be an issue we have to tackle. Sometimes it requires seeing their situation from a higher vantage point, so that we can identify other factors in their lives that aren't syncing with the LORD's ways. Maybe they are still engaged in worldly pursuits that are inconsistent with godliness. Maybe it's the abusive way they are treating their family relations or community members. Maybe they are gripping onto something and need to let it go. Or maybe they are just going through the motions of having a relationship with God. Seeing the bigger picture of their life can show where the disconnect with God is. This is why it is important to stick with your struggling person for a while, maybe in a discipleship walk, because comforting, healing, and restoration often require seeing more of their life than just the surface and offering a more holistic assessment.

That being said, we should probably do some self-assessment on our own lives, lest we fall into the trap of being hypocritical and self-righteous. When we feel like God isn't answering our prayers (or our fasting), we often default to the belief that God is saying "no" or "not yet" because it is not His timing, without taking a serious look at why God is delaying His response. Sometimes, it is because we are being selfish, abusive, or uncompassionate in a way that is offending Him.

Q: What are some stumbling blocks that prevent us from doing effective self-reflection?

A Final Thought on Fasting

While Jesus was with His disciples, His disciples did not fast, at least not the way the Pharisees fasted, nor the way that John the Baptist's disciples fasted. Jesus explained that when the bridegroom is with the bride, it will be a time of feasting, not fasting (Mark 2:18-20).

Q: Who are the bridegroom and bride in Jesus's analogy?

Q: Fasting was a part of the old kingdom practices. Do you think there will be fasting in the Millennial Kingdom to come?

LESSON 24

The Comfort of Confession and Closure

READ

Isaiah 59:1-21

DISCUSSION

In Part 1 of this study, God proved that He is fully able to save His people. In Part 2, He provided a way for grace to be extended to them through the death of the Sin-bearing Servant. Israel's restoration hinged on that pinnacle act of the Servant's death. Now, in Part 3, the kingdom that should have come about immediately after the Servant's death has been delayed and a kingdom full of darkness, wickedness, idolatry, and oppression emerges in its place. Israel is still sinning, and God cannot let her sinful thinking and behavior come into His kingdom of light and peace until she understands, acknowledges, and turns from it. For this reason, He takes her to task for inappropriate fasting in the last chapter, which revealed all the carnal cravings and abusive behaviors of which she still has not let go. She is still grasping selfishly after earthly pleasures and hoarding these things. She has completely missed the point.

In this chapter, the prophet explains to Israel that it is not that God is unable to save her or that He does not hear her. What is delaying the restoration project is her continued sin and lack of repentance. She has been operating under the misconception that her redemption and restoration would happen automatically when the kingdom was realized because her sins would be reckoned to her past. She thinks the LORD will now grant her grace simply on the merit of having endured affliction in the Babylonian captivity. But even as the LORD gave her that promise in Isaiah 57:17-18, He warned her that there would be no peace for the wicked. They would not come into the kingdom.

God isn't just going to pretend that the past is over and grant Israel grace going forward, because her inward motivations haven't changed. As we saw in the last chapter, contrition doesn't always reach the heart. Sometimes it is only an outward face that is put on without the much-needed spiritual transformation. She has made a show of contrition the way an alcoholic would, begging and pleading for forgiveness and grace, while still in bondage to the inner cravings of the flesh. Today will be a candid discussion of Israel's need for spiritual rehab.

Isaiah 59 is divided into a three-part dialogue:

1. The prophet's rebuke of Israel
2. Israel's national confession
3. God's response to the confession

Isaiah 59:1-8 (The Rebuke)

Verses 3-4 outline the sins that have earned Israel this rebuke.

First, Israel has not kept her hand from evil. She has not kept her lips from evil, either. She has spoken lies and perversities. Perversities describe doing someone an injustice in how you speak about them. You don't speak about them justly or rightly. You skew your words to paint them in a false light for your own purpose. Hands, fingers, lips, tongue, feet, and thoughts—her whole body is following its natural, sinful bent toward evil and carnality.

Secondly, Israel has abandoned truth and, with it, justice. There is no justice without truth. She trusts in empty words and lies. What she conceives in her heart she then gives birth to in her actions. God gives the repulsive analogies to hatching vipers' eggs and weaving spider's webs. Let's consider those images.

The viper's power is in its poisonous mouth. There are antagonists in this world actively hatching viper's eggs—creating, promoting, and feeding the people with poisonous messaging, lies, and puffed-up words, and when those are taken into the community body, people begin to die. We have seen this in our own country. The poisonous messaging and hate-filled speech being blasted over social media and news stations has led to violent protests in communities and schools, random acts of violence, murder, assassination attempts, and terrorist attacks. The viper's eggs beget a new generation of vipers, but even trying to crush one to prevent the spread of poison spawns a verbal backlash. The analogy to the serpent is appropriate. All of these vipers are the spawn of the Serpent, Satan, who is Himself a liar and murderer, and the father of these (John 8:44).

Then there is the spider's web. A web doesn't just snare with one strand. The snare is set by weaving a network of strands that work together. When corruption grows to involve a network of participants, sorting out that network to get to the source of wickedness can be very difficult. This, too, has happened in our own country, where antagonists at a high level have funded community outreach groups who funnel the money to contractors, sub-contractors, shell corporations, and services who engage and support activists on the ground to agitate against the government authorities. It can be very hard to uncover the source because of the network the antagonist has built up around him or her.

God says, the spider's webs will not become garments that cover them. The word for garments here is significant. It is the Hebrew word, *beged*, which refers to underclothes worn beneath the outer wrapping—things that are worn close to the man and his heart in such a way that they mold to his body and, figuratively, to the shape of his character. For instance, when a person is mourning, they tear their *beged*, that which is close to the heart, as a way of illustrating that their heart is rent. A priest changes into new, clean *beged* before he enters the LORD's tabernacle to serve. But *beged* can be used to mislead and disguise, particularly in war, and it becomes a spoil of war—something taken by force, treachery, or pillaging. The more nefarious side to the *beged* is drawn from its Hebrew root, *bagad*, which means to act treacherously, deceitfully, unfaithfully, covertly, or fraudulently. It speaks of the hidden acts that go on behind the scenes or beneath the sheets, so to speak. Isaiah says that sinning Israel has woven a *beged*-like web of lies and deception around her, and she carries out her schemes behind the scenes and under the sheets. But God says her *beged* doesn't hide anything. In fact, it reveals her character and heart.

Israel begs to enter the kingdom of peace, but how can God let this kind of organized crime and corruption enter His kingdom? He can't. Her thoughts and ways are in complete conflict with the ways of righteousness and justice that make for peace. She has made crooked paths that must be straightened before she can enter the kingdom.

Isaiah 59:9-15 (The Confession)

Notice that the speaker changes in these verses. The rebuke was phrased in the third person (*your* iniquities, *your* sins, *your* hands, *your* feet). The response is phrased in the first person and plural (*we* look, *we* grope, *our* sins, *our* transgressions). These verses also begin with the word "therefore," meaning it is in response to the verses before it. This is Israel's response to the rebuke.

> **Q:** How does Israel describe being in that crooked place? What does she acknowledge about herself and her condition?

She agrees that she has so twisted and profaned the cause of justice that it is far from her now. She has completely forgotten the right way—the way life was meant to be—and this wicked way has become her new norm.

When you have fallen this far off the right path, how do you get back?

Notice the light and dark theme. This theme carries into the next chapter where Israel comes into the light, but at this point, she is in darkness. She gropes like a blind person for something solid to guide her and stumbles because she cannot see. She growls—the Hebrew word describes the noise of crying aloud in frustration, like a trapped bear banging at its prison bars and roaring in desperation and despair. She mourns pitifully like a dove. She looks for someone to plead her case, but there is none. She is the victim of her own twisted justice system. Salvation (Hebrew: *yeshua*) is far from her.

She agrees that she has sinned and that the charges God brought against her are true. She lists them, beginning with her sins against the LORD Himself. She has rebelled and faithlessly denied Him and turned away from Him. To that she adds her sins against others in oppressing them and inciting revolt. Inciting revolt carries the sense of encouraging people to turn aside from legality and morality, or, in the religious application, inciting apostasy. She conceives and utters lies. Notice, these are premeditated acts. She thought about them before she said them, and she said them deliberately, knowing they were wrong. Under the Old Covenant laws, there is no sacrifice prescribed for premeditated sin, only unintentional sin. These are grievous sins Israel is confessing, sins worthy of death.

She then acknowledges the consequences of these sins. Her lies have circumvented the truth, which has fallen away, and there is no integrity.

> **Q:** What is integrity? What are some of its values? (Google it and see what you find.)
>
> **Q:** What are the consequences of a loss of integrity?
>
> **Q:** Have we lost this quality in our culture today?

When integrity in a structure's fabric or foundational support is compromised, the structure collapses. When the value of truth in human dealings is lost, the community collapses. Integrity is gone in Israel, and there is no straight way out of the mess into which it has gotten her. When a person's life finally implodes and they decide that they are going to turn their life around and start doing what is right, often they become prey for the wicked and victims of a broken justice system.

In verse 15, the New King James translation says that the lack of integrity and justice displeases the LORD. "Displease" is a pretty tame translation of the Hebrew. In the Hebrew, it means to be evil in His eye. It enrages Him to the point where He begins to deliver some eye-for-an-eye, evil-for-evil justice. God is not evil, but He is not above bringing calamity on people in order to correct behavior, as Israel has now experienced firsthand.

Isaiah 59:16-21 (God's Response to Confession)

In response to Israel's corporate confession, the LORD puts an end to the delay of the kingdom program and extends His Arm again to gather His repentant people.

Verse 16 says that the LORD saw that there was no one to intercede [Hebrew: *pagah*]. Think of a story or movie scene where one king is approaching a city, and the prince of that city sends a greeting party out to assess the approaching king's intentions. The greeting party are the *pagah*, the intercessors, and they can meet the approaching king with different goals or attitudes. They can welcome him with rejoicing and goodwill; they can greet him with supplication and an appeal for mercy; or they can meet him with hostility and a declaration of war.

The Great King is coming, the highway has been prepared (or it should have been). He expects someone, a representative or envoy, to come out to meet Him on the highway, but there are none. No one greets Him with welcome and goodwill. No one comes to beg His mercy out of a desire for peace. There is no one to intercede.

    Q: How does the Great King react to that?

The Arm of the LORD made His first appearance as an intercessor back in Isaiah 52-53. Isaiah 53 described the Servant in His *pagah* role.

> *"All of us, like sheep, have gone astray, each of us has turned to his own way; but the LORD has caused the wrongdoing of us all to fall [**pagah**] on Him . . . Therefore, I will allot Him a portion with the great, and He will divide the plunder with the strong, because He poured out His life unto death, and was counted with wrongdoers; yet He Himself bore the sin of many, and interceded [**pagah**] for the wrongdoers."*
> – Isaiah 53:6, 12 NASB20

The Arm of the LORD, who was representative of the LORD's strength, gave up His strength to become an offering for sin. He became Yeshua, the salvation. He was the Shepherd who allowed Himself to be struck in order to strike peace between humanity and God. He was the intercessor who faced the sword of the King's wrath in order to end the conflict between the two parties. That was the first picture.

We now have a second picture of Him. This is the same Arm of the LORD who brought salvation before, and He is still in His intercessory *pagah* role, but His attitude has changed. (Remember, an intercessor can *pagah* with different attitudes and goals.) This time He is clothed as a warrior and His task is to make war, take vengeance, and deliver a recompense to His enemies. His purpose in God's Highway Project has been to end the conflict for God's people, first on the spiritual front and then on the physical front.

    Q: Christ is the intercessor, but who are the warring parties this time?

On one hand, there is the King who is coming, and is sending His own envoy ahead of Him. He is met with antagonists bent on war. The last several chapters have been wholly focused on Israel's wickedness that is delaying the kingdom, but there has been no discussion of the outside nations who are her antagonists. The nations are still in the background picture, and they play a role here. But some of the enemies of God have also been in Israel's camp. So far, Israel has been a mixed bag of the faithful and faithless, and the LORD now begins the process of identifying and separating those two camps within Israel herself. In verse 20, He comes now to wage war on behalf of the repentant remnant who turn from transgression. To these, He promises a covenant of peace.

Q: What is the Holy Spirit's role in all of this? (59:19, 21)

Depending on which English translation you are using, you will get different renderings of verse 19. The actual words in the Hebrew go something like this:

"... *For he will come* ... ["he" is not specifically defined]

"... *like a stream, rushing* ... [a torrential stream or river]

"... *which the ruakh of the LORD* ... [*ruakh* can either be translated as breath or spirit]

"... *drives.*" [Hebrew: *nus*, to drive something away, to impel it to flee]

The differences in the English translations stem from the use of the pronoun "he." "He" will come. Who is "he"? Is "he" the enemy or the conqueror? Whoever "he" is, he comes with the force of a flood, like water being driven by wind. The driving aspect is what the Spirit of the LORD does. Just as a gust of air blows on the water and drives it along, so the Spirit impels the inundating flood backward and causes it to flee. Thus, the King James and New King James versions translate this as the "enemy" coming in like a flood and the Spirit withstanding and pushing back against an them, like a commander lifting a standard against them in battle. But in other translations, "he" is cast as the conqueror, Christ, who goes out to wreak vengeance against Israel's enemies. The Spirit carries him along to victory like one borne along by a flood. Either way, the two floods meet in this grand battle. The enemy pours in like a flood, and the

Isaiah 59: The Comfort of Confession and Closure | 273

Spirit-driven Conqueror drives them back with a more powerful flood. That is the epic picture here in Isaiah.

The Spirit is very much a part of the battle against the enemy as the Arm of the LORD takes vengeance against the LORD's enemies. He plays an intercessory role in restraining the enemy—of pushing back and maintaining the line that the enemy seeks to overrun.

According to verse 21, the Spirit also remains after the battle. The indwelling, witness-bearing Spirit becomes part of the new covenant that the LORD makes with the faithful remnant of the nation of Israel when they come into the kingdom. Remember, Isaiah did not see the Church Age, or the giving of the Spirit in this age. This picture is of the Spirit being granted to Israel remains a future event.

The Purpose of Recompense

Dealing out recompense and repayment to the LORD's enemies is one of the Arm of the LORD's main tasks, and it is part of providing closure for victimized Israel. Let's dig into verse 18 a little.

> "According to their deeds, so will He repay [Hebrew: **shalam**], wrath to His adversaries, repayment [Hebrew: **gemul**] to His enemies; to the coastlands He will render [**shalam**] repayment [**gemul**]."
> – Isaiah 59:18 ESV

In other versions, the words repay and repayment might appear as recompense, retribution, reward, but they all basically describe the same thing—getting what is due for a deed, for better or worse, to a man's benefit or punishment. That is the meaning of Hebrew word *gemul*, which the ESV renders as "repayment."

But there is a second word for "repay" used in this same verse. It is the Hebrew verb *shalam*, from which the noun *shalom* springs. *Shalam* is more than just a matter of repaying something. It is the act of restoring peace and well-being by making restitution or compensation for the damage done. This word shows up throughout the books of the Law when it talks about things being stolen from a person or damages done to his person or property. The damage or lost item was to be replaced with an additional amount added (usually one-fifth) for restitution. Think of being reimbursed for the cost of a damaged car with an additional award for pain and suffering.

Compensation is needed for recovery from physical damages, but the physical damages are only part of what victims like Israel lose. There are other, less tangible damages that come with physical loss or abuse such as a loss of peace, loss of trust, fear, anxiety, anger, and humiliation. These are all stumbling blocks to healing that must receive some form of restitution before the person can be restored to wholeness and well-being. Someone who has been victimized or suffered loss needs this kind of closure in order to be restored again, and *shalam* is about getting closure. It's about bringing the victim's external and internal conflict to an end, which was God's goal at the onset of this highway project. The comfort that He offers here is the restoration of what was taken from her physically, mentally, and emotionally, and He accomplishes it by taking vengeance on His enemies.

Notice that the LORD is taking recompense from the "coastlands," that is, the Gentile nations in which Israel has been oppressed and abused. When the LORD *shalams* His enemies, it is vengeance at its most brutal. We talked about the comfort of vengeance in Isaiah 47 when God explained how He would deal with Babylon. This vengeance is for the abuses and oppression heaped on His people, and it is what Israel needs to restore her value and dignity. It is part of the comfort provided by the Arm of the LORD in His intercessory capacity. Israel cannot take vengeance herself. Vengeance belongs to God and is meted out according to His justice and His judgment.

God is impartial in dealing with His enemies. Just as His wrath fell upon Israel for a time when she was at enmity with Him, so it falls on her enemies now. Moses warned the children of Israel of the LORD's repayment plan when they were preparing to enter the Promised Land.

> *"Therefore know that the LORD your God, He is God, the faithful God who keeps covenant and mercy for a thousand generations with those who love Him and keep His commandments; and He repays [**shalam**] those who hate Him to their face, to destroy them. He will not be slack with him who hates Him; He will repay [**shalam**] him to his face."*
> – Deuteronomy 7:9-10

Having taken vengeance against His enemies and provided the necessary closure, the LORD establishes a new covenant with a Spirit-filled presence within the remnant of the nation of Israel. This is for the nation as a whole, not individuals. The next few chapters will present pictures of glorified Israel in the fully realized kingdom at the culmination of God's Highway Project.

GOD'S HIGHWAY PROJECT

The Comfort of Confession

As I considered the analogies of vipers and spiders' webs, my heart sank to see such tangible evidence of the same degradation in my own country and culture. Social media, public broadcasting, school curricula—all have become venues for viperous tongues that poison the people's thinking. The network of wickedness has paid, extorted, or otherwise influenced its way into governmental channels at all levels, into the justice system, the education system, and even into charity organizations who pay lip-service to helping the people but, in fact, only bog down the restoration process while taking a fat cut of the resources. Even when righteous people agree that something needs to be done, they are powerless to fight the system and become victims of it. We have followed in Israel's footsteps.

Q: What will it take to put things right?

Q: Why is confession such a vital step in God's Highway Project?

Q: What comfort comes from confession?

There will be a final, literal battle waged at the end of Israel's historical timeline when she will confess her sin before God as a nation and be restored. In the meantime, there have been Jews and Gentiles alike who have accepted the Servant's atonement for their sins and are engaged in confession as they face not just the social battle front, but the spiritual warfare driving it.

This description of the Savior arming Himself for battle is echoed in Ephesians 6, where we as His disciples are exhorted to put on similar armor.

Read Ephesians 6:10-20.

> **Q:** For what battle are we arming ourselves?
>
> **Q:** What role does the Spirit play in this battle?
>
> **Q:** How does confession help defeat the enemy?

The prophet's warning to Israel to repent is much like the prophetic warning to repent given to the churches in the book of Revelation.

> **Q:** Of what sins are the various churches called to repent before the Redeemer returns? (Read Revelation 2–3.)
>
> **Q:** What comfort does God offer to these churches?

The Comfort of Closure

The closure that comes with *shalam* (recompense or reward) is part of the comfort for the faithful. As we move forward into the final chapters of Isaiah, the recompense will be the focus of the text and is, itself, the final comfort offered.

Victims of abuse and oppression need closure, and not just a return of property or restoration of physical damages, but closure on the emotional and psychological levels. They need validation, vindication, and even vengeance to restore their wholeness and well-being.

> **Q:** Is this something that we as comforters or intercessors can provide, or is this something that only God can provide?
>
> **Q:** How do we help them find closure?

LESSON 25

Out of Darkness, Into Light

READ

Isaiah 60:1-22

DISCUSSION

Isaiah 60-62 bring us to the culmination of our theme of God's Highway Project. Having resolved the spiritual conflict between Israel and God, the Servant now ends the physical conflict between Israel and her enemies as He brings her out of exile's darkness and into the fully-realized kingdom of light. In these chapters, Isaiah extensively details the promises given to Israel that are specific to her restoration first as a nation, and then as individuals, so we will go through the bulk of verses fairly quickly, just to get a grasp of the overall picture. Then we will pull out some applications.

The intent of Isaiah 60-62 is to show the reversal of conditions for the Jews and Gentiles. Where Israel once served, now she reigns. Where the Gentiles once reigned, now they serve. Their positions have been switched. There are only two classes of people presented in these chapters: Israel and the Gentiles. The "Gentiles" include the following:

- The ***goyim*** or nations. These represent the physical, non-Hebrew nations who have been Israel's antagonists throughout Isaiah. They are Gentiles, physically speaking.

- The ***nekar***, or sons of the foreigners. These are also Gentiles, but they are Gentiles spiritually speaking. They are alienated from a spiritual relationship with God and serve foreign gods. The focus is on their spiritual identification and not their association with a physical nation. Note: The sons of the foreigners were mentioned back in Isaiah 56. There was a subset of these Gentiles who joined themselves to the LORD to serve Him, and the LORD promised them that they would be accepted and honored in His kingdom.

They are Gentiles physically and yet not Gentiles spiritually. In our passages today, the sons of the foreigner will be mentioned, but they will not be the redeemed Gentiles of Isaiah 56. They will still be this heathen version.

- The **zur**, or stranger, who is someone who has "turned aside" or has "strange" or heathen ways. These also are Gentiles in a spiritual sense like the *nekar*.

These all become servants of Israel who now reigns over them. She is moving from darkness into light, from that which was inferior to that which is superior. This is the grand reversal of fortune and ultimate validation and vindication for her as a victim. This is her closure.

But what is it like, making that transformation from darkness into light? Is it only about the victim gaining ascendancy over her antagonist, or is there a deeper spiritual change that happens in the victim herself as she sheds that persona of darkness and becomes a reflection and instrument of God's light to a darkened world? That is where our application will be today.

In the previous chapter (Isaiah 59), Israel cried out from the darkness and, in response, the Redeemer came and dealt with her enemies. Isaiah 60 now opens with a call to her to arise and step into the light.

Isaiah 60:1-3

Arise and shine! Your light has come! The address is actually to Zion, the City of the LORD which personifies corporate Israel at a national level, which we discover later in verse14. Jerusalem, her reigning city, is now glorified above the Gentile nations. These nations are drawn to her light, and they bring gifts to her.

Isaiah 60:4-8

Verses 4-11 focus heavily on the wealth of the Gentiles pouring into the city. Certain tribes are singled out for honorable mention. Midian, Ephah, and Sheba bring gold and incense. Sheba is known for her frankincense (Jeremiah 6:20). Kedar and Nebaioth bring flocks and rams for offerings. Interestingly, all of these tribes spring from Abraham. Midian, Ephah, and

Sheba were descendants of Abraham and Keturah who Abraham sent to the East to keep them from infringing on Isaac's inheritance (Genesis 25:1-6). Kedar and Nebaioth are descendants of Ishmael. So, this is the in-gathering of blessing that originated with Abraham and comes from his own progeny.

This picture of riches being brought to a king and kingdom is a pattern in Scripture. It happened previously in the days of Solomon, when the Queen of Sheba brought him vast gifts of gold and spices in return for knowledge and enlightenment (1 Kings 10:1-13). The gospels record another fleeting instance when three wise men from the East came to Jerusalem, following the light, seeking the king, and bearing gifts of gold, frankincense, and myrrh (Matthew 2:9-11). This same pattern will be fully realized in the future as an ultimate act of glorification.

Isaiah 60:9-16

Verses 9-16 focus on the rebuilding of the city, physically. Verse 9 mentions the coastlands and the ships of Tarshish. The ships of Tarshish were the merchant ships who sailed around the Mediterranean marketplaces, buying and selling luxury items. They were the ones that Solomon engaged to bring the building materials for the Temple and palace. Here, the same ships bring luxury materials from Lebanon to beautify the sanctuary, and the sons of the foreigner rebuild the walls. The gates are open continually to receive these gifts.

Israel is built up physically, but also in prestige. Any nation or kingdom that does not serve her will perish and suffer utter ruin. The aggressors who afflicted her will bow to her. Where she had once been forsaken and hated, she is now an eternal excellence and a joy of many generations.

Isaiah 60:17-18

We began with a contrast between light and darkness. Verses 17-18 now set up a second series of contrasts between the superior and inferior, described this way:

> *"Instead of bronze I will bring gold, instead of iron I will bring silver, instead of wood, bronze, and instead of stones, iron. I will also make*

your officers peace, and your magistrates righteousness. Violence shall no longer be heard in your land, neither wasting nor destruction within your borders; but you shall call your walls Salvation, and your gates Praise." – Isaiah 60:17-18

Bronze, iron, wood, and stone are the inferior materials. God replaces them with the superior materials of gold, silver, bronze, and iron, respectively. Violence, wasting, and destruction are replaced with righteousness and peace as a new administration is put in place. The city is encompassed by salvation (again, the word, *yeshua*), and the gates—the mouths of the city—declare its praise.

Isaiah 60:19-22

The picture now changes focus from the city to the God who dwells in her and is, Himself, her light. The sun and moon were only fleeting, external sources of light for a dark world. These have been replaced by a superior, eternal light that lights from within, and it has a transforming effect on God's people. This is something to which we as believers in this age can relate because we, too, have been giving an indwelling Spirit who transforms us into a people of light.

GOD'S HIGHWAY PROJECT

Light and Dark

The chapter begins and ends with this motif of light and dark. These terms become part of our Christianized vocabulary that non-Christians around us may not understand, so let's flesh out these terms.

> **Q:** When we talk about a people of light or a city of light, what does light describe?
>
> **Q:** By contrast, what does darkness describe?

Jerusalem represents a kingdom that is materially rich and full of abundant life, but the kingdom's true wealth and power lies in its enlightenment (moral guidance, truth, knowledge and instruction), justice, and peace. That is the same kingdom picture that we studied in Isaiah 54-55, only this time, the kingdom is fully realized.

The darkened world isn't drawn to Jerusalem so much as it is drawn toward God's light that shines through Jerusalem. Remember, this city isn't just a bunch of buildings but a body of people—living stones—who embody God's light before the world. That is her role—to walk in light and to bring light to a darkened world. When she functions as this kind of intercessor, she reaps a blessing from that. Once-victimized Israel is now overflowing with power, riches, and royal prestige, but more than that, she has been so restored that she is able to minister to others who are themselves in darkness.

In the big picture, there are two paths to take in pursuit of this higher state of being and blessing. One is superior and the other, inferior. One is the superior path of light according to God's ways and His grace. The other is the inferior path of darkness according to the world's way.

The darkened world pursues its own inferior version of the power and wealth that God's kingdom offers, and it pursues these along darkened paths—through wickedness, oppression, degradation of others, and by inciting divisions, hatred, and violence. What the world pursues is an inferior kind of wealth because it is fleshly and temporary. It is like bronze compared to gold or iron to silver when compared to the royalty and wealth enjoyed by those who walk in the light of God's presence.

There are also two paths to take once glorification is achieved. The darkened world boasts and brags and treads down the enemies it has overcome, perpetuating its darkness with counter-oppression and vengeance.

> **Q:** How do a people of light conduct themselves going forward?

The Stumbling Block of Our Carnal "Dark" Side

God's people are called to walk in light and spread God's light to the world. We are called to be children of light, to value and pursue the things that are of eternal value, but we can, instead, walk in a way that brings darkness to the world instead of light.

Q: How does that happen?

Like Israel here in Isaiah, we, as believers in the Church Age, are called to remember the darkness from which our Savior saved us and how He brought us into His light. Like Jerusalem, we have God's glory dwelling within us in the form of His indwelling Spirit. In His Sermon on the Mount, Jesus said,

> *"You are the light of the world. A city that is set on a hill cannot be hidden. Nor do they light a lamp and put it under a basket, but on a lampstand, and it gives light to all who are in the house. Let your light so shine before men, that they may see your good works and glorify your Father in heaven." – Matthew 5:14-16*

When God's light truly shines in a believer, that light touches lives and draws people to Him—not to the believer but to Him. That is an important distinction to make. We are merely intercessors. But even as children of light, we still grapple with our carnal "dark" side—the sin nature that still dwells in our flesh—and we will until such time as we fully enter into the glory of His kingdom. That carnal sin nature is perhaps the biggest stumbling block that we must overcome because it wars continually with the Spirit who is also dwelling within us and wrecks our fellowship with each other.

The apostle, John, uses this light and dark motif heavily in his first letter. Let's look at a couple of those passages.

Q: How does John say our darkness is manifested? (Read 1 John 1:6-7 and 2:7-11.)

Paul also talks about comporting ourselves as children of light.

Q: How do we "put on" light? (Read Romans 13:11-14.)

Q: How do we step out of darkness and into light? What is involved in the transformation? (Read Ephesians 4:17-32 and 5:8-14.)

LESSON 26

Comfort Fulfilled

READ

Isaiah 61–62

DISCUSSION

Isaiah 60 talked about Jerusalem's transformation from a city of darkness to light. Jerusalem is symbolic of corporate Israel, and the passage detailed her restoration at the national level. Isaiah 61 begins with a sweeping inaugural address from the Servant, her King, to His people. Before we begin, let's review what we know of the Servant's work from what has been presented so far in Isaiah.

The Servant-King

The Servant was first introduced in Isaiah 42:1-7. God put His Spirit upon Him as He tasked Him with bringing justice and law to the Gentiles and establishing justice on the earth. This kingly task connects Him with the king described in Isaiah 9:6-7 who establishes a kingdom of peace. There He is called Wonderful Counselor, Mighty God, Everlasting Father, and Prince of Peace. In Isaiah 42, He is simply the Servant. In addition to bringing justice, He is given the task of enlightening the people—being a light to the Gentiles, opening blind eyes, and bringing prisoners out of prisons of darkness. He is the embodiment of light and enlightenment for the people, both Jew and Gentile.

In Isaiah 49:1-9, the Servant spoke for Himself of His own tasking. He was to be the Savior not just for Israel but for the entire world. Again, He was cast in a kingly role as He was called to restore the earth, to reestablish Israel, and bring light to the Gentiles and all people imprisoned in darkness. His voice mingled with the voice of the LORD as He addressed Israel in her dark despair.

In Isaiah 52-53, He became the manifestation of the Arm of the LORD, who sacrificed Himself to bring His people into a kingdom. He is granted the kingdom as His reward, and He divides that reward with the strong. Under His rulership, the kingship is democratized (Isaiah 55:5) as He extended the honor of royalty and rulership to the people of His kingdom.

The Servant-King goes silent when the kingdom is delayed, but now, in Isaiah 61, He speaks once more. Again, His voice is mingled with the LORD's voice in this inaugural address.

Isaiah 61:1-9

The phrasing of verses 1-4 is very much like Isaiah 49, but the focus changes a little. Again, the Spirit of the LORD is upon the Servant-King. He is anointed. The Hebrew word for anointed here is *mashach*, from which we get the word *mashiach* or *messiah*. This messianic anointing is given to Israel's kings and priests, both of which roles He plays. But in this passage, His administrative role is downplayed as He stretches out His hand to comfort His people. He preaches good tidings to the poor, heals the brokenhearted, opens prison doors, proclaims the year of the LORD's favor—and His vengeance, which is part of the comfort. Overall, His role is to comfort His own people Israel. Notice: There is no mention of Gentiles in the passage at all.

Unlike the previous chapter, Israel's physical restoration is mentioned only briefly in verse 4. Instead, the passage focuses more on the inner spiritual healing of people. In verses 5-6, we are given the comparison of "strangers" and "sons of foreigners" tending the flock and harvest while Israel is named the priests of the LORD. In Isaiah 59, I pointed out the different classifications of Gentiles in the kingdom. The *zur* (stranger) and *nekar* (foreigners) were part of the *goyim* (Gentiles) but their distinction was more along the spiritual lines. They were alienated from a spiritual relationship with God because they served foreign gods. Isaiah uses them now to create this comparison with Israel, who is corporately referred to as priests of the LORD. Just as the kingship was democratized in Isaiah 55:5, we now see the democratization of the priesthood in verse 6. The redeemed are not just royalty but a royal priesthood. A new class of citizen is defined as part of the emerging kingdom.

From the way Isaiah contrasts Israel and the Gentiles in these passages, it wouldn't seem like any Gentiles would be part of this new citizen class, but the apostle Peter tells us very clearly that Gentile believers are included in it (1 Peter 2:4-10). The reason for the disconnect is two-fold:

1. Isaiah only sees the remnants of Israel and the nations who survive the Tribulation and come into the kingdom still in their mortal bodies. Nowhere does Isaiah address those of the "first resurrection" as John writes in Revelation 20:4-6 who come into the kingdom in immortal bodies. The prophetic pictures that Isaiah describes only follow the timeline of Israel as she comes through the time of "Jacob's trouble" described in Jeremiah 30:7.

2. Isaiah's authorial intent is to emphasize the reversals of Israel's condition in relationship to the Gentile nations who are her oppressors during her exile. (But we know from Revelation 13:17-19, that another similar exile will happen to her in the future under the kingdom of the Beast and the then reigning city named Babylon.)

So, when we see Isaiah speaking about the Gentiles serving Israel almost as slave labor, we should make that distinction between Gentile believers who died for the faith and join the ranks of the royal priesthood (the immortals) and the unbelieving Gentile nations who survive the battle and are forced to bow the knee before Christ as He takes His throne (the mortals). Remember, Isaiah did not see the Church Age. He only sees the mortal elements of Israel and the nations who survive the Tribulation and live to see Christ come into His kingdom while still in their mortal bodies. Putting these oppressors beneath Israel's feet is part of granting closure to the victim of the Tribulation.

The Servant-King goes on to say that the people's shame is now removed, and they receive not just honor but a double honor. In their land, they will possess not just a single portion from the LORD but a double portion. The double portion is something reserved for the firstborn son in a family. They have a blessed status that is acknowledged by the Gentiles, and, I think, even within the royal priesthood itself. Israel is head of the governing body just as the firstborn son is head over the greater family.

Isaiah 61:10-11

In verses 10-11, the Servant adds His own rejoicing over His glorification from the LORD. That glorification is described in His being clothed as royalty but also as a bridegroom. This imagery spills over into Isaiah 62, where His people are described in similar terms as a royal bride.

Isaiah 62:1-9

We now zoom back out to the vision of Jerusalem at the national level. She is a city of light set on a high hill and a lamp set on a lamp stand. She is a gem of royalty (62:2-3). She is the Bride whose shame over being forsaken and left desolate is now put away (62:4-5). She is restored to her relationship with her Husband as promised back in Isaiah 54. After the delay caused by her continuing sin in Isaiah 57–59, the kingdom pictures of Isaiah 54–56 now burst to life again.

A roar goes out from the LORD, or the Servant, or perhaps both.

> "For Zion's sake I will not hold My peace [keep silent], and for Jerusalem's sake I will not rest, until her righteousness goes forth as brightness, and her salvation as a lamp that burns." – Isaiah 62:1

Just as the LORD does not keep silent, He calls His watchmen to not keep silent as well, but to give Him no rest until He establishes Jerusalem and makes her a praise in the earth. We have already talked about the watchmen in a couple places. In Isaiah 52, these were the ones who lifted their voice to proclaim the good news of salvation to Israel. In Isaiah 56, the wicked watchmen who did not keep justice or guard righteousness were dismissed. They did not warn God's sinning people of the judgment on the horizon, but fattened themselves on abundant living they had from oppressing the people. As a result, they had no part of the kingdom. God now replaces them with a new generation of watchmen who are commanded not to keep silent.

Isaiah 62:10-12

The final verses in Isaiah 62 wrap up the vision of Israel and Jerusalem in their glorified state at the completion of God's Highway Project. We see the glorification and granting of the reward of royal priesthood to the redeemed who pursued holiness and righteousness before the LORD. Where God's people were once forsaken and sent away, they are now the ones who are sought out. This echoes the promise in Isaiah 55:5:

> "Surely you shall call a nation you do not know, and nations who do not know you shall run to you, because of the LORD your God, and the Holy One of Israel; for He has glorified you." – Isaiah 55:5

Isaiah 62:10-11 are a reiteration of the opening statements from the very beginning of our study. They are the closing bookends for the themes of 1) preparing the way and 2) the reward for works.

Remember the dual inclusio:

> "The voice of one crying in the wilderness: '<u>Prepare the way</u> of the LORD; make straight in the desert a highway for our God . . . Behold, the Lord GOD shall come with a strong hand, and His arm shall rule for Him; Behold, <u>His reward is with Him, and His work before Him</u>."
> – Isaiah 40:3, 10

> "Go through, go through the gates! <u>Prepare the way</u> for the people; Build up, build up the highway! Take out the stones, lift up a banner for the peoples! Indeed the LORD has proclaimed to the end of the world: 'Say to the daughter of Zion, "Surely your salvation is coming; Behold, <u>His reward is with Him, and His work before Him</u>."'" – Isaiah 62:10-11

We have been focusing heavily on the first theme of preparing the way throughout this study, but we have a few more chapters to go, so I will save my final thoughts on that until God finishes His closing statements in the chiastic structure. The secondary theme of recompense and reward becomes a major focus here in the final chapters of Part 3, so let's gather the various threads we have already studied and frame them in a New Testament understanding of reward and recompense before we delve into the final chapters. The key question I would like to answer is:

> **Q:** How does the concept of recompense tie back to the original goal of comforting people? Why would it be a necessary part of that?

The Reckoning of Rewards

The topic of rewards or recompense has already cropped up in various places in Parts 1 and 2. We talked about the reward of a crown that is granted to both Cyrus (Isaiah 45:14) and the Servant (Isaiah 49:4). Unlike Cyrus, the Servant shares His spoil with the strong (Isaiah 53:12) and the kingship in His kingdom is democratized (Isaiah 55:3-5). Thus, the pinnacle reward, by Isaiah's definition, is the right to rule and enjoy the blessings and distinction accorded with royalty. We bring this definition of the reward into New Testament teachings on pursuing crowns. This reward isn't just for Israel but for all the faithful who are called by Christ's name and pursue His kingdom even at the cost of their own life. The Lord has promised to extend the glory of royalty to us if we endure even as Christ endured, as Paul explains:

> *"The Spirit Himself bears witness with our spirit that we are children of God, and if children, then heirs—heirs of God and joint heirs with Christ, if indeed we suffer with Him, that we may also be glorified together."*
> – Romans 8:16-17

> *"This is a faithful saying: For if we died with Him, we shall also live with Him. If we endure, we shall also reign with Him. If we deny Him, He also will deny us. If we are faithless, He remains faithful; He cannot deny Himself."* – 2 Timothy 2:11-13

The reward fits into the greater framework of recompense or *shalam* which we talked about in Isaiah 59. Recompense carries with it the idea of being compensated for your works, whether good or evil. You reap what you sow, figuratively. Recompense is a vital part of God's Highway Project because it is needed to resolve the conflict between victims and oppressors, provide closure to victims, and return to them a sense of material, emotional, mental, and spiritual wholeness.

Now, as we move into the final chapters of Isaiah, the discussion of recompense and rewards shifts focus a little. It is no longer about comforting victims specifically. Instead, it is applied broadly and without partiality to both God's enemies and His people.

Before we begin this discussion, we should clarify some doctrinal points. First of all, the reward for works does not equate to salvation. It has been emphasized repeatedly in Isaiah's discourse that Israel cannot save herself by her own hand. In fact, her works are as wicked and unclean as the nations around her. The only hope she has of entering the kingdom is based on the merit of the Servant's work on the cross, not her own works, and certainly not on the merit of her suffering. She brought that judgment upon herself as recompense—wages earned—for her sin, and we know that the wages of sin is death, not eternal life in the kingdom (Romans 6:23). Neither her works nor her suffering save her or make her righteous before God. From this we derive the doctrinal understanding that salvation is granted by grace alone and not according to works (Ephesians 2:8-9). It is a gift that was purchased by the sacrificial death of the Christ, the Sin-bearing Servant, and it is offered to all men, Jew and Gentile alike.

Because of their opposing natures, grace-based salvation and works-based rewards have separate applications, and, in fact, they govern different aspects of the kingdom experience. Salvation by grace determines citizenship and entrance into the kingdom; the reward for works determines placement within the kingdom's community structure based on a merit system.

But the reward for works is not limited to those in the kingdom, nor is it only for the righteous. All people, believers and unbelievers, those in the kingdom and those outside of it, will be judged according to their works and given some kind of recompense, as Jesus promised,

> *"And behold, I am coming quickly, and My reward is with Me, to give to every one according to his work."* – Revelation 22:12 (cf. Isaiah 40:10, 62:11)

This promise applies to all people across all ages, and pursuing the reward isn't something that you can choose to do or not. However you live your life, it is going to reap a reward according to the LORD's judgment in the end. Everyone will come to that moment of standing before the King and having their lifetime achievements reviewed and rewarded, for better or worse. It is a necessary closure to end all conflict and create health and wholeness in the eternal kingdom.

As Israel is learning here in Isaiah, attaining the reward of royalty involves more than simply believing in the Messiah. It requires action on her part.

The crown and right to rule isn't just given automatically. God won't let her step into the position of authority without having learned the lesson of submitting to authority first—understanding what it is like to be subject to both kind and harsh masters. When God glorifies the victim of a harsh master by putting that master under their feet, it is tempting for the victim to rule as harshly and oppressively as they were once ruled. That is the way that people still sunk in darkness act. They perpetuate oppression in that way, and that is why the transformation into being a people of light is important. The inner heart must be sorted out and established in alignment with God's thoughts and ways before that crown can be awarded. There can be no oppression or injustice in the coming kingdom. Those who would rule must know how to discern and judge issues by right values, how to wield authority correctly, and how to be a leader and example. God has already passed judgment on Israel's wicked leadership in Isaiah 56 for their failure in this. The apostle Peter builds on that example with this warning:

> *"Shepherd the flock of God which is among you, serving as overseers, not by compulsion but willingly, not for dishonest gain but eagerly; nor as being lords over those entrusted to you, but being examples to the flock; and when the Chief Shepherd appears, you will receive the crown of glory that does not fade away."* – 1 Peter 5:2-4

Glorification in the eternal kingdom is the end result of God's Highway Project as Isaiah saw it, and the high point of the chiastic structure for Part 3. But there are still four more chapters in Isaiah with two major pictures in them. The closing arguments in Isaiah 63–66 will revisit not just the opening arguments in Part 3 but the opening picture of God's sovereignty at the very beginning of this study (Isaiah 40). The courtroom scene in Isaiah 41 will now reconvene to deliver God's final judgment on both the victim and the antagonist, and it will be without partiality. The verdict will be pronounced and the determination of reward and recompense made. To demonstrate His claim to sovereignty over Israel's idols, the LORD will predict the creation of a final "new" thing that will put all of His rivals to an end. It will be the final closure and comfort for His people.

GOD'S HIGHWAY PROJECT

The Stumbling Block of Keeping Silent

Keeping silent was one of the stumbling blocks in God's Highway Project that we talked about in light of facing fury, and it runs contrary to the LORD's command here. The more a culture degenerates into violence, hatred, the suppression of truth, and promotion of skewed values, the more necessary it becomes to speak up in defense of justice and righteousness according to God's vision. Speaking up is a fearful thing to do, especially when addressing sin, but the healing and restoration of a community cannot take place in silence. When we speak up, there will be backlash, but like the Servant, we do not seek a reward from this world but from the LORD's hand. The LORD is the only one whose validation we need to seek, and the only one of whom we should truly be afraid if we fail to speak the truth, whether in our witness to the world, about the sin in the world, or even the sin within ourselves. Speaking up is what reveals the darkness and drives it away.

The end is drawing near. I will remind you again of the questions for reflection that I asked before.

Questions for Reflection

Q: Have you remained silent at a time when you should have spoken the truth? Why?

Q: Is there something about which you should speak up now?

Q: Have you remained silent when given an opportunity to witness to someone? If so, why?

Q: Is there someone to whom you need to witness today?

Closing Arguments

The last four chapters of Isaiah present God's closing arguments in the chiastic structure, so we might think that the content is merely looping back to previous statements to resolve certain points in the opening arguments. That would make Isaiah 61–62 the end of the study. Thematically, Israel's glorification in the kingdom is the end of her journey from brokenness to restoration.

The content seems to loop back on itself, and yet, it doesn't. The prophetic pictures have been unfolding in a progressive order, producing a linear timeline, and the timeline does not end at Isaiah 62. In fact, to view the Millennial Kingdom as the final step in the prophetic timeline runs contrary to the eschatological timeline presented in the book of Revelation. The Millennial Kingdom isn't the eternal kingdom. It has a thousand-year cap, and there are other events that happen after it. So, it is not the end picture, not in the book of Revelation and not in the book of Isaiah. The picture series continues until the very end in Isaiah 66 and it will be in keeping with the book of Revelation.

As we move forward into the final chapters, I will first compare the closing arguments to the opening argument as we have been doing previously and finish the discussion according to the thematic chiastic structure. It is correct hermeneutic practice to examine the literal text and its application first. And yet, we know that there is also a deeper, prophetic side to the Old Testament texts which must also be considered. Once we finish the thematic discussion, we will step back and look at the grand sweep of prophetic pictures that span Isaiah 53–66 and discuss the timeline they describe. We will consider what parts of the eschatological timeline Isaiah saw and what he didn't see, and how the omission of the hidden parts impacts the interpretation of his text.

The next stop is the picture of treading out the s.

LESSON 27

Treading the Winepress

READ

Isaiah 63:1–64:12

DISCUSSION

I explained at the beginning of Part 3 how the opening and closing arguments revolve around the central picture of the glorified kingdom of peace. As we now move into the final chapters, we will see a mirroring not just of the arguments, but also of events. There is another battle similar to the one the Redeemer fought, another penitent prayer from Israel, and another judgment sequence. We saw all of these in Isaiah 58–59. We will see them again in chapters 63–65a, complete with a verdict. Then, a final picture of the righteous kingdom described as the "new heaven and new earth" will be juxtaposed with the previous wicked kingdom in Isaiah 57 as the chiastic structure closes.

But the closing arguments and pictures aren't an exact rehash of the opening ones as the chiastic structure would suggest. They fit the pattern of one another, and yet, there are some significant differences that suggest that the closing elements are unique events in their own right. In this lesson, we will flesh out the judgment sequence in Isaiah 63-65a, which is described as treading the winepress. It opens with the battle.

Isaiah 63:1-14 (The Battle)

Isaiah 63:1-6

The chapter begins with a dialogue between the prophet and God. The prophet poses the question: Who is this figure coming from Bozrah of Edom, clothed like a victorious warrior-king returning in splendor and majesty after his battle? Whenever the narrative includes specific names of places, it is helpful to consider the meaning of those names because they are part of the picture. Obviously, The LORD isn't coming from Bozrah of Edom in a literal sense. He is coming from the enclosure or sheepfold (Hebrew: *bozrah*) with His clothes stained red (Hebrew: *edom*). The proper names spring from common words, and the common words help build the picture. The *bozrah* or enclosure will reinforce the idea of a winepress in the next verse, although the idea of a sheepfold is also very evocative, considering that the LORD calls Israel His flock.

The LORD answers the prophet, saying, I am coming. Notice how He characterized Himself: He speaks righteousness, and He is mighty to save. The victorious King declares His supremacy.

The prophet then invites the LORD to tell of His battle, prompting Him with the question, why is Your apparel stained red (Hebrew: *adom*) like one who treads the winepress?

The LORD explains that He has trodden the peoples in His vengeance and caused them to drink the cup of His wrath. The year of redemption has come. Verse 5 is worded very much like Isaiah 59:16, so much so that you can't help comparing this picture of God treading the winepress to the picture of the Redeemer coming to save Israel back in Isaiah 59. And so, we have our chiastic pairing:

Opening Argument: (Isaiah 59:16–60:22) The battle: The Redeemer comes in vengeance to deliver Israel from her enemies
Closing Argument: (Isaiah 63:1-14) The battle: The LORD comes in vengeance to tread the winepress of "the peoples"

As with all chiastic structures, there is a comparison between the opening and closing statements, and yet, there are some differences in those statements that we should consider. The closing statements usually resolve the opening arguments, but they can also expand the picture (such as a national Savior becoming a universal Savior) or present a reversal.

> **Q:** If we look at it as if it is the same battle, as the chiastic structure suggests, what does that tell us about the relationship of the Redeemer-King and the LORD?

> **Q:** In Isaiah 59, the Redeemer fought against the nations who oppressed Israel. Is the LORD arrayed in battle against the same people? Who are "the peoples" in verse 6?

The treading of the winepress is a vivid picture that should not be unfamiliar to us as New Testament students. The same phrase is mentioned in Revelation 14:17-20 and 19:11-21.

> **Q:** Who is the one treading the winepress in these passages?

If we incorporate our understanding of who treads the winepress according to the book of Revelation, we would identify the treader as Christ, who is God Himself, but also God's agent for accomplishing this task. Thus, this first chiastic pairing seems to be speaking of the same battle. In Isaiah 59, the Redeemer did the work. In Isaiah 63, God gets the glory for it.

Isaiah 63:7-14

The prophet now gives a rather lengthy address, which he begins by recounting the victorious King's character qualities. This picture of God is a sharp contrast to the angry, vengeful warrior who trod the winepress a few verses earlier. Here, the prophet urges the LORD to remember His mercy, praising Him for His loving kindness and great goodness to Israel. The LORD became their Savior and was afflicted in all their affliction (that hearkens back to the Sin-bearing Servant's death in Isaiah 53:4-5). The LORD came to them as a Savior, thinking that they would not deal treacherously with Him, but we know from the gospel accounts that Israel did just that. The prophet does not mince words in saying that they rebelled and grieved His Holy Spirit. The people's actions so grieved His Spirit that they provoked the LORD to wrath, and He battled them as He would His enemy, but then, in verse 11, there is a movement away from wrath back to grace again, prompted by a series of rhetorical questions. It is not clear in verse 11 who is doing the remembering and asking the questions. In the Hebrew, it simply says, "the days of old were remembered," without assigning that to a speaker. The purpose of the questions is what is important. That purpose is to urge the LORD to act according to His character of loving kindness and mercy, and to remember His promise to redeem those who return to Him, if only for the sake of His glory.

Notice that there is no mention of the nations in all of this, unlike there was in the opening argument. In the opening argument, the Redeemer comes to avenge Himself specifically on the coastlands, that is, the Gentile nations oppressing Israel. The only enemy mentioned in this passage is Israel herself.

> **Q:** Is Israel part of the "peoples" being trodden down in the winepress along with the nations?

From Israel's response, it seems that she is. She has been counted as the enemy in His eyes for her faithlessness and treachery. So, that is a difference between the opening and closing arguments. Where Israel herself was previously portrayed as a victim, she is now portrayed as an enemy and is lumped together with the rest of God's enemies. As the prophet points out, this has been her pattern of behavior since the "days of old."

The prophet's intercessory address to the LORD is followed by a penitent prayer from Israel.

Isaiah 63:15–64:12 (The Penitent Prayer)

Opening Argument: (Isaiah 59:9-15) The penitent prayer
Closing Argument: (Isaiah 63:15–64:12) The penitent prayer

Isaiah 63:15-19

Again, this picture in the closing argument is very similar to the opening argument, but there is a sour note about it. In verse 15, Israel questions why God has restrained His hand as if He is not seeing her plight. This hearkens back to the very beginning in Isaiah 40:27 where she complains that God has passed over her just claim. Does a Father do this to a child? And then she makes a rather shocking statement in verse 17:

> "O LORD, why have You made us stray from Your ways, and hardened our heart from Your fear?..." – Isaiah 63:17

Israel admits she has a hardened heart and is in a state of continuing sin (which was the reason God delayed the kingdom in Isaiah 57–58), but look at what she says. She lays the charge squarely on the LORD for having hardened her heart. What an outrageous charge, to blame God for her own straying, saying it was His fault! Is it His fault? Did the LORD harden Israel's heart? Interestingly, Paul confirms Israel's words in Romans 9–11.

> **Q:** Why did God harden Israel's heart so that she continued in her blindness and sin?

Israel bemoans the fact that she had possessed her land but a little while, and now the adversaries have trodden down the sanctuary. She claims she has been dispersed to the Gentile nations over whom God never ruled or called by His name. After this rather petulant, self-pitying opening, Israel's confession now continues into the next chapter.

Isaiah 64:1-12

"Oh, that You would rend the heavens!" Israel still wants the shock and awe treatment for her enemies, and she goes on in this vein for four verses. Finally, she admits her own condition and takes responsibility for that condition. The phrase, *"We all fade as a leaf,"* hearkens back to the opening statement in Isaiah 40,

> *". . . All flesh is grass, and all its loveliness is like the flower of the field. The grass withers, the flower fades, because the breath of the LORD blows upon it; surely the people are grass. The grass withers, the flower fades, but the word of our God stands forever."* – Isaiah 40:6-8

She needs salvation and cleansing. God has hidden His face from her because of her iniquities. Again, this wording is similar to Isaiah 59:

> *"But your iniquities have separated you from your God; and your sins have hidden His face from you, so that He will not hear."* – Isaiah 59:2

Israel pleads for mercy. She appeals to God as her Father. She appeals to Him as her Creator. He is the Potter; she is merely clay in His hands. He was the one who made her (and He is the one who hardened her in the furnace of affliction). She closes her prayer with final appeals on behalf of herself as His people who are scattered, His land which is a wilderness, Jerusalem which is desolate, and His Temple which is lying in burnt ruins.

How can He continue to restrain Himself? Will He remain silent and punish her beyond measure? Again the tone of the ending questions is accusing, as if He is being unfair or unjust.

The penitential prayer is very much the same in both the opening and closing arguments, but I see the following differences:

- Last time, Israel took full responsibility for her failure. This time, she blames God for hardening her.
- Last time, Israel appealed to God when her own justice system failed her. This time, she complains that God's idea of justice has failed her as well.

GOD'S HIGHWAY PROJECT

Israel's penitential prayer reveals that she is still grappling with the same victim-like mentality we saw earlier. It is almost as if she is blaming God for not acting quickly enough, and she rationalizes that God's failure is why she has lost hope and fallen back into her sinful ways. She is in this cycle of sin leading to punishment, punishment leading to hopelessness and disbelief, and disbelief leading to sin again.

    Q: What was supposed to break that cycle?

    Q: When we are grappling with a struggling person caught in this mentality of blaming God, how do we break them out of it? Can we break them out of it, or is this something God has to address?

In the opening argument, when Israel confessed, the Redeemer responded by coming to save her from her enemies. How does God respond this time?

LESSON 28

The Final Recompense

READ
Isaiah 65:1–66:24

DISCUSSION

In the previous chapter, the closing argument disclosed that God's enemies are not just found in the Gentile nations. They are among Israel's ranks as well. She is not all pure and innocent. Quite the contrary. Many among her are still entrenched in a victim mentality that blames God for hardening her heart and remaining silent in spite of her pleas for mercy.

As we move into these final chapters, God begins to separate all the people of the world collectively, and the division line no longer falls between Israel and the nations. There are only two categories: the wicked and the righteous. God separates the faithful from the unfaithful in Israel's ranks and adds the unfaithful to the "wicked" category. He does the same for the Gentile nations, drawing out the righteous who seek Him from the rest of the wicked. He addresses the wicked category first, and then the righteous, and grants each the recompense that their works have earned.

Isaiah 65:1-16 (Address to the Wicked)

Opening Argument: (Isaiah 58:1-14) Israel seeks God, but God does not answer her, followed by (Isaiah 59:1-8) God's charge against her

Closing Argument: (Isaiah 65:1) God is found by those who do not seek Him, followed by (Isaiah 65:2-16) Judgment of the wicked and righteous of Israel

The opening and closing arguments have dual parallels. The initial statement focuses on seeking and finding (or not finding) God, which is then followed by judgment.

Isaiah 65:1-5

Chapter 64 ended with Israel's scathing rebuke of God over remaining silent while His people, land, city, and Temple were in ruins. Now, in Chapter 65, He comes roaring out at her like a lion. "I will NOT keep silent. I will repay!"

He begins with the apostates among Israel. In verse 1, He makes a rather scathing comparison between the Gentiles, who had once been the high-water mark for heathen practices, and His own idolatrous people. The Gentiles sought Him and He allowed Himself to be found by them. They had not been a nation called by His name, but now they are. By contrast, His own people have been calling to Him and seeking Him with their penitential prayers, and yet He has not answered them because they are still sunk in idolatry and hypocrisy. Think about the journey we have come through. How many times has He rebuked them for idolatry? Their heart was already hardened against Him, even before He decided to harden it further for His own purposes.

The LORD remarks on their continued idolatry (the main issue of Isaiah 57) and their hypocrisy (the main issue in Isaiah 58). Both involve sacrificial service, but not the kind that honors God. Israel's idolatrous sacrificing is a sin against God Himself. Her hypocritical sacrificing—making a show of sacrificing while oppressing her own kin—is a sin against her fellow men. Verse 5 records her hypocritical words, *"Do not come near me, for I am holier than you!"* Holier than who? She is wicked and idolatrous! Her self-righteousness and idolatry infuriate Him.

Isaiah 65:6-16

The LORD did not answer Israel back in Isaiah 58, even though she sought Him. He delayed His response to her and answered the Gentiles instead. But now, there will be no more delay. He will not be silent any longer but will answer His people—with judgment. He launches into the wicked with five "behold" statements (65:6, 13-14).

The main thrust of His address is against the wicked, and yet we find that not all of Israel falls under judgment. In the middle of delivering His verdict against the idolaters, the LORD identifies a remnant among them—a "cluster"—who are righteous. These He claims as His servants, as opposed to the rest of the apostates who haven't sought Him, who did not answer when He called, and did not hear when He spoke. This is what separates the sheep from the goats, so to speak—how they responded to the Shepherd and what were their sacrifices. The sheep are brought into the pastures of the kingdom. The goats are numbered for the sword and slaughter.

Idolatry is addressed with the first "behold" statement (65:6), then the hypocrites are judged. As they did to Him and to their fellow men, so the LORD does back to them. Their recompense is revealed with four more "behold" statements.

- They shall be hungry while the righteous eat (65:13)
- They shall be thirsty while the righteous drink (65:13)
- They shall be ashamed while the righteous rejoice (65:13)
- They shall sorrow of heart while the righteous sing for joy (65:14)

The imagery suggests the picture of a celebration banquet table at which the righteous sit while the wicked look on from a distance. The hypocritical "fasting" in which the wicked once indulged themselves has now become a true and permanent fasting.

In addition to all this, the LORD's righteous servants are given a new name while the names of the slain apostates become the new curse words and epithets (kind of like calling someone a Neanderthal or a Cretin as a comment on disgusting or base behavior. The apostates will become the new derogatory example.)

Verse 16 ends with God refuting Israel's claim in the previous chapter that He was being unjust and unfair and that He hadn't kept His promises. To this, He responds that the blessings and promises have and will be kept because He is the God of truth. The Hebrew word for truth is *amen* (the same word with which we close our prayers). The use of this word is significant because it hearkens back to the curse passages in Deuteronomy 27:

> *"'Cursed is the one who makes a carved or molded image, an abomination to the LORD, the work of the hands of the craftsman, and sets it up in secret.'*

Isaiah 63–66: The Final Recompense

> *And all the people shall answer and say, '**Amen!**'"*
> *"'Cursed is the one who treats his father or his mother with contempt.'*
> *And all the people shall say, '**Amen!**'"*
> *"'Cursed is the one who moves his neighbor's landmark.'*
> *And all the people shall say, '**Amen!**'"*
> *"'Cursed is the one who makes the blind to wander off the road.'*
> *And all the people shall say, '**Amen!**'"*
> *"'Cursed is the one who perverts the justice due the stranger, the fatherless, and widow.'*
> *And all the people shall say, '**Amen!**'"*
> *"'Cursed is the one who lies with his father's wife . . .'*
> *And all the people shall say, '**Amen!**'"*
> *"'Cursed is the one who attacks his neighbor secretly.'*
> *And all the people shall say, '**Amen!**'"*
> *"'Cursed is the one who takes a bribe to slay an innocent person.'*
> *And all the people shall say, '**Amen!**'"*
> *"'Cursed is the one who does not confirm all the words of this law by observing them.'*
> *And all the people shall say, '**Amen!**'"* – Deuteronomy 27:15-20, 24-26

"Amen . . . amen . . . amen!" The curses have come upon the unrepentant idolaters and hypocrites as God recompenses them for their deeds according to the perfect justice and truth of His Law, just as He warned them He would. Their own words have confirmed their fate.

Verse 16 ends with the remark that the former things would not be remembered. We talked a lot about the "former things" and "new things" back in Part 1 where God challenged Israel's idols to prove their godship by predicting and bringing events to fruition. God's sovereignty was proven by His ability to point to His works of old as well as declare new things. He previously declared the coming of Cyrus (Isaiah 41:21-24) and brought it to pass. He declared the coming of the Servant (Isaiah 42:9) and brought that to pass. He now declares more new things with two final "behold" statements.

Isaiah 65:17-25

The sixth "behold" statement in Isaiah 65 declares His creation of the new heavens and the new earth. This is the supreme act of sovereignty and power that reestablishes God as the Creator of all things. The arguments for His sovereignty with which this study began are put to rest.

The seventh "behold" declares the creation of a new Jerusalem. Thus, we have a new kingdom established that is a complete reversal of the wicked kingdom with which we began Part 3, and the final closing picture in the chiastic structure.

Opening Argument: (Isaiah 57:1-21) The old wicked kingdom where the righteous perished and the wicked flourished
Closing Argument: (Isaiah 65:17–66:24) The new heaven and new earth where the righteous flourish and the wicked perish

The new Jerusalem is described as a place where there is no more weeping or tears (65:19) and a long life (65:20). Its citizens will enjoy the fruit of their labor that had once been taken from them by their oppressors (65:21-23). There is perfect communion between God and His people (65:24), and all creation will be at peace, with no more hurting or destruction (65:25). It is presented as a return to Eden, and yet, it is not without flaw.

Death may be delayed in this kingdom, but it is not a kingdom without death, which means there is still the potential for sin here. Not all Bible translations include the word sinner in verse 20, but that is the meaning in the Hebrew—one who has missed the mark. These die an unnaturally early death as a consequence of their sin. The presence of sinners isn't what you would expect in a picture describing the new heavens and new earth, is it? The phrase "new heavens and new earth" frames a particular picture in our understanding of the End Times that seems to be at odds with Isaiah's words here. This is why it is important to understand what Isaiah saw and what he didn't see of the prophetic timeline. Let's get through Isaiah 66 and God's address to the righteous, and then we will look at the timeline. There are still more pictures.

Isaiah 66:1-5 (Address to the Righteous)

Isaiah 66 opens with a dialogue similar to Isaiah 65, only this time the LORD addresses the righteous while the wicked are only a secondary mention. Verse 1 is a rhetorical comment on God's dwelling place. All heaven is His throne and the earth His footstool. All earthly things have been put beneath His feet, and yet He elevates the lowly—those who are poor and contrite and who tremble at His word (cf. Isaiah 57:15). He will address them personally in verse 5, but first He declares another action against the wicked—those who did not answer when He called and did not hear when He spoke. This phrase is almost a repeat of Isaiah 66:4, but now the LORD adds to that previous statement. Not only are the wicked numbered for the sword and slaughter, He will also choose their delusions for them and bring fear on them. He will throw the stumbling blocks of blindness and fear in front of them, so that the wickedness of their hearts will be hardened further.

In verse 5, God returns to His validation of those who tremble at His word. Their brethren taunted them, *"Let the LORD be glorified, that we may see your joy,"* even as they persecuted them. That is like an abuser scoffing at a victim, saying, *"Count it all joy when you fall into trials,"* even as they are abusing the victim. It's like the men of Israel scoffing at Christ as He hung on the cross, saying, *"Save Yourself! If You are the Son of God, come down from the cross!"* There is a viciousness in it. It is a humiliation. God promises a reversal—the righteous victim will not be ashamed. And in a way, their humiliation is likened to the humiliation the Sin-bearing Servant once endured. They have shared that experience with Him.

Isaiah 66:6 (The Final Battle)

This is a very condensed picture of a battle. We have seen two previous battle scenes that were paired together in the chiastic structure, but this one is out of sequence and something of a one-off. It is its own self-contained picture.

The word "voice" (Hebrew: *kolh*) is used three times in quick succession in this one verse: the voice of uproar in the city, the voice in the Temple, and the voice of the LORD who repays His enemies. It describes a tumult, a roar, or a rushing sound; by implication, the sound of destruction or the sound of victory and jubilation. This word, *kohl*, appears 36 times in Isaiah. Here are some examples to help flesh out the context of this particular verse.

> *"The noise [**kolh**] of a multitude in the mountains, like that of many people! A tumultuous noise [**kolh**] of the kingdoms of nations gathered together! The LORD of hosts musters the army for battle." – Isaiah 13:4*

> *"You will be punished by the LORD of hosts with thunder and earthquake and great noise [**kolh**], With storm and tempest and the flame of devouring fire." – Isaiah 29:6*

> *"The LORD will cause His glorious voice [**kolh**] to be heard, and show the descent of His arm, with the indignation of His anger and the flame of a devouring fire, With scattering, tempest, and hailstones." – Isaiah 30:30*

> *"At the noise [**kolh**] of the tumult the people shall flee; when You lift Yourself up, the nations shall be scattered;" – Isaiah 33:3*

So, you get the picture. This is the battle scene in which an enemy multitude rushes upon the city of Jerusalem and the LORD roars back at them from the Temple. (It is about as briefly described as the Gog-Magog rebellion in Revelation 20:9, hint, hint.)

Isaiah 66:7-13 (The New Jerusalem)

As in Isaiah 65:18-25, we have another, similar call to rejoice over Jerusalem as a nation is born. This picture of a righteous nation is the complete opposite of the wicked, idolatrous kingdom pictured in the opening arguments (Isaiah 57). Israel, previously pictured as a barren and bereaved woman, bears children—and without the pain of laboring for them. This act is solely by the LORD's hand. Miraculously, she becomes a flourishing mother of many children overnight.

In the previous chapter, the LORD Himself declared that He would rejoice in His people (65:19). Now, He commands everyone else to do the same. Rejoice is an imperative command. Those who rejoice with her share in her abundance, glory, peace, and comfort. Comfort is mentioned three times in verse 13. The threefold declaration of comfort represents His final completion of the comforting process. God's people have been saved, physically and spiritually. They have been vindicated, validated, avenged, and recompensed. So, we have the end of God's Highway Project. It began in exile, in a place of brokenness and despair. It ends in restoration to a kingdom of peace, wholeness, abundant life, and royal blessing.

The chiastic structure ends here. The courtroom arguments that began in Isaiah 41, when God convened court, have been heard; the verdict is in.

Isaiah 66:14-21 (The Final Judgment of All Flesh)

"When you see this..." This is the defining moment. It will be a moment of rejoicing for some, terror for others. In the previous chapter, the LORD declared the reward set aside for both the righteous and the wicked. Now the judgment commences.

Verses 15-18a describe the nature of the LORD's judgment. It is characterized by fire and sword. It is against His enemies, but the wicked apostates are particularly singled out, as promised in the previous chapter.

In verse 18b, the LORD gathers the nations for a display of His glory. This Hebrew word for "gather" doesn't just mean to collect or gather them, but to take them in hand. When the LORD takes the nations in hand like this, it is often to make war with them. So, this carries forward the sense of a battle playing out in conjunction with a final judgment.

In verse 19, the LORD says He will set "a sign" among the nations. What is the sign? We don't know exactly. It is some signature act that is miraculous, perhaps disastrous, but whatever the display of sovereign power is, it will convince all flesh that He truly is LORD. The text intimates that there will be survivors from this who will carry the news to the nations, and notice which nations are named: Pul (aka Put or Libya, the coastlands of North Africa), Lud, Tubal, and Javan (all nations to the north in Asia Minor and the coastlands of Greece) and Tarshish, which is an epithet for the merchant ships that plied the Mediterranean. Some distinctive disaster happens in the midst of this mercantile Mediterranean alliance. We see something like this foretold with the destruction of Babylon at the end of the Tribulation. She is described as a mercantile power who sits on many waters, and she is destroyed in a day.

> *"In the measure that she glorified herself and lived luxuriously, in the same measure give her torment and sorrow; for she says in her heart, 'I sit as queen, and am no widow, and will not see sorrow.' Therefore her plagues will come in one day—death and mourning and famine. And she will be utterly burned with fire, for strong is the Lord God who judges her."* – Revelation 18:7-8

This is an example of the kind of "sign" that the LORD might set among the nations. The sign is God singling out a particular faction of whom He then makes an example by pouring out His wrath on them to hallow His name. A similar sign was once made with Pharaoh in the Exodus. Another sign is accomplished with the Gog-Magog war in Ezekiel 38–39.

In verses 20-21, the nations bring back the exiles as they would an offering to the LORD. God reckons this offering as being of like kind to the offering that Israel herself brings Him. There is a mingling of righteous Gentiles and Jews in this imagery. Where it says, *"And I will also take some of them as priests and Levites,"* even Jewish scholars remark that there are two possible interpretations of this. Either the LORD is saying that He will take some from the nations and make them priests and Levites, or He will take some from the returning exiles and make them priests and Levites. The Jewish scholars note that either interpretation goes against Levitical law which limits the priesthood to the Aaronic line.[1] According to 1 Peter 2:9, both righteous factions are combined into a royal priesthood.

Isaiah 66:22-24 (The Universal Recognition of the LORD)

The LORD makes a final statement about the new heavens and new earth, detailing the separation of all souls into two categories, but we should note very carefully how they are separated. Verse 23 defines the "all flesh" category. They are the living who come to worship the LORD from New Moon to New Moon and Sabbath to Sabbath. Those in the "all flesh" category look upon those in the other category described in verse 24. These are the dead, the corpses of men who rejected the

---

1 Adele Berlin and Marc Zvi Brettler, editors ; Michael Fishbane, consulting editor. The Jewish Study Bible: Jewish Publication Society Tanakh Translation. (Oxford ; New York : Oxford University Press, 2004), 916, commentary in side note attached to verse 21.

LORD and rebelled against Him. These are given over to an eternal destruction where their worm does not die nor their fire is not quenched. This is no longer a matter of separating Israel from the nations. The LORD is dividing all flesh on the more universal grounds of believers and unbelievers, those who accept Him and those who reject Him, and evaluating them according to their works. *"For I know their works and their thoughts,"* the LORD says in verse 18.

It is important to understand that all flesh will be judged by their works, but none will be justified by them. Even we as believers cannot stand on our own works. Only those who are justified according Christ's works and merit and have His blood covering their sins are the ones written into the Book of Life.

GOD'S HIGHWAY PROJECT

This is God's idea of closure—recompense for all people across all ages, according to their deeds and according to His sovereignty and sense of justice. It is horrifying and glorious in its impartiality and finality. Like the verdict in a court case, the recompense puts an end to the physical conflict between both parties, but unlike human courts, it also puts to rest the victim's need for further vindication, validation, and vengeance. It is a definitive end to all conflict.

This is the final comfort.

Conclusion

We have now come to the end of Isaiah and the end of God's Highway Project. The main theme of "preparing the way" formed the bookends for this lengthy portion of Scripture that delved into the process of healing people—people who have struggled with sin that has brought antagonists and hard circumstances into their lives, who have suffered abuse or victimization (rightly or wrongly), and who need a way out of the crooked places in which they find themselves.

The overall goal was to comfort people, and that comfort could only be achieved by bringing an end to the physical, mental, emotional, and spiritual conflict in their lives. As we worked our way through Isaiah 40–66, we marked God's progress with Israel toward these ends as it unfolded in stages. The first stage was to remove Israel from her antagonists' hands, something which Cyrus accomplished; but that was all that Cyrus did. He did not help resolve the spiritual conflict or provide any lasting release. He was merely the stop-gap measure to take her out of harm's way and calm life down enough to where God could begin to talk with her on a more intimate level. The major milestones with which she grappled in the first stage of the process were understanding and acknowledging God's sovereignty over her life and letting go of her own ways of empowering herself. When we struggle or when we are comforting a struggling person, we run into the same stumbling blocks of fear, frustration, and the need for vindication, validation, and even vengeance. We studied all of that in Part 1.

Taking a person physically out of harm's way is a necessary first step, but it doesn't provide a permanent comfort. Once God had Israel's attention, He began the more difficult process of addressing the raging conflict inside her which was the focus of Part 2. Together with the Servant (Christ), He began to address the issues of despair, self-pity, shame, anger, and her withdrawal into silence. The key to resolving her internal conflict revolved around the "good news" of the Servant's work. He instilled the hope of her future restoration and reward if she pursued His path and aligned herself with His ways and thinking.

The way that Part 2 ended made it seem like all was well in struggling Israel's life and she was on the road to recovery; and some of her people were. But others persisted in a worldly, idol-worshiping lifestyle that was not aligned with God. Still others put on a show of righteous living without having any transformation of heart. God adjusted His responses accordingly. He rewarded those who stuck to the highway and pursued Him in spite of the difficulties and persecution. With those who adamantly rejected His comfort, He simply walked away and left them to their fate. With the ones in between, who make a show of righteous living without transforming their thinking, He waited to see if there would be self-reflection and self-correction.

There were two responses to God on Israel's part, represented by the two rounds of confession. The first round of confession was made by those who reflected and truly repented. The Redeemer answered them, and they were counted among the righteous. The second round of confession revealed a rebellious heart that still blamed Him for their struggle and goaded Him over remaining silent. These the Redeemer also answered, but with judgment. Part 3 focused heavily on the responsibility of the struggling person to actively pursue the sanctification journey, and the LORD's sorting out of those whose hearts are truly His from those that aren't.

When we have been on the journey with our struggling person for a while, there comes a point, as it did with Israel, when that person has to make a decision for themselves as to which path they are going to take in their relationship with Christ. Their choices fall into three basic categories. There are those who will truly pursue a relationship with Christ and righteous living, and so we continue the sanctification journey with them. There are those who will depart from the effort entirely—and from us. We let those go. The third category is a little hard to identify. They look like they are pursuing a relationship with Christ, and yet that relationship hasn't had any impact on how they treat others. They are still abusive, oppressive, contentious, swift to anger, self-absorbed, and pursuing their own desires without seeing what is wrong with what they are doing. Thus, there is a disconnect between loving God and loving others. We may or may not see the evidence of this, but if we do see it, perhaps we mention it to them and wait to see if there is any self-correction. If we count this person as a brother or sister in Christ, then perhaps it becomes necessary not to keep company with them until the behavior is corrected. Paul advised this in 1 Corinthians 5 and again 2 Thessalonians 3. If they self-reflect and repent, that's wonderful! Our brother or sister is restored to us. If they don't, then we put them into God's hands to judge their heart and let them go.

That is a broad summary of the stages of the journey from brokenness to restoration that God modeled for us with Israel. As those stages of relationship unfolded, various issues cropped up in progression, and there was a four-step highway-building process for dealing with those. The highway-building process represented actions on the comforter's part. God modeled all of them with Israel, who is a worst-case scenario. I asked this question in the beginning, and I will ask it again:

> **Q:** When we seek to comfort or help a struggling person, why is it important to remember that we, too, are like the grass and only the Word of God is eternal?

When we seek to apply God's model, we must begin with acknowledging that whatever healing comes in our struggling person's life will come from God through Christ. There will be limitations to how much we can do because we are not God. He allows us to help in the restoration effort, but there will be parts that we have to leave in His hands alone. Nevertheless, we should consider what we can apply. Let's make a high-level pass through some of the key elements.

Step #1: Lifting up the valleys

> **Q:** What are some ways God lifted up His down-trodden people that we can also do?

> **Q:** Our current culture places a high value on being supportive and empowering people, but what are some potential pitfalls in casting ourselves in that role?

Step #2: Bringing down mountains

Israel's enemies were mountain strongholds in her life that needed bringing down.

> **Q:** Is this something we are called to do, or should this task remain in God's hands? Why?
>
> **Q:** What problems might arise when we take up our struggling person's cause?

Israel is also her own worst enemy. Victimized and oppressed people need lifting up, but sometimes they lift themselves up and seek their own empowerment instead of letting God lift them and relying on His power.

> **Q:** Where do victimized or oppressed people often turn for empowerment?
>
> **Q:** What kind of walls or relational barriers do they build in their lives that prevent them from progressing toward healing?
>
> **Q:** What were some of Israel's self-comforting behaviors, attitudes, or coping mechanisms with which God had to grapple?

God responded to Israel with rebukes, exhortations, and warnings, while at the same time offering love, long-suffering faithfulness, and reassurances.

> **Q:** Why is a balanced response necessary? What happens when we offer only positive affirmations or negative condemnations?

Step #3: Making crooked places straight

Proclaiming the "good news" was the key action that satisfied God's command to comfort His people. The Sin-bearing Servant's death released Israel's conflict on the spiritual level but also went a long way toward relieving her inner emotional and psychological conflicts.

> **Q:** How does our witness of Christ play a part in resolving our conflicted person's struggles?
>
> **Q:** Christ should be the way out of a crooked place but more often He presents a stumbling block to struggling people. Why?

Straightening crooked places involved realigning a person's thoughts and ways with God's thoughts and ways, particularly in regard to what He considers valuable—His sense of justice, righteousness, and how life ought to be. We can find ourselves battling the cultural messaging around us as we try to draw our struggling person back to God's way, and often our struggler falls back into old ways of thinking and acting.

- **Q:** How has our current culture skewed our perception of what is valuable in life? How has it caused brokenness in our community?

- **Q:** How has our current culture skewed the picture of how life ought to be? How has it caused brokenness in our community?

- **Q:** How has our current culture skewed justice and truth?

Our effort to comfort and restore someone can be made very difficult by disillusionment caused by their unrealistic expectations, distrust of authority and truth, and their acceptance of social norms that run counter to God's ideals. We may draw them out of that oppression, but the world can draw them back.

- **Q:** How do we respond when our struggling person falls back into an old, worldly lifestyle or coping habit?

- **Q:** How do we respond when they blame others or even God when their idea of how life ought to be isn't realized?

Step #4: Smoothing the rough places (removing stumbling stones)

Empowerment was a foundational issue at the beginning of the highway project. When people are oppressed or victimized, a sense of powerlessness overtakes them, and they have different reactions to that feeling. Some try to take back their power by force. Others give up entirely and withdraw behind their walls into silence. The desire for empowerment can become a consuming pursuit because empowerment provides the comforts of validation, vindication, and vengeance.

- **Q:** How can we present God as a better source of empowerment?

Despair can morph into self-pity, which is a destructive means of empowerment that our current culture validates.

- **Q:** How can we keep from enabling self-pity?

Stumbling stones such as fear, despair, anger, silence, and shame can linger long after the original antagonist or difficult circumstances are gone and cause problems in future relationships. It is hard to address these in a study like this because each person's struggle is different. This is why personally identifying with a person's specific struggle is helpful to be truly effective. Reflect on your own life journey and think of one difficulty with which you have grappled in your personal life.

> **Q:** How did you find your way through the experience? (Perhaps I should ask first, have you found your way through it?)
>
> **Q:** Did the experience equip you uniquely to comfort someone by offering empathy or guidance?
>
> **Q:** How did you find comfort in the Word of God?

Many times, we can try to "smooth things over" by offering platitudes, but platitudes can kill the comforting effort.

> **Q:** What are some typical platitudes that people offer when comforting struggling people?
>
> **Q:** Why aren't they comforting?
>
> **Q:** Not all platitudes are bad. Many come from the Word of God. How do you offer comfort from God's Word in a way that doesn't sound like a platitude?

God's Highway Project has been a lesson in how God comforts His people and brings the conflict in their lives to an end. In the vast timeline of Israel's history, the process is still going on. For all intents and purposes, Israel is still in exile today. Her national restoration will continue to be delayed until such time as she, as a nation, acknowledges her brokenness before the LORD and accepts the salvation of her Messiah who died for her sin. But this restoration process isn't limited to national Israel on the grand scale. God's approach to healing and restoration is universal and can be applied in the lives of individuals even today. God the Father, Christ the Son, and the Holy Spirit all work together in this process to deal with each person's individual situation, and they bring us into the process as we minister to one another. This is why we study Isaiah, to learn from God's methods.

The Prophetic Timeline

We have finished our discussion of Isaiah 40–66 from the thematic standpoint. It is a journey from the brokenness of being exiled from God to the peace and well-being of being restored to Him. Establishing a righteous kingdom of everlasting peace was the ultimate goal of God's Highway Project and the final peak in Isaiah's timeline. Thus, in a thematic sense, the Messianic kingdom represents a final, eternal state of being because once a person accepts the salvation of Christ's death on the cross, entrance into His kingdom and inclusion in that citizenship is assured from that point forward into eternity. But in the literal timeline of historical events, the Messianic kingdom is not the end of the timeline. Far from it. We know from prophetic writings that come after Isaiah's prophecies that there are other events that happen. There is much more to the eschatological picture.

The beauty of the LORD's omnipotence and omniscience is that He can create a linear historical timeline that plays out with a symmetry that mimics a chiastic format, and by mimicking it, He can hide information in plain sight and keep His enemies groping for understanding until it pleases Him to reveal it.

The chiastic structures in Isaiah order the prophetic pictures by building them in a very linear fashion up to a focal point—the kingdom. This peaks in Isaiah 60-62. But from that point on, we question whether the next battle or judgment sequence in the linear progression is a new event or if the writer is merely revisiting the previous events with closing remarks. If everything revolves around the Messianic kingdom as the final, "everlasting" kingdom, then according to the chiastic structure, the battles mentioned on either side of that kingdom picture are really the same battle, as are the two judgment sequences and Israel's two penitential prayers. They are paired in the chiasm, therefore, they must be the same event, right? That is not necessarily the case. The battle on one side of the kingdom picture may follow the pattern of the battle on the other side, but that doesn't mean they are the same battle. They are merely a pattern of one another. In Scripture, similar events can play out numerous times according to a pattern, and yet not reach complete fulfillment until some time in the future. This allows for more information to be added to the picture over time until the full picture is finally revealed. God uses patterns in this way to connect the dots for us as He brings events to fulfillment.

I would argue that the prophetic pictures in Isaiah 40–66 employ both a chiastic structure and a linear timeline to accomplish their purpose. The theme of restoration is built in cascading chiastic structures culminating in Chapter 62, but the argument for God's sovereignty is made in the unfolding linear timeline which ends in Isaiah 66. When God was making the argument for His sovereignty in the opening chapters, He talked extensively about the former and latter things, and the new things He would do that would bear witness of His Godship over His people and His creation. Hidden within the chiastic structure is an unfolding timeline full of "new" and unprecedented events that build a case for His sovereignty. The book of Isaiah ends on this final picture.

We have explored the theme of restoration in the chiastic structures. Now, let's look at the theme of God's sovereignty as it plays out in the linear timeline. The kingdom picture is not the end in the linear timeline. Instead there is going to be another battle, another judgment sequence, and another level of kingdom experience that will eclipse even the Messianic kingdom. Instead of viewing these events as reiterations of the previous events, we are going to look at them as new events—"new things" through which the LORD displays His Godship. We will begin with the death and resurrection of the Servant in Isaiah 53 and move forward on the timeline from there. Keep in mind, these future events are merely high points in the eschatological timeline, not a complete picture. There were things that Isaiah saw and things he didn't see. Isaiah's vision is similar to Daniel's in that it is Israel-centric and only follows the periods of time relevant to Israel's national redemption program.

What Isaiah Saw and Didn't See

I will begin with what Isaiah saw and then add New Testament references from the book of Revelation and other prophetic books for comparison to reveal what he didn't see. Let's get started.

We pick up the timeline in **Isaiah 53** with the **death of the Sin-Bearing Servant** (who we know is Jesus Christ in His first coming).

Isaiah 54-56 then presents a picture of **the Messianic kingdom**. Pictures of grace upon grace abound as both Jews and Gentiles are brought into abundant life in the glorious kingdom. This is the kingdom as it should have been realized at Christ's resurrection, but it wasn't. As Isaiah observes, something went wrong.

Isaiah 57 reverts abruptly to the picture of a **wicked kingdom** in which the wicked flourish while the righteous perish (that is, they are taken away to spare them from the coming calamity). Israel's restoration program is delayed while the sin issue remains unaddressed.

> Let's pause for a moment and consider these pictures from a New Testament standpoint.
>
> After Christ's death on the cross and His resurrection, He should have come into His kingdom, but the Messianic kingdom was not realized at that point because corporate Israel rejected Him as their King. Instead, the Church Age ensued. **Isaiah did not see the Church Age**, nor did he see the inauguration of the **New Covenant**. The New Covenant only came into view in later prophecies like Jeremiah's, and it isn't explicitly defined until Christ Himself explains it at the Last Supper.
>
> Isaiah skips over the intervening Church Age and fast-forwards to the picture of the wicked kingdom that arises in the End Times. His description goes hand-in-hand with the description of the **kingdom of the Beast** and a **future Babylon** in **Revelation 13, 14, 17, 18, and 19**. Therefore, the righteous who Isaiah describes as being "taken away" are the martyrs who die during the reign of the wicked kingdom. They may also foreshadow the rapture of the Church at the beginning of that time. First Thessalonians 5:9 explains that because of our

identification with Christ's atoning sacrifice on the cross, we are no longer appointed (or destined) to experience God's wrath with the rest of the unbelieving world, which is why we are raptured out of the world before that time of judgment unfolds in all its fury. Paul explains this in 1 Thessalonians 4:16. The rapture of the saints also fits with Isaiah's picture of the righteous being "taken away" to spare them from the calamity to come as the wicked kingdom begins to flourish.

The Kingdom of the Beast and future Babylon portrayed in the book of Revelation follow the pattern of the wicked kingdom in Isaiah 57 and also agree with what Jeremiah describes as the time of Jacob's trouble in Jeremiah 30:7. So, we can connect all those dots according to the pattern.

Now, let's return to the picture we are building in Isaiah.

From the wicked kingdom in Isaiah 57, we move to the **judgment sequence** in **Isaiah 58**. The sequence plays out in conjunction with the reign of the wicked kingdom. Thus, the wrath of God's judgment is the "calamity" from which the righteous are spared. God charges backsliding Israel with sin.

In **Isaiah 59**, Israel responds with a **penitential prayer**. She confesses her sin corporately as a nation and asks for mercy. The LORD then responds in by sending the Redeemer. Isaiah 59 ends with the **epic battle** as the Redeemer wages war against Israel's enemies and avenges her.

> We see some parallels to this in the New Testament as well. In the book of Revelation, the Tribulation Age fits the pattern of this judgment sequence in Isaiah. Isaiah describes it strictly in terms of Israel's experience as the conflict that drives her to return to God. At the end of the Tribulation, when Christ the Redeemer returns, the remnant of Israel who are left will experience that moment of national repentance and mourning as they turn and acknowledge their Savior. Where they once rejected Him, they now embrace Him. This same picture is further supported by Zechariah 12 which also describes a time of Israel's mourning and national turning. This battle is easily labeled as the battle of **Armageddon** at Christ's second coming

mentioned in **Revelation 16**. Armageddon fits the pattern of the battle in Isaiah.

Back to Isaiah . . .

In the wake of the battle, the **Righteous Kingdom** under the Messianic King is inaugurated in **Isaiah 60-62**. From Isaiah's perspective, this kingdom is the final, everlasting kingdom and its citizenry consists of the remnant of people who survive the time of judgment. The remnant of the Gentile nations who once oppressed Israel are now made to serve her while she reigns as a royal priesthood. This is the grand reward that was promised to her when she returns to God.

It is important to note what Isaiah did *not* see in these visions.

First of all, he did not see that the Messianic kingdom would only last a thousand years. John tells us in **Revelation 20:1-8** that it is defined as a specific period of time when **Satan is bound**. Isaiah did not see this spiritual side of the kingdom dynamic.

Secondly, Isaiah did not envision the **return of the resurrected saints** at the time of Christ's second coming. He saw the righteous perishing in the wicked kingdom, but he did not see them reigning as a royal priesthood along with the remnant of mortal Israel in the Messianic kingdom. The only Gentiles that he foresaw being brought into the kingdom are the mortals who survive the battle of Armageddon and are made to serve Israel.

Back to Isaiah . . .

The **Messianic kingdom** in **Isaiah 60-62** is the high point of God's Highway Project and the end point in Isaiah's timeline. The follow-on pictures of another battle, another prayer, another judgment sequence, and the new heaven and new earth are not presented as unique events in their own right but as the recounting of earlier pictures according to their chiastic pairings. Thus, the **treading of the winepress** in **Isaiah 63** is also a picture of the battle of Armageddon.

When we consider the imagery of treading the winepress, it is important to consider who is doing it. In **Revelation 19:15**, Christ treads the winepress at His second coming when He charges forth into battle to strike the nations. The same winepress imagery also appears in **Revelation 14:19-20**, where the angel is commanded to thrust in the sickle and reap "the vine of the earth" and throw it into the great winepress of the wrath of God, who then treads it out. On one hand, Christ treads the winepress. On the other hand, God (the Father) does. As it is in the book of Revelation, so it is in Isaiah. The battle on one side of the Messianic kingdom features the work of the Redeemer. The recounting of that battle on the other side shows the LORD Himself taking action.

Following the battle in Isaiah 63, Israel offers another **penitential prayer** in **Isaiah 64.** This is followed by an extensive **judgment sequence** in **Isaiah 65-66**. On the surface, the before-and-after pictures of battle, prayer, and judgment may follow the pattern of one another, but Israel's tone of voice and the LORD's response are radically different in the final sequence. These differences set the closing pictures apart as unique events. This is where the linear event timeline diverges from the chiastic loop. So let's consider the events as an ongoing timeline.

The prayer and judgment follow the pattern of the previous prayer and judgment, but they are presented in the reverse order. Previously the LORD charged Israel with sin, for which she then repented, and then the Redeemer came. *After* the battle of Armageddon, the Messianic Kingdom is established. The battle that is described after the kingdom is a mere recounting of the treading of the winepress.

Why, then, would Israel suddenly lift her voice in another penitential prayer? There doesn't seem to be a need or reason for this, or at least no reason that Isaiah relates. But notice that the tone of the prayer is radically different from the previous one. It seems that there is still a sinful element in the kingdom's citizenry that has a hardened heart. Their prayer is less penitent and more accusatory against God.

In response, God doesn't send the Redeemer this time. Instead, He roars back at them in wrath and judgment. This judgment is all consuming and affects the totality of Israel and the Gentile nations. All flesh is gathered before God to be judged wicked or righteous. It may fit the pattern of the previous judgment sequence, but the judgment is now a universal judgment as opposed to a national judgment of Israel alone.

Isaiah 65 ends with the glorious picture of **the new heaven and new earth**. This is established in conjunction with the **final judgment sequence**, which continues to the end of the book in **Isaiah 66**.

Within that judgment sequence, there is the fleeting mention of a **final battle** in **Isaiah 66:6** that does not have a parallel in the chiastic structure. That, too, indicates that we are shifting away from the chiastic loop and into a linear timeline.

In summary, the flow of pictures goes like this, beginning with the Messianic kingdom:

After the Messianic kingdom is established, there is a recounting of the Savior's exploits. That appears to be the end of things, but then something happens in kingdom—an event that is unexplained in Isaiah but is described in the book of Revelation. In the wake of this event, we find a cross-section of people with hardened hearts crying out against God. God then responds with a final, universal judgment. In the midst of this judgment we see another battle break out, which the LORD Himself puts down, and a vision of the new heaven and earth in which the righteous now flourish while the wicked perish.

The end pictures are a little jumbled together, but they straighten out when put into the timeline of **Revelation 20-22**. Let's compare Isaiah vision with John's vision in the book of Revelation, and consider what Isaiah didn't see.

> The Messianic Kingdom is our starting benchmark in Isaiah 62 and also Revelation 20:1. Remember, Isaiah saw only the physical side of the conflict as it related to physical Israel; John saw the spiritual conflict going on behind the scenes. Thus, John gives us an opening statement in **Revelation 20:1-3** that **Satan is bound** at the beginning of the Messianic kingdom.
>
> In **Revelation 20:4-6**, John goes on to reveal a second element of the kingdom that Isaiah did not see—the return of the righteous who had died and now come into the kingdom in their resurrected form. Isaiah only saw the mortals who survived the Tribulation. John sees the immortals which he identifies as those of the "first resurrection" over which the coming judgment has no power.

The Prophetic Timeline

According to **Revelation 20:7**, Satan remains bound for the duration of 1,000 years. Thus, the Messianic kingdom is free of His influence. At the end of the 1,000 years, **Satan is unbound** and begins his work again. I believe this is the unforeseen event in Isaiah that explains why the kingdom seems to come under attack again, spurring the next penitential prayer for deliverance. But the prayer is different in nature this time. There is an accusatory tone to it. Rebellion is fomenting.

Revelation 20:7-9 describes a rebellion instigated by Satan, which then ends in a pitched battle with two entities described as Gog and Magog. These represent the totality of the nations in this conflict. **The Gog-Magog rebellion** and **the battle** in **Isaiah 66:6** are the pattern of one another, but they are *not* reiterations of Armageddon. This is a unique battle that arises at the end of the Messianic Age.

Revelation 20:10-15 then goes on to describe the judgment of all souls at the **great white throne of judgment**. This parallels the judgment sequence of **Isaiah 65-66** which is all-consuming in character. The judgment before the Great White Throne is a unique event. It fits the pattern of judgment similar to the Tribulation, but it should not be confused with the judgment at the time of Christ's second coming as Isaiah's chiastic structure would suggest. These two judgments follow the same pattern, but they are unique events and the final judgment eclipses the first. Now, *all* the dead, including those who die during the Messianic kingdom, are presented in resurrected bodies before the Great White Throne to be judged according to their works. In both Isaiah and Revelation, the wicked are consigned to the fire. Revelation 20:14-15 describes it as a lake of fire into which all are cast except those found in the Book of Life.

Isaiah orders the events so that the vision ends on the picture of judgment. This is to reinforce the chiastic structure. The chiasm began in Isaiah 57 with a picture of a wicked kingdom and now resolves with the judgment of the wicked in Isaiah 66. The book of Revelation lays out the events chronologically, reversing Isaiah's order. The judgment in Revelation 20:10-15 comes first, then gives way to the picture of **the new heaven and new earth**, along with the **new Jerusalem** in **Revelation 21-22**.

What Isaiah did not see is that life in the new heaven and new earth is a separate kingdom experience from the Messianic kingdom. We know this because Isaiah 65:20 tells us that citizens in the Messianic kingdom will still experience death, whereas those in the new heaven and new earth do not, as John reveals in Revelation 20:14. According to John's vision, death is removed from the picture at the final judgment before the Great White Throne, which fully purges the everlasting kingdom of sin and its recompense. All mortality is brought to an end.

Isaiah ends with the picture of recompense being determined for both the wicked and righteous. The book of Revelation ends with a similar final warning from Christ Himself in Revelation 22:12-15 which echoes Isaiah's words. He says,

> *"And behold, I am coming quickly, and My reward is with Me, to give to every one according to his work. I am the Alpha and the Omega, the Beginning and the End, the First and the Last. Blessed are those who do His commandments, that they may have the right to the tree of life, and may enter through the gates into the city. But outside are dogs and sorcerers and sexually immoral and murderers and idolaters, and whoever loves and practices a lie."*

When we look past the chiastic structure and consider the final pictures in light of an eschatological timeline, we see the full display of God's sovereignty in declaring the "new things" He will do. These are unique things that mankind has never seen before nor will it see again. The chiastic structure describes the restoration of man, but the linear timeline declares the glory of God.

When we look at the full sweep of these events, they are equally terrifying and thrilling—and comforting. The fact that God has declared the end of these things should bring us comfort when we are faced with an increasingly hostile and oppressive world. Things will get worse, but then they will get better—much, much better.

Paul gives us this encouragement in 1 Thessalonians 5:1-11:

> *"But concerning the times and the seasons, brethren, you have no need that I should write to you. For you yourselves know perfectly that the day*

of the Lord so comes as a thief in the night. For when they say, 'Peace and safety!' then sudden destruction comes upon them, as labor pains upon a pregnant woman. And they shall not escape. But you, brethren, are not in darkness, so that this Day should overtake you as a thief. You are all sons of light and sons of the day. We are not of the night nor of darkness. Therefore let us not sleep, as others do, but let us watch and be sober. For those who sleep, sleep at night, and those who get drunk are drunk at night. But let us who are of the day be sober, putting on the breastplate of faith and love, and as a helmet the hope of salvation. For God did not appoint us to wrath, but to obtain salvation through our Lord Jesus Christ, who died for us, that whether we wake or sleep, we should live together with Him. Therefore comfort each other and edify one another, just as you also are doing."

Comfort each other, as the LORD commanded and as He Himself has modeled for us. Comfort yourself and each other not just in the grace of His salvation purchased by Christ, but in His sovereignty over your life, pursuing the reward of the crown that He has reserved for those who pursue His righteousness. Comfort, comfort His people!

Thank you for joining me for this study! It helped me tremendously as I worked through it, and I hope it gives you some insight as you pursue your own efforts at comforting and being comforted.

Christy Voelkel

www.ingramcontent.com/pod-product-compliance
Lightning Source LLC
Chambersburg PA
CBHW051400070526
44584CB00023B/3232